ENGLISH LANGUAGE LEARNERS
Day by Day, K–6

ENGLISH LANGUAGE LEARNERS
Day by Day, K–6

A Complete Guide to Literacy, Content-Area, and Language Instruction

Christina M. Celic

HEINEMANN
Portsmouth, NH

Heinemann
361 Hanover Street
Portsmouth, NH 03801–3912
www.heinemann.com

Offices and agents throughout the world

Library of Congress Cataloging-in-Publication Data
Celic, Christina M.
    English language learners day by day, k–6 : a complete guide to literacy, content-area, and language instruction / Christina M. Celic.
       p. cm.
    Includes bibliographical references and index.
    ISBN-13: 978-0-325-02682-4
    ISBN-10: 0-325-02682-3
   1. English language—Study and teaching (Primary). 2. Language arts—Study and teaching (Primary). 3. Content-area reading.   I. Title.

LB1528.C45 2009
372.6—dc22
                                                                    2009025713

Editors: Yvonne S. Freeman and David E. Freeman
Production: Patricia Adams
Typesetter: Eric Rosenbloom, Kirby Mountain Composition
Cover design: Bernadette Skok
Manufacturing: Steve Bernier

Printed in the United States of America on acid-free paper
13 12 11   VP   2 3 4 5

To my mother,

Sharon Celic,

a master teacher whose passion and

talent for educating children inspired me

to follow in her footsteps.

Contents

PREPARATIONS FOR INSTRUCTION

Foreword

The education of language minority students in the United States has received much attention in the past forty years, especially since the passing of the Bilingual Education Act in 1968. But in the past ten years, as a result of greater accountability measures and an increase in immigration, all teachers throughout the United States have had to grapple with how to educate children who are developing academic English. Increasingly, the onus to educate these language minority children is not just on specialized teachers—bilingual teachers and ESL teachers—but also on all other teachers. It is in this larger context of what to do inside any classroom to meaningfully educate these emergent bilingual students with varying proficiencies in English that this book becomes important. This is not a book written from the outside in—what specialists and bureaucrats say should be done. Instead, this is a book about how one talented educator goes about the business of organizing her classroom space and planning lessons so that every child learns.

Many books have been written on strategies for teaching language minority children. But this book makes a unique contribution. Perhaps the most distinguishing characteristic of this book is that it asks teachers to look at classrooms through the eyes of a child who is developing academic English. The gaze of the emergent bilingual child blends with that of the teacher as they look around the room together to ensure that there are resources and spaces for learning. The gaze and voice of student and teacher blend, as the author, Christina Celic, asks questions such as "Are there books and other texts about topics and people you can relate to?" "Are there resources available that would help you start writing in the new language?" and "Is your native language seen as something that can help you learn the new language?" Celic speaks directly to teachers, telling them: "When you think about the language demands of the curriculum, you put yourself in your English language learners' shoes. You understand how difficult it would be to keep up with the academic work without the appropriate language structures and vocabulary to express your learning."

It is this positioning of the teacher seeing through the eyes of the language minority child (and standing in his shoes) that makes this book so successful. Celic's pedagogical philosophy and practices rest on the fact that good teachers must build on language minority children's strengths and that teachers must learn to assess and use students' strengths, including their home language practices, to educate them—intellectually, but also linguistically, as they develop English.

My reading of this book parallels in process Celic's intertwined gaze, voice, and steps between teacher and students in the classroom. Many years ago, Christina Celic came into my teacher education classroom at Columbia University's Teachers College as an experienced ESL (English as a second language) and bilingual teacher. I was privileged to supervise her and visit her own classroom. I was immediately astounded by her ability to plan and deliver instruction in ways that made the children successful and happy learners of sophisticated academic content but also of English. Although her classroom then was considered an ESL classroom, Celic supported students' learning through the use of languages other than English. Celic stretched definitions and structures that were handed down to her by the administration, as she creatively responded to the students' curiosity about learning, their imagination, their energy, and their interests. I quickly became the student, learning from Celic how to put into practice conceptual understandings. I encouraged her to document her practices and to write in order to share her know-how with others. Celic's writing of this text and my reading of it bring our teacher-student relationship full circle. My gaze intertwines with hers in a cycle of respect for her deep understandings and practical knowledge. Like the links in Celic's classroom chain of accountability, teaching is about adding links to a chain of learning that relates teachers to students, people to other people, and people to new knowledge and understandings. This book is one more link that connects all of us who care about the education of bilingual children in the United States. I am proud to be another link in the long chain of which she's also a link.

Besides the great empathy that Celic's practical advice shows, there are three other reasons why this text is unique: (1) it offers hope and is not solely centered on problems; (2) the advice is grounded and makes students and teachers feel secure; and (3) it is about educating children, not simply teaching them English. Just as Celic offers detailed treatment of each of her practical suggestions, I would like to pause to consider each of these reasons separately.

The gaze that Celic's book communicates is one that reflects light, possibility, hope, confidence, and security, for both teachers and children. It is as if the light of the children's eyes illuminates the teacher's work. While other texts are centered around problems in teaching these emergent bilinguals, Celic's text is full of possibilities and offers a better future of teaching practice and learning. Just as she raises the bar of confidence for her students, Celic raises the self-assurance of teachers to facilitate the meaningful education of these students. By sharing practical steps on how to set up the classroom first, then the first week of instruction, and finally the entire cycle of lessons, curricula, and assessment, Celic offers a pathway to success. For second language assessment, she helps teachers identify both "secure" and "developing" language structures. Her choice of words leaves no question but that teaching and learning will be secured in the future. The gaze that Celic maintains is one of confidence in development.

Because this practical guide is based on Celic's actual classroom experience both as a teacher and as a staff developer and coach, the examples are real, authentic, and meaningful. Not only does the book provide us with examples from Celic's own classrooms, but at times we hear her own words, as she shares classroom scripts with us. Just like her stoplight example, the advice she gives teachers is to make all systems go.

The light is green as she shares her own teaching confidence with others. And Celic also shares of herself as a second language learner. A fluent English-Spanish bilingual, Celic has recently learned Portuguese as a result of her move to Brazil. With confidence, she shares those experiences, again putting herself in the shoes of the language learner.

Finally, this book is not just about teaching English, but about educating language minority children as they expand their linguistic repertoire and become users of academic English. Celic makes evident that teaching these children English is important, but this cannot be the main goal of education. Thus, of the eight Keys to Success that Celic develops, seven have little to do with teaching English per se. Only one focuses on English language development, and even that principle does not isolate language from content. Language is developed in a meaningful and rich classroom context where curriculum, instruction, and assessment practices support content-area knowledge as well as academic language and literacy.

Celic says that the classroom must function "like a team." It is interesting that half of the eight Keys to Success raise the possibility of collaboration, sometimes among people, other times among contents and structures: *involve* families, *connect* learning to students, teach language and content *together*, *integrate* instruction thematically. This collaborative spirit is then raised and made meaningful through two other key principles that provide the classroom team its stature and stability: *raise* the bar, and be *consistent*. And all of this is then anchored by the key principle that keeps the whole structure balanced: use students' native language to support learning. And yet, Celic's approach is not a simple recipe that can be followed for success for all. The last key principle is to differentiate instruction, thus acknowledging differences in individual children and their learning.

One of the greatest challenges in U.S. education today is how to teach language minority children, especially those whose bilingualism is emerging as they are developing academic English. With elegance of style, and precision in descriptions of practice, Celic's book offers a way to see through a language learner's eyes, a way to walk in her shoes. No longer does the *caminante* not have a *camino*. Celic does not solely offer us a road that we can make upon walking; she also shares the steps that we can all follow. And she offers us her firm hand as she transforms classrooms to meaningfully and creatively educate language minority children day by day.

Ofelia García
Graduate Center, City University of New York

Acknowledgments

There are many people who influenced the creation of this book and who were a part of its publication. I would first like to thank my mentor, Dr. Ofelia García, who encouraged me to write this book after spending time in my classroom and seeing the work my English language learners were doing. As teachers we often get caught up in the day-to-day details of our classrooms, and it was her perspective from the outside looking in that helped me see the importance of sharing these practices with other educators.

This book became a reality thanks to many talented and dedicated professionals at Heinemann. Thank you to my editors, Yvonne and David Freeman, for coaching me throughout the writing process. Their support and feedback, grounded in their years of experience teaching and writing in the field of ESL and bilingual education, were truly invaluable. I would also like to thank Patty Adams, Production Editor, for transforming the manuscript into a professional and attractive book. Her expertise and attention to detail made a world of difference. Thank you to Elizabeth Tripp for her careful copyediting and helpful suggestions to fine-tune the manuscript. A special thanks to Maura Sullivan, Director of Editorial, for enthusiastically supporting this book from the beginning.

I feel very fortunate to have worked for John Bernardino and Margaret Dounis, who in 2000 founded P.S. 212, a public elementary school in a diverse immigrant community in Queens, New York. As principal and assistant principal of P.S. 212, they firmly believed that all the students at their school, including English language learners, should be academically successful. Thank you for giving me the freedom to implement different instructional practices in my classroom and for supporting my professional development to help make those high expectations a reality for my ELLs.

The students I taught at P.S. 212 are at the heart of this book. It is their written work, class discussions, and photographs that bring to life the teaching practices I describe in each chapter. Their work shows the background and capabilities they brought to our classroom at the beginning of the school year, and how they evolved from one month to the next while learning the grade-level content and learning English. I'm very proud of these students and the effort they put into learning on a daily basis! I would especially like to thank my students' families for letting me include their children's work in this book.

My former colleagues at P.S. 212 are an incredible group of teachers, and I'm grateful to have been able to work with and learn from such dedicated educators. Our planning meetings, book study groups, curriculum development projects, and conversations over lunch helped me improve my teaching practice. I appreciate their continued friendship and support.

I would like to thank Linda Chen for giving me the opportunity to work as a Literacy Coach at P.S. 165, a dual language bilingual school in Manhattan. I would also like to thank the teachers at P.S. 165 for welcoming me into their classrooms so that together we could think about how best to meet their English and Spanish language learners' needs.

While much of my teaching career has been in New York City, my first years of teaching were in Illinois at Johnson School in the East Aurora School District and at Einstein School in the Schaumburg School District. Both areas have a large community of English language learners, and it was through the strong professional development I received in these two school districts that I was able to start implementing more effective teaching practices in my classroom.

The learning community at Teachers College Columbia University has also influenced my teaching, and in particular the Bilingual-Bicultural Education program where I did my Masters in Education. I would like to thank again Dr. Ofelia García, as well as Dr. María Torres-Guzmán, Dr. Victoria Hunt, Patricia Velasco, Maureen Matarese, and Dr. Yi Han for stretching my thinking about the theory and practice of teaching students in different kinds of language programs. Thank you also to my colleagues from the Bilingual-Bicultural Education program; the conversations we've had over the years have certainly made my teaching stronger.

I come from a family of educators. My grandfather, John Fleming, my aunts Pam Danielian and Kathy Theis, my godmother Geri Shouba, and my mother, Sharon Celic, all showed me as I was growing up what it means to be truly dedicated to students and the teaching profession. This has helped me keep in perspective that teaching must always be about doing what's best for the students.

Thank you to my parents, Ken and Sharon Celic, for being a constant source of love and support throughout my life. I appreciate their willingness to listen to me talk about my ideas for this book and for sharing in my enthusiasm.

Finally, this book would not have been possible without the support of my husband and best friend, Rafael López Lorenzo, who always encouraged me to pursue this dream. Thank you for being by my side for the past ten years.

Christina M. Celic
August 2009

Introduction

When I first began teaching in a bilingual classroom, I felt completely overwhelmed. I realized very quickly that my language education coursework, and even my student teaching experiences, hadn't fully prepared me for the reality I faced in my classroom. I was at a loss for how to implement instruction with my students, who were all at different stages of learning English and had a wide range of reading, writing, and content-area skills in English and Spanish. I was also discouraged by the challenges many of my English language learners (ELLs) faced that were out of my control: starting the school year with below-grade-level skills in literacy and the content areas, having limited formal education from their home countries, or lacking academic support at home, often because their parents worked multiple jobs or didn't know how to help with schoolwork in English.

But I knew the one thing I *could* control was what went on inside my classroom—the way I organized the physical space for learning, the way I designed my units of study and lessons, and the way I differentiated instruction. So, I decided to become proactive about the situation. I descended upon the local bookstores and bought every professional book I could find that related to either best practices in teaching or to working with English language learners. I spent my free time devouring these books and thinking about how I could piece together the research and practices from each field. The question I was determined to answer was "How can I teach the grade-level curriculum in a way that makes my English language learners successful?"

It was this question that guided me from one year of teaching to the next as I tried out new approaches to teaching language through reading, writing, and the content areas. Each year I reflected on what had worked and I planned what I'd do differently the next time around. This trial-and-error process was frustrating at times, but I was encouraged to see that each year my English language learners were in fact experiencing greater levels of success in reading, writing, math, social studies, and science. I also saw a difference in their self-concept. Once they realized they could succeed in school, they became proud of their accomplishments and were more motivated to keep working. This confirmed for me what I had read during my first year of teaching in Thomas and Collier's

(1997) research: the *approach* we use to teach English language learners is a greater predictor for their success than any of the other factors that are out of our control.

When I began doing professional development work with bilingual, English as a second language (ESL), and mainstream teachers in grades K–6, I found that I wasn't the only one grappling with this task of teaching language and the grade-level curriculum. In writing this book I wanted to share the specific teaching practices I've found to be successful with English language learners. These practices are based on what the research has shown to be effective for ELLs, which I summarize in Figure I–1 as the *Keys to Success*. No matter what I change about my teaching from year to year, it's always grounded in these research-based principles about what works with English language learners. In each chapter of this book I include step-by-step examples of teaching practices that illustrate these Keys to Success in action. These practical examples show how you can help your ELLs improve academically and linguistically when you're preparing for a new school year, planning units of study, and implementing instruction with your students.

What Will You Find in This Book?

All of the suggestions I provide are based on my experience with teaching English language learners in different bilingual and ESL programs in the elementary grades, and from working with bilingual, ESL, and mainstream teachers who have English language learners in their classrooms. Throughout the book there are suggestions for adapting different practices for different types of language programs and settings.

This book is divided into two main sections. The first section of the book details how to prepare for teaching English language learners. Chapter 1 provides specific ideas for setting up a classroom that is designed to support ELLs in learning language and content. In Chapter 2 I detail how to plan assessments and initial instruction for the first weeks of school that will help you get started quickly with appropriate, challenging instruction for your ELLs. Chapter 3 addresses the topic of classroom management with ELLs, including how to set up a daily schedule, routines, rules, and homework procedures.

The second section of the book focuses on developing effective instructional practices for the rest of the school year. Chapter 4 explains how to integrate literacy and content-area instruction throughout the school day to give ELLs a familiar context for developing academic language, literacy skills, and content-area knowledge. Chapter 5 discusses how to plan instruction that teaches academic language and content at the same time. Finally, Chapter 6 gives snapshots of classroom instruction in action that illustrate how all of the elements from the previous chapters come together to help ELLs be academically and linguistically successful.

At the end of each chapter I include a section that outlines which Keys to Success were shown in action, giving you a chance to reflect on how you're currently implementing these research-based practices in your own classroom.

It's impossible for this book to detail every aspect of current best practices in reading, writing, and the content areas. To provide a more in-depth understanding of particular instructional approaches, I refer to resources I've found helpful in improving my own teaching practice at the end of each chapter.

1. **Raise the bar.**
   a. Teach the same rigorous and challenging curriculum expected for the grade level.
   b. Align all your instruction to state standards.
   c. Hold all ELLs accountable for their learning through continual assessment.
2. **Teach language and content together.**
   a. Recognize that language and content must be developed simultaneously.
   b. Create language objectives that help students meet literacy and content objectives.
   c. Focus on developing the *academic language* ELLs need to be successful with the curriculum.
3. **Integrate instruction.**
   a. Weave together content-area studies and literacy throughout the day and throughout a unit of study.
   b. Provide *multiple opportunities* for ELLs to hear, speak, read, and write academic language related to a content-area topic.
4. **Differentiate instruction.**
   a. Balance whole-class, small-group, and individual instruction to meet ELLs' varying linguistic and academic needs.
   b. Provide academic interventions when necessary based on your continual assessments.
   c. Use a visual approach with pictures, graphic organizers, sketches, media, and realia (real-life objects).
   d. Explicitly model what you are teaching and what you expect students to do.
   e. Use a hands-on approach.
   f. Use collaborative learning structures.
5. **Connect learning to students.**
   a. Activate students' background knowledge and experiences to contextualize new learning.
   b. Build background knowledge when necessary to understanding new information.
   c. Create a valued place in the classroom for students' backgrounds to foster an accepting learning environment.
6. **Use students' native languages to support learning.**
   a. Understand the positive effect this has on academic performance in English.
   b. Use the first language(s) as a resource, whether you have a bilingual, ESL, or mainstream classroom.
7. **Be consistent.**
   a. Structure a consistent daily schedule, routines, rules, and procedures so ELLs know what they're expected to do in the classroom.
   b. Use the same words or phrases consistently to signal instructional directions.
8. **Involve families.**
   a. Provide ways for all family members to participate actively in their children's education, regardless of their English language proficiency or academic background.
   b. Keep families informed of their children's progress and ways they can support learning.

Figure I–1 Keys to Success *with English Language Learners*

Terminology Used in This Book

Although there are many different ways to refer to an ELL's level of proficiency in English, in this book I use the levels developed by TESOL (Teachers of English to Speakers of Other Languages): Level 1: *starting*, Level 2: *emerging*, Level 3: *developing*, Level 4: *expanding*, and Level 5: *bridging* (Gottleib et al. 2006). When talking about my ELLs' English proficiency in more general terms, I use the terms *beginning*, *intermediate*, and *advanced*. To talk about an ELL's native language, I often use the term *L1*, and to talk about his second or additional language, English, I often use the term *L2*.

How Should You Read This Book?

Every year it seems there are more demands on teachers' time. While the ideas in this book build upon each other from chapter to chapter, you can certainly skip to the parts that address your most urgent needs as a teacher. New teachers will likely find it helpful to read the book from beginning to end since it is organized sequentially from what to do on the first days of school through the rest of the school year.

My hope is that this book provides you with a practical foundation for addressing your own English language learners' academic and linguistic needs on a daily basis, and that the specific examples help you envision your classroom as a place where your ELLs can be successful, motivated, and confident in their abilities.

CHAPTER 1

Setting Up a Classroom for English Language Learners

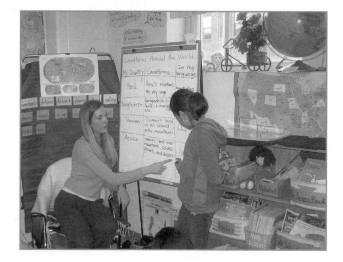

*T*here was nothing more terrifying for me, professionally speaking, than when I was a first-year teacher unlocking the door to what would be my future classroom. It was six weeks into the school year and I had been hired to take over a bilingual fourth- and fifth-grade class whose teacher had unexpectedly moved to another state. Two languages, two grades, two curricula, and twenty-eight ELLs on my roster had turned me into a totally overwhelmed beginning teacher, and I had only one weekend before my first day with the students. To make matters worse, the classroom wasn't at all organized. Everywhere I looked there were stacks of boxes and piles upon piles of materials, supplies, and papers invading every learning space in the classroom.

I didn't know where to start, but I knew I had to get the classroom space under control before my first day with my new class. I began by unpacking the boxes and organizing the books. I found storage places for all the materials and supplies and created different centers in the classroom. I brought in a rug and a rocker to create an attractive reading area, and I put some plants on the windowsill. By the end of the weekend I looked around the room and was happy to see how welcoming it looked. I began imagining all the amazing things that were going to take place in the room that year with my group of ELLs.

However, when my class arrived and instruction began, I realized that I hadn't considered how the classroom itself could be a teaching tool to support my ELLs' learning. Instead of just being visually attractive and organized, I wondered how I could tailor each area of the room to help my ELLs learn both English and the grade-level content. As a new teacher, my to-do list that year was endless, but little by little I began a classroom makeover to turn it into a resource that would facilitate my ELLs' language learning and academic development.

I begin this book with a chapter on setting up the classroom because no matter how many times I start a new school year, I always feel like I have to get my physical space under control before I'm mentally ready to tackle anything else. As teachers who work with ELLs, when we begin the task of setting up the classroom it's important to consider how we can design each area to maximize our ELLs' ability to develop both linguistic and academic skills.

In this chapter I show how you can

- take into account the needs of your ELLs when you design your classroom
- plan a layout for your classroom that makes sense to ELLs
- form a classroom library with appropriate resources
- provide collaborative work areas
- create centers that help ELLs learn both language and content

Examining Your Room Through the Eyes of an English Language Learner

As you set up your classroom, it helps to think of it as an environment that should support your ELLs in learning language and grade-level content at the same time (Freeman and Freeman 2007; Gibbons 2002). It may be difficult to determine whether or not your classroom is truly a place where ELLs can achieve this dual focus of learning language and learning content. Imagine for a moment that you're an English language learner, trying to learn English and keep up academically with your classmates. As you look around your classroom from this perspective, think about the following:

- the written language (on charts, the board, posters, word walls)
  - Is the written language supported with pictures, photos, examples, or graphic organizers that would give you clues to understanding the content?
  - Does the written language include familiar words that you have been explicitly taught during lessons?
  - Would you even know what content area or topic the writing is related to?
- vocabulary development
  - Are there any visual resources like word walls, charts, or labels in the classroom that would help you learn important vocabulary words and understand their meaning?
  - Are there ways you could meaningfully practice the vocabulary?
- the resources available for reading
  - Are there books and other texts at an appropriate level that would help you develop your reading skills in English? Or would you be expected to wait to read in English until you'd learned more of the language?
  - Are there books in your native language that would help you continue to develop your reading skills?
  - Are there books and other texts about topics and people you can relate to?

- Are there resources such as a listening center that would let you listen to the language as you were reading?
- Are there language charts in the classroom that would help you learn the letters and sounds of English?
- the resources available for writing
  - Are there resources available that would help you start writing in the new language (modeled writing displayed on charts, word walls, bilingual picture dictionaries, a variety of paper choices)? Or would you be expected to wait to write in English until you'd learned more of the language?
- the spaces for learning
  - Are desks and other areas set up so you could collaborate with your peers in learning English and grade-level content? Or would you be expected to always work alone?
- your native language
  - Are there any materials or resources available in your native language to help you understand new concepts and build literacy skills?
  - Have you been partnered up with anyone who speaks your native language?

When you think about a classroom from this perspective, you can begin to see what it would be like for an English language learner, particularly in the early stages of language development, to learn the language and keep up academically with the rest of the class. Once you're aware of how the classroom can be a resource to support your ELLs' progress, you can begin transforming it into a place where all students can be successful in their learning. Remember that organizing a classroom with the needs of ELLs in mind is an ongoing process. The beauty of teaching is that every year is a chance to start fresh, reflecting on what could be done differently as well as what you want to keep the same.

Creating a Layout

The layout of your classroom should be logical and organized so your ELLs know where to find information and resources for each subject. For example, my math word wall, math charts, and math manipulatives are all grouped together in one section of the room. My ELLs know they can find anything they need related to math in that area. This is particularly important for beginning ELLs who don't understand most of the environmental print in the classroom. When ELLs know where they can consistently look for information, vocabulary, or materials related to a particular subject, it supports their ability to learn in the classroom. Figure 1–1 shows an example of how I structured my classroom layout one year. In the layout you can see how resources for each subject are clustered together. As I describe how to set up each part of the classroom with ELLs in mind, you can refer to this layout to see how the areas can all fit together. Finding a space for everything can be a challenge because classrooms range widely in size and shape. But with a little creativity and input from other teachers you can usually find ways to make it all fit. In this layout you can see that about a quarter of the space was sectioned off to be an office for an out-of-classroom teacher, so I didn't have a full room to work with.

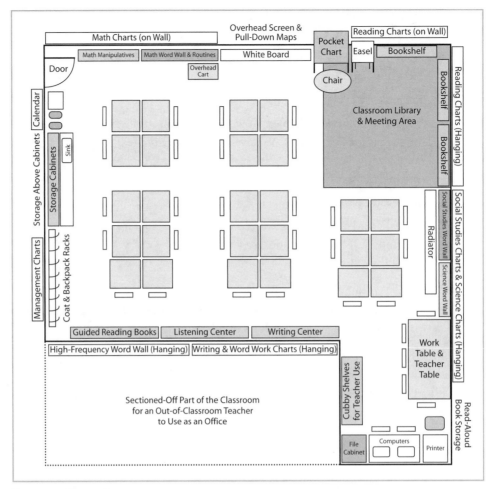

Figure 1–1 *Classroom layout*

Establishing the Classroom Library

I typically begin by setting up the classroom library because this large space affects where everything else in the room is placed. This is the heart of the classroom where you'll be gathering students for minilessons, read-alouds, and possibly shared reading, shared writing, interactive writing, and class meetings (Taberski 2000; Calkins 2001). There are certain resources and materials you can include in this area that will improve your ELLs' ability to understand what you're teaching in your minilessons, develop their literacy skills, and develop their language skills.

Easel with a Whiteboard

When you teach minilessons in the classroom library area, it's essential to have resources that make the instruction visual for your ELLs. An easel with a whiteboard next to your chair gives you a place to write down examples of the reading or writing strategy that you're modeling for ELLs. Instead of relying purely on listening skills, ELLs can see the strategy in action. This scaffolds the language for ELLs with early levels of L2 proficiency, increasing their comprehension of the strategy. If you're using a big book during a minilesson, read-aloud, or shared reading, the easel can be a place to display it so ELLs are able to see the enlarged text as they're hearing the language. The easel can also support chart paper tablets that you can use for shared writing, interactive writing, and shared reading.

Near the easel I keep a basket with materials I may need during instruction. I have a supply of differently colored dry-erase markers to make my writing on the whiteboard more visual and comprehensible for my ELLs. The variety of colors also helps me make more realistic sketches on the board to clarify the written language. Highlighting tape or highlighting markers are useful during literacy instruction to help ELLs focus on a particular letter, word, or sentence in a text that you have written on chart paper. For shared reading texts that I display on the easel, I always keep a stock of sticky notes that I can use to cover up key words or parts of words. That way my ELLs can predict what's missing based on context clues and what they know about the language. If a particular shared reading text has a rhythm or rhyme I want my ELLs to pay attention to, I pull out some maracas and tambourines from the materials basket. Hearing the rhythm of the text with the percussion instruments helps ELLs build fluency in the language and is a great way for them to physically participate in the reading. Finally, I keep a stock of extra pens and pencils so I can take note in my assessment binder of how my ELLs are using the language during instruction and how they're progressing with their literacy skills (see Chapter 2).

Pocket Chart for Language Development

Many primary-grade teachers have pockets charts in the classroom library where they develop vocabulary with the class or build a text with sentence strips. However, a pocket chart is a great resource to have in *any* grade with ELLs. I hang a pocket chart in the classroom library to display vocabulary or language structures my ELLs need to know for our literacy and content-area studies. In a basket next to the pocket chart I keep a supply of index cards, sentence strips, and markers so I can easily add new words or sentences to the pocket chart during instruction.

Stuffed Animals and Finger Puppets

In the classroom library I also have some physical objects close at hand to help my ELLs understand the texts we're reading. I keep a bin with a wide variety of small stuffed animals so that whenever we read a fiction or nonfiction text related to animals we can act out the different parts or demonstrate the information we're learning. I also collect stuffed animals and dolls of characters from books that I read to the class. Frog and Toad, Corduroy, and Ramona have been some of my ELLs' favorites, which they've used to retell the important parts of the story or to re-create the dialogue between the characters. Finger puppets also work well for this kind of activity. All of these hands-on resources are a great way for ELLs at different L2 proficiency levels to participate in the reading and to increase their comprehension of the text. It also helps beginning ELLs take more risks with the language because they're not the ones speaking; the stuffed animals or finger puppets are.

Literacy Charts

Whenever I create visual examples on the whiteboard during reading and writing mini-lessons, I later re-create them on chart paper so my ELLs can refer to the literacy concept, the language structures, and the vocabulary in the future. I try to make the charts as visual and as clear as possible so ELLs at any L2 proficiency level can understand the concept. For charts to be most effective, they should be based on the examples that

ELLs are familiar with from the minilessons. Debbie Miller (2002) has excellent examples of visually oriented reading comprehension charts that can easily be adapted to upper grades as well. Hanging or mounting your reading charts in the classroom library area will help your ELLs know exactly where to look to find everything related to reading. Instead of preparing charts before the first day of school, make them as you teach new strategies throughout the year so your ELLs are familiar with the concept and the language. As the year goes on, you'll replace earlier charts with new ones, but it helps to keep all the charts for reference. One way to do this is to staple the first charts to the bottom of a bulletin board and then staple others on top in a way that lets you and your ELLs flip through them.

Language Charts

There are certain premade language reference charts that you can have set up in the classroom library area by the first day of school. These include an alphabet chart, a vowel chart, and a blends and digraphs chart. While primary classrooms traditionally have these as instructional staples, upper-grade classrooms should also have them available as ELLs learn the letters and corresponding sounds of the new language. Bilingual classrooms will have these charts in both languages, but ESL and mainstream classrooms can also have bilingual alphabet and sound charts to help ELLs compare and contrast sounds and letters in the L1 and the L2. Explicitly drawing attention to the connections between languages helps ELLs transfer what they know from one language to another (García 2006; Cummins 1981). I like to refer to these language charts when I work with ELLs during shared reading and word study, as well as when we create texts during interactive writing and shared writing.

Leveled Books

Having books in your library that support ELLs in developing their L1 and L2 literacy skills is a critical aspect of setting up your classroom. When you begin organizing the books in your classroom library, you'll want to think about how to divide them into *leveled* and *nonleveled* book baskets. Figure 1–2 shows the library in my self-contained ESL classroom with a section of leveled book baskets in English, using the Fountas and Pinnell levels, and another section of nonleveled book baskets organized by topic and genre. There is also an area with baskets for bilingual books, picture books in Spanish, and a range of leveled chapter books in Spanish.

Many of the classroom library books should be leveled so ELLs can read texts that are appropriate for their current reading ability, also referred to as their independent reading level. Providing students with books at their independent reading level is an essential way to help them improve their reading ability (Calkins 2001; Fountas and Pinnell 2006). It ensures that they're reading texts that are neither too easy nor too challenging, which develops their decoding, comprehension, and fluency skills. Since each student reads books at her independent level, it's a key way to differentiate instruction for your ELLs' diverse literacy needs. These just-right books also build ELLs' vocabulary base in English and provide models of how the language is structured (Chen and Mora-Flores 2006). Many schools pass along students' reading levels from one grade to the next, which lets you know what levels you'll need to have available in your library. Chapter 2 details how you can determine your ELLs' current reading levels through assessments.

In a mainstream classroom with ESL students, you'll have leveled book baskets in English, but you can also provide baskets of picture books and chapter books in your

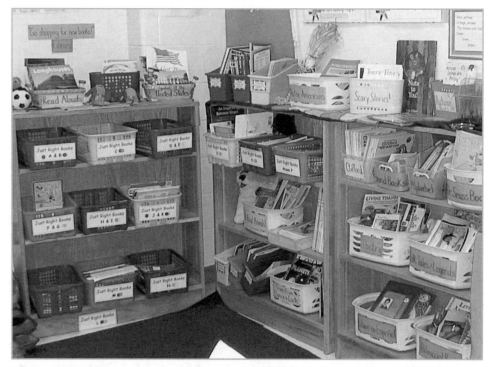

Figure 1–2 *Classroom library with leveled and nonleveled book baskets*

ELLs' native languages. Encouraging ELLs to read in their native language is important because it helps them continue to develop higher-level reading skills in the L1 while working on more basic reading skills in English. Studies show that the literacy skills ELLs develop in one language transfer to another, so any time invested in building literacy skills in the native language will increase ELLs' ability to read successfully in English (Goldenberg 2008; August, Carlo, and Calderón 2002; Thomas and Collier 1995). It also affirms for ELLs that their native language is an asset, not a detriment, and that it's valued in your classroom. In addition to the leveled books your ELLs read in English, set up a system where they can choose several books in the native language each week to read independently or with their family.

When setting up a leveled library in a bilingual or dual language classroom, separate the book baskets by language. One section of the library should have baskets of leveled books in the L1, and another section can have baskets of leveled books in the L2. That way, students can easily choose books in each language depending upon their reading level in the L1 and the L2. You can do the same for nonleveled book baskets. Many teachers color-code language in bilingual classrooms, using one color for the L1 and another for the L2. You can use this same color-coding system with the color of your book baskets as well to help students keep the two (or more) languages separate.

Building a Leveled Library

Gathering enough books that reflect the entire range of your ELLs' reading levels is a common problem, especially when first establishing a leveled classroom library. If you have beginning ELLs in your classroom, you'll need books in English starting at the earliest reading levels. While this doesn't pose a problem for kindergarten and first-grade teachers, most second- through sixth-grade teachers don't have books at those early levels. In a classroom with ELLs spanning all L2 proficiency levels, it's quite possible that you'll need books ranging from Level A all the way to the highest reading levels for your grade.

Once you know your ELLs' reading levels you can approach your administration about ordering independent reading books at the levels you need. This doesn't help in the short term, however, since getting funds and ordering books can be a lengthy process. In the meantime, one solution is to enlist the help of other teachers who have books at the levels your ELLs need. When I started teaching in a fourth- and fifth-grade self-contained ESL classroom, I had ELLs at every English proficiency level and spanning reading levels from A to P. Unfortunately, my new classroom didn't have any leveled books below Level H. Until I was able to get my own books for the missing levels, I paired up with several first-grade teachers. They agreed to let my group of ELLs who were reading at those earlier levels come to their rooms once a week to borrow just-right books. A few months into the year, the school was able to order the leveled books I needed for my classroom library.

Near the end of the school year, another issue surfaced as a number of my ELLs with an advanced English proficiency level approached grade level in reading. Although this was certainly a good issue to have, I found myself scrambling for books from Levels Q to T. This time around I coordinated with several upper-grade teachers, who let these ELLs borrow books from their leveled libraries on a weekly basis.

Another way to expand your leveled library is to print off leveled books from a website such as Reading A–Z (www.readinga-z.com/). With a subscription you get access to hundreds of illustrated fiction and nonfiction texts at every reading level that you can print out and staple together to make your own books. These leveled books are available in English, Spanish, and French. Another website to try is Scholastic Mini-Books (minibooks.scholastic.com/minibooks/home/), which has fiction and nonfiction leveled books in English that you can print with a subscription. This website has some leveled books in Spanish as well. While printing leveled books from websites certainly doesn't replace having real books in your library, it can be a way to quickly get your ELLs reading books that match their reading abilities. And, with the wide variety of topics that the books touch upon, you can easily find books that coordinate with different content-area units of study. Another benefit to using these books is that you can print off multiple copies and use them for instruction with guided reading groups.

Assembling books you print from websites can be time-consuming if you're relying on them to make up a substantial part of your classroom library. To get around this, I occasionally invite small groups of ELLs to have lunch with me in the classroom, and after eating we spend the rest of the time cutting the pages, putting them in order, and stapling them into books. You can also ask ELLs' families to help assemble the books at home, which is a wonderful way for them to get involved in an important part of their children's learning. Families don't have to speak the L2 to put together the books, and they know they're making a significant contribution to the classroom.

Organizing Leveled Books

Although there are different systems for leveling books, one that's widely used in classrooms across the United States is Guided Reading (Fountas and Pinnell 2006, 1999). Each grade has certain corresponding alphabetic reading levels, ranging from A to Z:

Kindergarten: A–C

First grade: D–I

Second grade: H–M

Third grade: L–P

Fourth grade: O–T

Fifth grade: S–W

Sixth grade: V–Y

Seventh and eighth grades: X–Z

If you're just beginning to level your library, use the resources in Figure 1–3 to find out the levels of certain common books. Many of these resources also indicate the correlation between A–Z levels and other leveling systems such as Reading Recovery and Developmental Reading Assessment (DRA).

In order to level books with any system, you need to have a strong understanding of exactly what distinguishes one reading level from the next. Knowing the characteristics a text has at each level lets you know what you'll need to teach students to help them improve as readers (Calkins and the Teachers College Reading and Writing Project 2002; Fountas and Pinnell 2006, 1999). Some characteristics of text include the amount of text per page, the complexity of the language and vocabulary, the use of repetitive patterns, and the amount of picture support. These all affect the difficulty level of a text.

One way to begin leveling a library is to start with some baseline books that are typical of a particular level that you can use to compare with other books. For example, knowing that *Rain* (Kalan and Crews 1991) is a Level C book or that *The Carrot Seed* (Krauss and Johnson 1945) is a Level G book, you can compare it with other books in your classroom and temporarily group together the ones that are similar. Likewise, knowing that Suzy Kline's Horrible Harry books are at Level L or that most Beverly Clearly books are at Level O lets you determine what other books are at a similar level of difficulty and group them together for the time being. As the school year progresses, level your books more accurately to provide ELLs with books that are the best match for their reading abilities. In Figure 1–3 I provide a list of books and websites that can help you level the books in your classroom library.

While there are many resources for leveling books in English, there is less available on leveling books in other languages. Many books in English are translated into other languages, particularly Spanish, but that doesn't necessarily mean they have the same reading level. For example, the Spanish translation may use a higher level of language complexity than the English version, making it more challenging to read. Or a translation may include less picture support or more text per page, which also alters the difficulty level. As a starting point, you can level a book according to its English counterpart, but be prepared to adjust the levels as you become more familiar with difficulties your students encounter with the books in the other language.

Most importantly, keep in mind that leveling a classroom library is a process. This could easily take up all your time before the school year begins, so as you sort and level books, know that you'll continue this organization as the year gets under way. Calkins (2001) recommends that if you level just 30 percent of your library, there will be enough books for students to get started with during independent reading.

Nonleveled Books

Other books in the library are nonleveled, giving ELLs the opportunity to read texts that are of interest to them, even if they're not precisely at their reading level (Cappellini 2005). This includes nonfiction books organized by topic, books relating to content-area units of study, seasonal books, books in particular genres such as poetry, folktales, biographies,

Books

Calkins, Lucy. 2002. *A Field Guide to the Classroom Library A–G*. 7 vols. Portsmouth, NH: Heinemann.

Fountas, Irene C., and Gay Su Pinnell. 2006. *Leveled Books K–8: Matching Texts to Readers for Effective Teaching*. Portsmouth, NH: Heinemann.

————. 2009. *The Fountas and Pinnell Leveled Book List, K–8+: 2009–2011 Edition*. Portsmouth, NH: Heinemann.

Websites

- Fountas and Pinnell Leveled Books K–8 (www.fountasandpinnellleveledbooks .com/):
  With a subscription, you'll have access to thousands of leveled books and other reading resources, including the levels of recently published books.

- Teacher Book Wizard (bookwizard.scholastic.com/):
  Search the company's book selection to find levels of English, Spanish, or bilingual books.

- Leveled and Guided Reading (rigby.harcourtachieve.com/en-US/lgr?=rigby):
  Search the company's book selection to find the Fountas and Pinnell levels of books in English and Spanish, as well as DRA and Reading Recovery levels.

- Beaverton School District Leveled Books Database (registration.beavton.k12.or .us/lbdb/):
  This is a free resource from a school district where you can search for reading levels of books in English or Spanish.

- Leveled Books Database (books.atozteacherstuff.com/leveled-books/):
  With this free resource you can search for thousands of A–Z leveled books (referred to also as Guided Reading levels) as well as Reading Recovery and Accelerated Reading levels.

Figure 1–3 *Resources for leveling books*

mysteries, and historical fiction, and books that examine the language such as alphabet books, sound books, or high-frequency word books (Miller 2002; Taberski 2000).

Encouraging ELLs to read nonleveled books is an important way to maintain their engagement in reading (Cappellini 2005). And tackling a high-interest, yet more challenging text can help ELLs stretch their reading skills. For example, when Joaquin started third grade with me, he was a Level 2 ELL reading at approximately Level E in English. Joaquin was fanatical about animals, and in particular he was an expert on sharks. Even though the nonfiction shark books I had in the library were higher than Level E, Joaquin was able to read and understand quite a lot of the text because he had such strong background knowledge on the topic. Reading a combination of Level E books and non-leveled books of interest helped Joaquin progress to increasingly higher reading levels throughout the year and at the same time stay excited about what he was reading.

The nonleveled book baskets you create in the classroom library will depend entirely upon the books you have available to you. As you're organizing books by level, be on the lookout for books that could be used in different nonleveled baskets. Whenever possible, add a multicultural focus to your book baskets so they represent the experiences and backgrounds of your ELLs. For example, if you have a book basket on families, try to include books that show how families from different cultures live. If you have a genre basket for poetry, look for collections written by authors from different cultural backgrounds. This gives all students a broader worldview and also shows your ELLs that their experiences are an important part of learning in the classroom (Kottler, Kottler, and Street 2008). Figure 1–4 gives examples of the types of nonleveled book baskets you could create for your classroom library, including ways to make them multicultural.

Nonfiction Social Studies Baskets

- families (representative of different cultures)
- communities (neighborhood, city, state, around the world)
- countries (one basket per country)
- regions of the world (South America, the Caribbean, the Middle East, Asia, etc.)
- jobs/professions
- geography (maps, landforms, atlases, etc.)
- U.S. history (Colonies, American Revolution, immigration, westward expansion, etc.)
- indigenous groups (from regions in the United States and around the world)
- explorers (to the United States and other parts of the world)
- sports and players (from around the world)

Nonfiction Science Baskets

- life cycles
- plants
- ecosystems (desert, rain forest, ocean, plains, etc.)
- animals (if possible, make more specific baskets like jungle animals, ocean creatures, etc.)
- insects (if possible, make more specific baskets like butterflies, flying insects, creepy crawlies, etc.)
- dinosaurs
- human body
- magnets
- simple machines
- solar system and Earth
- experiments/how-to books

Seasonal Baskets

These can be a combination of fiction and nonfiction books.

- holidays and celebrations (in the United States and other countries)
- fall, winter, spring, summer

Read-Aloud Books

This basket contains books you've previously read-aloud to the class. These books can also be recorded on tape for ELLs to listen to and read in the listening center.

Other Genre Baskets

Choose books for these baskets that represent a range of cultures whenever possible.

- poetry
- folktales/legends/fairy tales
- biographies
- mysteries
- historical fiction
- nursery rhymes

Concept Books

These are common in early primary grades but also helpful for beginning ELLs in any grade to acquire basic vocabulary in the L2.

- alphabet/sound books
- shape books
- color books
- opposite books
- number books

Author Baskets

Try to include collections of books from authors who write about different cultural perspectives.

- Arthur Dorros
- Allen Say
- Alma Flor Ada
- Tomie dePaola
- Gary Soto
- Eve Bunting

Bilingual Books and Native Language Books

If you teach in a mainstream classroom with ESL students, you can create baskets of picture books and chapter books in students' native languages (Freeman and Freeman 2007; Herrell 2000). Development of native language literacy skills improves your ELLs' reading skills in English (Goldenberg 2008).

Figure 1–4 *Examples of nonleveled book baskets for ELLs*

Choosing Books

It's important to develop a system where students can "go shopping" for books, or choose new books to read from the library on a regular basis. Many teachers like to have students store these books in a sturdy plastic book bag to keep them organized. From a management perspective, scheduling this book exchange once a week can be an easy solution. It could be that each group of students has a specific day when they choose new books, or all students could do it on the same day, such as Friday.

The number of books ELLs need to borrow each week depends entirely on their reading level. ELLs reading at a lower level, whether they're in primary or upper grades, are reading shorter books and therefore need a much higher quantity to be able to sustain independent reading throughout the week. On the other hand, ELLs reading at a higher level may need only one or two leveled chapter books to sustain their independent reading for the week. Since the amount of books will be different for every ELL, when you initially assess their reading levels you can let them know what leveled book basket they should take their books from and how many they should take each week. Students in bilingual programs typically have this quantity of leveled books split between the two languages they're reading in, whereas students in ESL programs will have most of their books in English with perhaps some books in the native language to continue progressing as readers in their L1. While the majority of books ELLs choose are from the leveled book baskets, they should also choose several books they're interested in from the nonleveled baskets.

Organizing Collaborative Work Areas

English language learners in both primary and upper grades benefit greatly from working with other students collaboratively (Hill and Flynn 2006; Freeman and Freeman 2001; Faltis and Hudelson 1998; García 1991). Working collaboratively provides ELLs with more models of the L2 because more language is directed at them as they work with their partner or group, and they also have more opportunities to practice the language because there is more interaction (Gibbons 2002). Since the language ELLs hear in collaborative situations is contextualized around a particular learning activity, it's also more meaningful for them, helping them develop their understanding of how the language works.

Collaborative Group Arrangements

Collaborative interaction can be facilitated when ELLs are seated in small groups (Freeman and Freeman 2001; Hill and Flynn 2006). Groups of four work very well because each student has a partner seated next to him. When groups are larger than four, some students will have classmates seated on both sides, which can be distracting. It's also more intimidating for ELLs to share ideas collaboratively when they are in large numbers. However, because of space issues, sometimes there is no choice but to make larger groups with six students.

When you get your ELLs' cumulative records, look through them to find out what level of language proficiency each student tested at in English. TESOL identifies the following levels of English proficiency: Level 1: *starting*, Level 2: *emerging*, Level 3: *developing*, Level 4: *expanding*, and Level 5: *bridging* (Gottlieb et al. 2006). See Chapter 2 for a more detailed description of how to determine an ELL's proficiency level. With this data, you can begin strategically grouping ELLs together. The goal is to create completely heterogeneous groupings of ELLs so that every student has someone in the group who can act as a linguistic support. Mixing ELLs with proficiencies from Levels 1 to 5 ensures that group members will be able to work collaboratively and maximize their learning. If you have any newcomers, seat them next to another student who speaks the same L1, if possible (Freeman and Freeman 2007; Gibbons 1991). Figure 1–5 shows some possible groupings of ELLs based on their L2 proficiency levels.

In each example in Figure 1–5 I have tried to ensure that ELLs are seated next to and across from someone with a slightly different L2 proficiency level (Chen and Mora-Flores 2006). Whenever possible, I don't seat a Level 1 ELL next to or across from another Level 1 ELL. This unsupportive arrangement would create unnecessary confusion as both newcomers attempted to understand the new language and content. I also try to avoid seating Level 1 ELLs next to Level 5 ELLs. There's such a vast difference between their proficiency levels that it can easily become frustrating for the more linguistically proficient ELL to constantly support the newcomer. Whereas Level 5 ELLs have little to gain, linguistically speaking, from being partnered with Level 1 ELLs, a Level 3 ELL can put her growing command of English to use in helping a newcomer learn the language. If there are several Level 1 ELLs in a group, I try to seat them on opposite sides of the group so they each have a different partner. Another consideration is that ELLs should never have newcomers seated on both sides of them. This arrangement limits how much they can help each newcomer, and most importantly they need to have another student nearby with a higher English proficiency level who will challenge and expand their own language use. So, if I seat a Level 1 ELL on one side of a Level 3 ELL, then I try to seat a Level 4 or 5 ELL on the other side.

Since dual language programs have students who are English language learners as well as native English-speaking students who are learning the second language, you'll need to mix these two language groups in your seating arrangements. The goal is to not only mix language proficiency levels but also mix native language speakers. For example, you would try to avoid pairing up a Level 1 English language learner with a Level 1 Spanish language learner because they wouldn't be able to support each other linguistically. However, a Level 1 ELL could be seated next to a Level 3 Spanish language learner, who could be next to a Level 5 ELL.

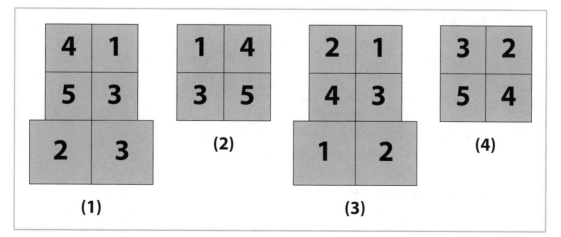

Figure 1–5 *Grouping ELLs based on L2 proficiency level*

Taking the time to purposefully place ELLs in collaborative groups will pay off later because they'll have the linguistic support they need to learn in the classroom. Create mock versions of your desk arrangements on paper and play around with combinations of ELLs until you strike a balance between their linguistic needs and, as you get to know them during the school year, their academic and behavioral needs.

Keep in mind that these heterogeneous groupings are designed for collaborative activities that ELLs engage in during different subject areas. However, there are also times when you'll create homogenous groupings for a particular purpose (Hill and Flynn 2006; Cappellini 2005), such as for guided reading groups, small interactive writing groups, and reading partners.

It's common for new ELLs to arrive during the first weeks of school, particularly at schools with a high population of immigrant students. Having several extra desks or table spots available at the beginning of the year is highly advisable. This (along with extra sets of class textbooks, materials, and forms to be sent home) makes the newcomers' transition into the classroom much smoother—for them as well as for you.

Collaborative Work Tables

Having one or more work tables in the classroom allows you to

- meet with guided reading groups
- work with a small group of ELLs who need extra help in a particular area
- have ELLs work together on a project
- have a push-in teacher work with a small group of ELLs
- meet with ELLs for reading or writing conferences

You can maximize the classroom space even further by using one of the work tables as your desk. A work table can be a perfect place to prepare lessons and do paperwork, and it eliminates the need for a bulky teacher's desk. However, to make this system work, set up an off-limits area near the work table where you can store all the supplies you'll need for lesson planning and completing paperwork. It's also helpful to have a file cabinet and personal cubbyholes nearby to store paperwork.

Making Effective Centers

With the classroom library, groups of desks, and work tables placed in the classroom, you can think about where to set up centers for different subject areas. Centers are areas of the room where ELLs can find everything they need to help them understand the language and content of a particular subject area, including interactive word walls to practice key vocabulary and class charts to refer to what they've learned in the subject area. ELLs rely on these visual aids to understand the content they're learning (Rea and Mercuri 2006; Freeman and Freeman 2007). They also depend on consistency to know where to find information related to a particular subject.

When looking for a space to put each center, think vertically. The center can include floor space for storing materials in a bookshelf or other piece of furniture, wall space for mounting a word wall or charts, and air space for hanging charts on a clothesline. Some centers, such as the listening center, may also have an area where ELLs can gather to work together.

Math Center

Interactive Math Word Wall

An interactive math word wall is one way for ELLs to practice the academic vocabulary they need to be successful in math. While there are a number of ways to set up and use a word wall, the interactive version I describe helps ELLs manipulate the words and develop a stronger comprehension of the language. The math word wall is created little by little as your ELLs learn new vocabulary in each math lesson.

1. Identify the math content words ELLs will be encountering in a particular unit of study.

2. Create two flash cards for each word: one with the math word written on it, which can be written bilingually in English and the students' L1, and another card with a picture or example representing that word.

3. After ELLs have encountered the words through the context of a math lesson, explicitly teach the words (as described in Chapter 5). Place the word and picture cards next to each other in a pocket chart.

4. On a regular basis throughout the rest of the math unit, have students interactively practice the math words and their meaning.

5. Refer to the word cards whenever using those vocabulary words in math lessons to help ELLs connect the spoken word with the written word and mathematical concept.

Repetition of practice helps ELLs internalize the content-area vocabulary. It's helpful for ELLs to be able to manipulate the word and picture cards through a variety of vocabulary activities, so I suggest using a pocket chart for your math word wall. Figure 1–6 on page 16 shows an example of my interactive math word wall during a unit on multiplication and division. I added the word and picture cards little by little as we learned the new vocabulary words in the context of the math lessons.

Math Charts

Math charts should summarize in a very visual way the key math concepts ELLs have already learned. You won't have any charts in the math center when the school year starts, but as you begin teaching different math concepts during the first weeks of school, the space will begin to fill up. Keep in mind that the charts should

- be focused on *one* concept ELLs have already learned
- provide several clear, visual examples of the concept
- if applicable, clearly outline the steps involved in solving a problem
- be mainly visual with a few key words or sentences summarizing the concept
- be referred to in future lessons to help connect the oral language with the written language and the concept

For example, I made a series of math charts during a unit on geometry. One chart was based on a picture-sorting activity my ELLs did with their collaborative groups. They first determined which shapes were polygons and which were not polygons, explaining the rules for what makes a polygon. Then they sorted the polygons into two categories: convex and concave. On the chart I put the definition of a polygon at the top and then drew how the class had sorted the shapes into the three categories. Another chart was a visual reminder of the difference between line segments, lines, and rays, with pictures of each on the left and definitions the class had developed on the right. I also included examples of how to name and label line segments, lines, and rays. A third chart used the universal symbol for *no* (a red circle with a diagonal line through it) to show which shapes are parallelograms and which ones are not. I also color-coded the parallel sides of the parallelograms to help ELLs identify this defining characteristic. Whenever we discussed these geometry concepts in later lessons, I consistently pointed to the charts to remind my ELLs of the language and the math concepts.

Wipe-Off Math Charts

One of the best materials I've found for math lessons with ELLs is a wipe-off math chart. You can see two of these charts in Figure 1–7: "What's My Rule?" and "Place-Value Chart." Each wipe-off chart I use targets a different math skill or concept, and you can create endless examples and opportunities for practice with ELLs, such as the list of examples my ELLs and I put on the place-value chart. This repetition of practice with place value helped my ELLs develop a fuller understanding of the math concept and learn the mathematical language involved in expressing large numbers in English. The visual support in these charts is also an excellent scaffold for ELLs. These wipe-off charts are available from the Everyday Mathematics program.

Math Routines

Many teachers, particularly in the primary grades, begin the day with a morning meeting that includes different math routines. Upper-grade teachers can also incorporate math routines, either as whole-class activities or as class jobs for different ELLs to complete each day. The benefit of using math routines is that the repetition of practice builds academic language skills as well as math concepts for ELLs. Figure 1–10 at the

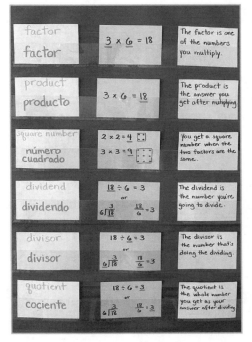

Figure 1–6 *Interactive bilingual math word wall*

Figure 1–7 *Wipe-off math charts and math routines*

end of the chapter shows how I set up a number of math routines on the bulletin board in my math center. Math routines can include, but are certainly not limited to, the following:

- Calendar activities: These can be used in a number of different mathematical ways in the primary and upper grades to help ELLs visually develop the concepts of counting, grouping, even and odd, patterns, finding factors of numbers, periods of time, or as a basis for number stories. I use a calendar where the days for each month have a different pattern for students to identify such as ABAB, AABB, or AABBCC, which is a skill they need to demonstrate on state testing (see Figure 1–10 at the end of this chapter).

- Number chart (to one hundred): This reinforces concepts of number, such as counting by ones, twos, fives, and tens. It's helpful for ELLs to practice different ways of counting in the L2 to learn the names of numbers and to make their recollection more automatic. This language development improves their comprehension during math lessons and their ability to orally participate in math activities. You can have a partner practice this counting with a beginning ELL on a daily basis during transition times.

- Clock activities: These reinforce the language connected with concepts of time. Have ELLs match the time written out in words with different clock faces or practice saying the time aloud. Phrases like *o'clock*, *half past*, *quarter past*, and *quarter to* are linguistically complex.

- "Days of the Week" chart: ELLs can label the days of the week with the sentence starters *Yesterday was*, *Today is*, and *Tomorrow will be* and practice saying the complete sentences.

- Tally chart: Students add to a tally chart daily, possibly to record data for the type of weather (*cloudy*, *sunny*, *rainy*). This builds weather-related vocabulary for ELLs and the math concept of how to create a tally chart.

- Bar graph: Students add to a bar graph daily, possibly to record data regarding students' daily attendance. You can also label the parts of a bar graph to help ELLs learn the language of what to include when making this type of graph (x-*axis*, y-*axis*, *title*, *labels*, *scale*).

- Line graph: Students add to a line graph daily, possibly to record data for the high temperatures predicted for the day. As with bar graphs, ELLs benefit from written labels of the parts of a line graph.

Group Baskets of Commonly Used Math Manipulatives

Using manipulatives is critical to help ELLs visualize math concepts (Coggins et al. 2007). However, it can be very time-consuming to organize these materials for each lesson. One way to avoid this is to create baskets of commonly used manipulatives for each group of students to use. This system works very well for managing the manipulatives you have students use frequently, such as pattern blocks, counting cubes, coins, base ten blocks, measuring tapes, rulers, and decks of cards. You can organize different types of manipulatives in zip-top bags inside the baskets. While not necessary for the beginning of the school year, having these group baskets of manipulatives cuts down significantly on prep time.

Overhead Transparency Manipulatives

Another resource that supports ELLs during math lessons is an overhead transparency version of the manipulatives. For example, during a unit on fractions I use transparent base ten blocks with an overhead projector to visually model the concept of fractions to the tenths and hundredths places. Then I have my ELLs practice the concept using the base ten blocks in their group baskets.

Writing Center

Writing Supplies

The writing center is a place to store supplies students need during the writing process, such as paper choices, extra pencils, pens for editing, staplers, pencil sharpeners, and materials for publishing writing like construction paper, markers, and colored pencils. Have the basics, like extra pencils, pens, and pencil sharpeners, ready by the first day, because some ELLs, especially newcomers, may not come with the necessary school supplies.

Paper Choices

English language learners benefit from having different types of paper to use during the writing workshop, depending on their proficiency in the target language (Calkins et al. 2006; Chen and Mora-Flores 2006). While this is a common practice in the primary grades, where students are just beginning to develop as writers, most upper-grade classrooms strictly use lined paper. Having choices available in every grade, and modeling for ELLs how they can use each type of paper, will help transition them into the challenging task of writing in a second language. These paper choices should be photocopied and available in the writing center by the first week of school so that all ELLs can be productive during independent writing time.

- Paper with a large picture box and a few lines: Allows Levels 1 and 2 ELLs in primary and upper grades to focus on drawing a picture related to the type of writing the class is doing, placing less emphasis on the unrealistic expectation of creating an extended amount of writing in the L2. You can show these ELLs how to use a picture dictionary to label parts of their drawing in the L2, if it's age appropriate.

- Paper with a small picture box and many lines: Appropriate for Levels 1 and 2 ELLs who already have a literacy base in their native language. You can have them write in the L1 and draw a picture that shows what the writing is about. You can again show these ELLs how to label their drawing in the L2 using a picture dictionary, if it's age appropriate. This type of paper is also appropriate for Levels 3 and 4 ELLs who still benefit from combining written language with a visual.

- Lined paper: Appropriate for ELLs with developed literacy skills in their native language. They can use the lined paper to write in the L1 in bilingual or mainstream classrooms. Lined paper can also be used with Levels 3, 4, and 5 ELLs for writing in the L2.

- Story sequencing paper: This graphic organizer can help ELLs plan how their story will go from beginning, to middle, to end. Depending on the grade level, it could have anywhere from three to six picture boxes, possibly with a few lines under each box. Any student, proficient English speaker, or English language learner, can benefit from using this graphic organizer. However, it particularly gives support to ELLs because it allows them to visually represent their story idea.

Bilingual Picture Dictionaries

Beginning ELLs benefit enormously from having picture dictionaries available in the writing center to use as a resource during the writing workshop. The thematic organization of the picture dictionaries can help ELLs add vocabulary into their beginning writing in the L2, greatly increasing the quantity of writing they are able to independently produce. The picture dictionaries are also a lifesaver for helping beginning ELLs stay focused on their writing for extended periods of time, once they know how to use them to label their writing with words from the L2 or use the words to fill in basic form sentences.

For example, when my class was writing narratives, one of my newcomers, Brando, drew a picture of himself seated on an airplane that was landing in New York. He had drawn all the new things he had seen when he had arrived. I wrote the basic form sentence, "I see _____," and I modeled how he could use words from the picture dictionary to complete the sentence. His eyes lit up, and he wrote an entire list of the completed form sentences that related to the things he had drawn, along with a little illustration next to each one to remember what the English vocabulary word meant in Spanish. After doing this writing in English, Brando wrote a detailed narrative in Spanish about the same topic of moving to New York.

Picture dictionaries are most effective if they're bilingual in English and the student's native language. Figure 1–8 shows Diana, a newcomer from Colombia, using a Spanish-English bilingual picture dictionary to add English words to her writing. This helped Diana work productively during independent writing and begin expanding her vocabulary base in English. One source you can try is the Oxford Picture Dictionaries for Kids. In addition to their monolingual English version, they have Spanish-English and Japanese-English bilingual versions for primary and intermediate grades.

High-Frequency Word Wall

The high-frequency word wall is a common element in primary-grade classrooms (Tompkins 1997), but many upper-grade teachers bypass a high-frequency word wall

Figure 1–8 *Diana uses a bilingual picture dictionary during independent writing*

since they feel students have already learned those words in the primary grades. Keep in mind that upper-grade ELLs have probably not learned all the necessary high-frequency words in the L2, and many English-proficient students in the upper grades also struggle with some of these words.

Primary-grade teachers often follow a set curriculum that dictates which high-frequency words they introduce each week. In the upper grades, the word wall can serve as a place to review whatever high-frequency words you observe your students misspelling during writing activities. You can start adding high-frequency words to the word wall during the first week of school, so have the space prepared with an area for each letter of the alphabet. This space could be on a wall, a bulletin board, or even chart paper hanging from a clothesline.

In addition to the word wall, you can also set up personal word lists for individual ELLs. This can be a two-page alphabetical reference where ELLs write down the high-frequency words you teach them through different literacy activities. In Brando's case, after learning and practicing the high-frequency words *I* and *see*, he added them to his personal word list as a reference for how to spell those words when independently writing in the future. He also added the basic sentence he used in his writing to remember how the high-frequency words could be combined together.

Writing and Language Charts

As you teach ELLs the routines of the writing workshop and different strategies for writing, you'll begin making charts they can refer to. Many of these charts will show models for writing certain kinds of text. These could be examples of writing you model during writing minilessons, shared writing pieces you create with the class, or interactive writing texts you create with the class. As with all the charts in your room, they should be made as you teach the concepts and skills so your ELLs understand the writing and can refer to them independently. Reserve a space for hanging these charts near the other writing resources.

Figure 1–9 shows some of the writing charts I hung as a reference for our unit on writing personal narratives (Calkins et al. 2006). The chart in the middle illustrates how to use a story sequencer to plan the rising action and resolution in a narrative. On the left is a model for how to take the story sequencer and turn it into a narrative. On the right is a writing chart that gives visual examples of how to add detail to a narrative through dialogue, emotions, thoughts, and sensory images.

You'll also be making charts that highlight important things the class has learned about how the language works. For example, below the hanging charts in Figure 1–9 is a pocket chart where the students brainstormed other words they could use in their narratives instead of *went* and *said*. Another language objective we had during this unit of study was to learn how to change regular and irregular verbs from the present tense to the past tense. We posted an ongoing language chart where ELLs added examples of past tense verbs from their narratives, as well as from the books they were reading.

Listening Center

A listening center is most common in primary-grade classrooms, but it's a wonderful resource for ELLs of any age. Listening to texts repeatedly can help students build fluency in reading (Rasinski 2003) and it helps ELLs connect the sounds of the new language with the print on the page (Fu 2003). This is particularly important for beginning ELLs so they can develop literacy skills in the L2 and sustain independent reading.

Figure 1–9 *Charts that model writing for ELLs*

Listening to these recorded texts also develops your ELLs' ear for the language, which supports their listening and speaking skills.

Tape Players

I invested in purchasing individual tape players for each of my Level 1 and Level 2 ELLs to use. That way they could take advantage of listening to recorded texts at a level appropriate for their L2 proficiency. I store each individual tape player in a separate bag in the Listening Center. At the beginning of independent reading time, my Levels 1 and 2 ELLs take their listening bag, which has the tape player they've been using and their books on tape inside. I make sure their books on tape are at early reading levels so they can more easily follow along with the text as they listen. I model for my ELLs how to listen to a text multiple times, how to quietly read along with parts of the text, and how to practice reading the text on their own (Fu 2003). I also teach them how to choose new books on tape each week from the leveled bins in the listening center. Listening to texts on tape is beneficial for Levels 3–5 ELLs as well. They can listen to a text that is slightly more difficult than their independent reading level to build reading fluency, word recognition, and comprehension skills.

I have found individual tape players to be a worthwhile purchase if your school doesn't have any because they allow each beginning ELL to listen to appropriate texts on a daily basis. If you have a large tape player with hookups for multiple students, which is typical in many schools, make sure you set up a system where beginning ELLs can use it frequently. In this case, the listening center should be located in an area where a small group of students can sit around the player.

Recorded Texts

For a listening center to be effective, you need to have a supply of recorded texts at a range of reading levels. Buying tape-and-book sets can be expensive, and recording your own texts can be very time-consuming. Try enlisting the help of your family members and friends to record books on tape. Having a variety of voices and accents can help your ELLs hone their listening comprehension skills. It's worth the time to offer your volunteers a brief training session, reminding them to read naturally but not too quickly, so your ELLs can follow along. Also have them give a recognizable signal for turning the page. Another time-saver is to record a text during literacy activities. For example, as you read aloud a book to the class, record it on tape, and later add that read-aloud book and tape to the listening center. You can do the same with a shared reading text you present to the whole class, or a shared reading text you work on with a small group of ELLs. Since your ELLs will have heard and practiced the text with you, they'll be able to use the tape to continue improving their ability to read that text.

Listening to recorded texts can also be very effective with ELLs who have limited formal education. One year I had a Level 2 ELL in my fifth-grade class who had sporadically attended school in the Dominican Republic and had limited reading and writing skills in Spanish. Since he faced the enormous challenge of learning English as well as learning *how* to read and write, he often felt frustrated and discouraged. I began recording texts for him based on what we had read together in class, and I let him take home the tape player every night to practice his reading at home. The following week when I took my class outside for dismissal, I saw his grandmother waiting for us. She came up to me and said that for the first time she saw her grandson excited about reading. She said that every evening while she was making dinner he would play the tape over and over again, practicing the sentences along with my voice and trying to read the books on his own. You never know what will connect with different students, but this interactive support can be engaging for even the most struggling readers.

Computer Programs

Most schools hold on to older technology, which is why I suggest the use of tape players in a listening center. However, there are also websites where ELLs can listen to texts and read along at the same time on the computer. One example is Raz-Kids (www.raz-kids.com/), which with a subscription gives students access to listen to and read books in English at every reading level. The audio recordings highlight words or phrases so ELLs can follow along as they listen, and they include different voices and sounds to make the books come to life.

Science and Social Studies Centers

Interactive Science and Social Studies Word Walls

These two word walls contain the specific content-area vocabulary that ELLs need to understand science and social studies concepts (Rea and Mercuri 2006; Freeman and Freeman 2007). I like to make the word wall interactive, as I described in the section on the math word wall. That way ELLs can match the vocabulary words with a corresponding image and then use those words for the different vocabulary activities I describe in Chapter 5. The images can be photographs, drawings, illustrations, or realia that you display next to the words (Calderón and Minaya-Rowe 2003). You'll start adding words during the first weeks of school as you begin your content-area units of study, so have a space set aside for each word wall. In addition to the word wall, you may also label bulletin board displays or reference charts with key vocabulary words. For example, on a world map I label the names of the continents and other geographical terms we're learning.

Science and Social Studies Charts

During integrated units of study, it's helpful to make charts that illustrate the key concepts or the relationships between concepts (Hill and Flynn 2006). ELLs can use graphic organizers during a learning activity to collaboratively summarize the key concepts and language they've learned, and then you can display them in the classroom on chart paper (Calderón and Minaya-Rowe 2003; Rea and Mercuri 2006). These graphic organizers could include webs, T-charts, and Venn diagrams. Appendix G gives examples of how to use these graphic organizers with ELLs in the content areas. I also like to create a time line that wraps around the walls of the classroom. When we learn something new about U.S. or world history, we use interactive writing to create a summary of the event and then add it to the time line, along with images my ELLs find or create. For example, during a unit on colonial life my ELLs helped me write the sentence, "1607: The English settled their first (1st) colony at Jamestown," and they included an image of Jamestown they found on the Internet. This helps ELLs put events into historical perspective and is a visual reference throughout the year when we learn about other parts of history. It's also a way to record important current events.

Science and Social Studies Resources

Science and social studies textbooks are one type of resource that supports learning throughout the year. You'll also want to collect other resources to use during your integrated units of study. For example, there are many nonfiction and fiction trade books that center around social studies and science topics. There are also poems, big books, and periodicals such as *National Geographic Explorer!*, *Scholastic News*, *Weekly Reader*, *Time for Kids*, and *Your Big Backyard*. *National Geographic Explorer!* translates some articles into Spanish on its website, which you can print out, and *Scholastic News* has a Spanish edition of its K–3 magazines. Chapter 4 explains how to use these resources throughout the instructional day in an integrated unit of study.

Computer Center

The computer center is traditionally made up of several desktop computers that students can access to support different areas of learning. Technology is of course constantly advancing, and many schools are replacing desktop computers with laptops and wireless Internet, which gives you more flexibility for where you can store and use the computers.

When you set up your computer center, think about what computer programs and websites will be most supportive of your ELLs' language development, literacy development, and content-area learning. English language learners benefit from using programs and websites that provide visual support, audio support, clear content, and bilingual materials. Supportive websites and computer programs also engage ELLs in activities that allow for repetition and reinforcement in developing skills and comprehension (Kottler, Kottler, and Street 2008). Following are a few examples:

- Kidspiration and Inspiration: These two computer programs help ELLs visually express their ideas and learning through graphic organizers and images.

- The International Children's Digital Library (en.childrenslibrary.org/): This website has over twenty-five hundred books in forty-eight languages that have been digitally scanned so ELLs can read them on the computer.

- Starfall.com (www.starfall.com/): On this website, ELLs can interactively learn the English alphabet, letter sounds, and phonics skills, and develop beginning reading skills, all with excellent audio support.

- National Geographic Kids (kids.nationalgeographic.com/): This website has a large collection of short videos related to science and social studies topics. If you connect your computer to an LCD projector, the whole class can watch a video together to support content-area learning.
- World Book (www.worldbookonline.com/): With a subscription, this highly visual encyclopedia provides resources for children in English, Spanish, and French.

Labeling the Classroom

When your classroom is set up, think about what things within the room should be labeled for ELLs. Labeling key areas, supplies, and objects helps beginning ELLs understand the basic vocabulary they'll be hearing you and the other students refer to in the classroom. Along with the label you can include a sentence that shows how the label can be used in context. Refer to the labels and sample sentences when talking to beginning ELLs, and later you can use those sample sentences as language models for them to practice producing the L2.

Figure 1–10 shows how I labeled areas and objects in one part of the classroom with orange sentence strips and how I put model sentences on blue sentence strips. In a bilingual classroom, labels and sentences should be in both languages, and in an ESL or mainstream classroom, you can consider labeling in multiple languages (Freeman and Freeman 2007). If you do this, make sure that all the languages spoken in the classroom are included.

Figure 1–10 *Classroom labels and model sentences for ELLs*

Final Thoughts

The photos in this chapter reflect the changes I've made over the years to the way I set up the learning environment, after I realized the important role the physical classroom could play in supporting my ELLs' linguistic and academic growth. When I think back to how I first set up my classroom as a new teacher, I realize how all of these little changes I've made have improved my ELLs' ability to learn both language and the grade-level content. I think my ELLs from that first year of teaching would have experienced greater success if I had thought about designing my classroom as a place where they could learn language and content, regardless of their L2 proficiency level. Since your classroom is a place for a unique group of students to learn, it's helpful to know a little about your ELLs' language proficiency levels and academic background before the school year begins so you can set up your room with those particular needs in mind. The next chapter explains how to find out this important information about your ELLs.

Reflecting on the Keys to Success

Raise the Bar

- Is my classroom designed to be a place where ELLs can learn the grade-level curriculum?

- Do I have the resources I need to teach the grade-level curriculum? If not, have I made a plan for how to get those resources?

Teach Language and Content Together

- Do I have interactive word walls in place that visually teach the language connected to math, science, and social studies?

- Do I display charts that clearly summarize key concepts using the academic language my ELLs have learned?

- Do I have a variety of fiction and nonfiction books at a range of reading levels that help ELLs learn about different content-area topics?

Differentiate Instruction

- Have I arranged desks in groups for collaborative learning?

- Do these groups have a mixture of ELLs with different L2 proficiency levels?

- Have I set up work tables or other areas for small-group instruction?

- Do I have leveled books in the classroom library that reflect the reading levels of all of my ELLs?

- Do I have listening center materials to support ELLs with varying reading levels in the L2?

- Have I made the classroom visually oriented for my ELLs through interactive word walls, charts, labels, and the materials I plan to use in minilessons?

- Have I organized math manipulatives to help my ELLs visualize new concepts?

Connect Learning to Students

- Do I have fiction and nonfiction books in the classroom library that are cultur-ally relevant to the ELLs in my class?

Use Students' Native Languages to Support Learning

- Do I have books in the classroom library in my students' L1 that they can read during independent reading or take home to read?
- Have I set up seating arrangements so that beginning ELLs are partnered with a native language peer whenever possible?
- Do I have bilingual picture dictionaries available in the writing center?
- Do I have bilingual word walls?
- Do I have websites available in the computer center that utilize students' L1?

Be Consistent

- Does my classroom have a consistent structure that helps ELLs know where to find information and materials related to different subject areas?

References for Further Reading

Organizing a Classroom Library and Making Reading Strategies Visual

Miller, Debbie. 2002. *Reading with Meaning: Teaching Comprehension in the Primary Grades.* Portland, ME: Stenhouse.

Taberski, Sharon. 2000. *On Solid Ground: Strategies for Teaching Reading K–3.* Portsmouth, NH: Heinemann.

Creating a Leveled Library

Calkins, Lucy, and the Teachers College Reading and Writing Project, Columbia University. 2002. *A Field Guide to the Classroom Library: Volumes A–G.* 7 vols. Portsmouth, NH: Heinemann.

Fountas, Irene C., and Gay Su Pinnell. 2006. *Leveled Books K–8: Matching Texts to Readers for Effective Teaching.* Portsmouth, NH: Heinemann.

Creating a Listening Center with ELLs

Fu, Danling. 2003. *An Island of English: Teaching ESL in Chinatown.* Portsmouth, NH: Heinemann.

CHAPTER 2

Getting Ready to Teach English Language Learners from Day One

*E*very school year brings its own challenges and intrigue, and this one was certainly no exception. The only thing the twenty-seven students in my class had in common was that they were all ELLs in the fourth grade. Aside from that, their differences in backgrounds, English proficiency levels, and academic abilities were incredible.

While most of the students spoke Spanish as their native language, they came from many different countries, including Colombia, Ecuador, Peru, Venezuela, Mexico, the Dominican Republic, Puerto Rico, and the United States. I also had a student from Nepal and a newcomer from India. As for their proficiency levels in English, my students were at each extreme: I had a large number of ELLs at a beginning stage of L2 proficiency and a large number at an advanced stage, but very few in the middle. This meant planning lessons that supported and challenged each type of ELL—no easy task.

When it came to reading in English, a few of my advanced ELLs were already approaching what was expected for fourth-grade students, but I was concerned about four others who had tested at an advanced proficiency level on the New York State ESL test but in actuality were reading at a beginning second-grade level. This kind of discrepancy is not uncommon, especially if the standardized test of English uses reading texts that are less demanding than what's expected for the ELL's grade level. I was also worried about two of my ELLs who had tested at a beginning proficiency level and were reading at Fountas and Pinnell's Level A in English, which is the lowest level, yet had been in our school since second grade.

In math I was pleased to see that a number of my ELLs demonstrated grade-level abilities, even when tested in English. Others, however, struggled to perform on math tests regardless of whether they were given in their native language or in English. My math *lessons had to teach the fourth-grade curriculum while also filling in my ELLs' gaps in knowledge.*

It was clear I faced some definite challenges in helping this group of students reach grade-level standards in literacy and the content areas. But the good news was that the school year hadn't even started yet! Through a little investigative work—glancing at cumulative records and portfolios and chatting briefly with former teachers—I had pieced together quite a bit of information about my new class. There was, of course, much more I needed to learn about the students in the weeks to come. But what I knew so far had given me a good idea of whom I would be welcoming into my classroom and how I could start assessing and teaching them from day one.

Doing this kind of proactive research before the school year begins gives me a head-start on understanding my ELLs' abilities and needs. With this insight I can set up the classroom with my ELLs' specific needs in mind. I can also plan appropriate assessments for the first weeks of school and quickly launch meaningful instruction that targets my ELLs' range of linguistic and academic needs. You may very well be thinking, "Is this just one more thing for me to put on my to-do list?" It's true that this kind of preparation takes up some of the limited time we have in our classrooms before the school year begins, but I've found that getting started right away with differentiated instruction more than compensates for the time spent up front. It also communicates a very powerful message to your ELLs: This classroom is a place where I expect each of you to be successful, and I'll help you achieve this, starting right now. The more you know about your ELLs, the more effectively you can create an instructional plan of attack to help them reach grade-level standards, or better yet, exceed them.

In this chapter I explain how you can

- gather important information about your ELLs before the school year starts

- assess your ELLs to know their current needs and plan appropriate instruction

- communicate with families to better understand your ELLs' backgrounds

Using a Whole-Class Profile

When I first began gathering information about my ELLs through research and assessments, I wanted a place where I could jot down everything I was learning and see the big picture of each ELL and the whole class. My handwritten checklists eventually turned into a more formal whole-class profile that had a space to record all of this information about their linguistic, academic, and cultural backgrounds. Figures 2–1 and 2–2 show examples of a primary-grade and an upper-grade version of the profile, which are the basis for this chapter. Throughout the rest of the chapter I explain how you can gather each piece of information and how you can use this data to launch instruction during the first weeks of school.

The categories I include in the profiles are based on the common data and assessments elementary schools use. However, the specific information you'll record will depend on the particular assessments your school administers and the categories that are relevant to your grade. For example, kindergarten and first-grade teachers will use the "Concepts About Print" category, whereas by second grade this may no longer be necessary for most students. In Appendix A I provide a partially blank profile so you can

Figure 2–1 *Primary-grade whole-class profile*

Student Names	Native Language(s)	Country of Origin	L2 Proficiency Level	# of Years Learning L2	Concepts About Print	Reading Level L1	Reading Level L2	Letter Name Identification L1	Letter Name Identification L2	Sound Identification L1	Sound Identification L2	High-Frequency Word Assessment L1	High-Frequency Word Assessment L2	Spelling Assessment L1	Spelling Assessment L2	Writing Level L1	Writing Level L2	Math Class Work	Special Services	Other
1																				
2																				
3																				
4																				
5																				
6																				
7																				
8																				
9																				
10																				
11																				
12																				
13																				
14																				
15																				
16																				
17																				
18																				
19																				
20																				
21																				
22																				
23																				
24																				
25																				
26																				
27																				

Student Names	Native Language(s)	Country of Origin	L2 Proficiency Level	# of Years Learning L2	Reading Level L1	Reading Level L2	Language Arts Standardized Test Results L1	Language Arts Standardized Test Results L2	Writing Level L1	Writing Level L2	Spelling Assessment L1	Spelling Assessment L2	Math Grade	Math Standardized Test Results	Science	Social Studies	Special Services	Other
1																		
2																		
3																		
4																		
5																		
6																		
7																		
8																		
9																		
10																		
11																		
12																		
13																		
14																		
15																		
16																		
17																		
18																		
19																		
20																		
21																		
22																		
23																		
24																		
25																		
26																		
27																		

Figure 2–2 *Upper-grade whole-class profile*

Figure 2–3 *Using the whole-class profile with a group of ELLs*

#	Student Names	Native Language(s)	Country of Origin	L2 Proficiency Level	# of Years Learning L2	Reading Level L1	Reading Level L2	Lang Arts Std L1	Lang Arts Std L2	Writing Level L1	Writing Level L2	Spelling L1	Spelling L2	Math Grade	Math Standardized Test Results	Science	Social Studies	Special Services	Other
1	Karen	Spanish	Ecuador	A	4 yr		N							2	3	3	3		
2	Debora	Spanish	Colombia	A	3 yr		P							3	3	4	3		
3	Vicente	Spanish	Mexico	A	4 yr		K							2	3	3	3		
4	Alicia	Spanish	Colombia	A	3 yr		N							3	2	2	2	counseling	
5	Juliana	Spanish	Ecuador	A	3 yr		M							3	3	3	3		
6	Miguel	Spanish	Dominican Rep.	A	4 yr		J							3	3	2	2		
7	Alejandro	Spanish	Mexico	A	3 yr		L							2	3	3	3	resource rm.	
8	Marcos	Spanish	Dominican Rep.	A	4 yr		L							3	2	3	3		
9	Francisco	Spanish	Ecuador	A	4 yr		P							3	3	4	3		
10	Carlos	Spanish	Colombia	A	4 yr		M							3	3	4	3		
11	Gracia	Spanish	Colombia	A	4 yr		K							2	2	2	2		
12	Marcio	Spanish	Colombia	A	3 yr		M							3	3	3	3		
13	Jesús	Spanish	Venezuela	A	4 yr		O							3	3	4	4		
14	Edwin	Spanish	Mexico	A	4 yr		N							3	3	3	3		
15	Julia	Spanish	Dominican Rep.	A	4 yr		K							3	2	3	3		
16	David	Spanish	Mexico	I	3 yr		L							2	2	3	2		
17	Ramón	Spanish	Colombia	I	2 yr		H							3	2	2	2		
18	Tamasi	Nepali	Nepal	I	EFL		J												Studied Engl. in Nepal
19	Conrad	Spanish	Colombia	B	2 yr		A							1	1	2	1		Intervention?
20	Fernando	Spanish	Dominican Rep.	B	2 yr		A							1	1	2	1		Intervention?
21	Samuel	Spanish	Colombia	B	3 mo		C							2		2	2		
22	James	Spanish	Colombia	B	3 mo		C							2		2	2		
23	José	Spanish	Puerto Rico	?															Newcomer
24	Diana	Spanish	Colombia	?															Newcomer
25	Angélica	Spanish	Colombia	?															Newcomer
26	Brando	Spanish	Ecuador	?															Newcomer
27	Sulekh	Hindi	India	?															Newcomer

1. Here I use the L2 proficiency levels provided from the New York State ESL test. The New York State ESL test: beginning (B), intermediate (I), and advanced (A). As I get to know my ELLs better, I refine these levels to the more specific TESOL proficiency levels: 1, 2, 3, 4, and 5.
2. Reading levels are based on the Fountas and Pinnell A–Z leveling system. None of my ELLs had language arts standardized test results from the prior year.
3. I wait to put in writing levels until I collect an initial writing sample on the first day of school.
4. Math, science, and social studies notations are based on the New York City grading system: 1 (far below grade level), 2 (below grade level), 3 (at grade level), and 4 (exceeds grade level).

31

tailor the categories to your grade and school, as well as reproducibles of the complete primary- and upper-grade profiles. The profiles can be used for any type of classroom with ELLs, including mainstream, ESL, and bilingual, because there's space to record information about your ELLs' abilities in the L1 and the L2.

During the first weeks of school I keep the whole-class profile on a clipboard so I can use it for a quick reference as I'm getting to know my ELLs. On the first day of school I carry the clipboard with me as I meet my ELLs and their families. I glance at the profile to remember where they're from, how long they've been in the United States, and what their proficiency level is in English. Then I adjust my interaction with each ELL accordingly. For newcomers, instead of initiating a full conversation, I simply give them a warm smile, introduce myself, and, if possible, speak to them in their native language. The profile is also an excellent resource to have on hand when assessing ELLs in class and when planning instruction for them. In the reading, writing, and math sections at the end of this chapter, I explain how I use the profile for instruction and assessment in the first weeks of school.

An Example in Practice

Figure 2–3 shows how I filled in the profile for the class I describe at the beginning of this chapter. The profile reflects the information I was able to gather about my ELLs before the school year began and how I highlighted the ELLs I had concerns about. I continued filling in the profile throughout the first weeks of school as I assessed my ELLs' current academic and linguistic abilities. The profile includes the ELLs who were on my original class list; once the school year began, several of them moved and four others arrived, so I had to update it accordingly. This is often the reality when teaching ELLs. Being flexible and having an organized system for keeping track of information about your ELLs helps keep your energies focused on instruction amid all the changes.

Native Language

One of the first pieces of information you'll want to record on the profile is the native language, or L1, of each of your ELLs. This is also referred to as their *home language* or *primary language.* You can find this data in each ELL's Home Language Survey, completed by parents when their child entered the school system. This is typically filed in a student's cumulative record.

It can be tempting to assume you know what a student's native language is based on his name. But since you never know the intricacies of a child's background, it's always a good idea to verify your students' L1. One year I had a student on my class list whose last name was Wong. I assumed she was Chinese, but when I glanced at her Home Language Survey, I was shocked to read that her family spoke Spanish. After meeting the girl and her family on the first day of school, I found out that her father was of Chinese origin and her mother was Peruvian, but the family exclusively used Spanish at home.

When you teach in a dual language bilingual program, taking the time to double-check students' native languages is absolutely critical. Since native English-speaking students and ELLs are combined together in one classroom, you have to clarify which students are learning which language as the L2. For example, you may have students with a Hispanic last name whose native language is English and who are learning Spanish as their L2. In some cases, both languages may be used in a child's home. If so, you'll want to investigate if one language is stronger for the student or if the student is a balanced bilingual with similar levels of proficiency in each language.

Once you know your students' native language(s), you can determine how to use the L1 as a resource to support their learning. If you aren't teaching in a bilingual program, you may be wondering why in the world you need to worry about finding ways to utilize your students' L1 in the classroom. You may also be questioning whether or not it would hinder their progress in English. This concern is understandable, because it seems logical that the more exposure an ELL has to English, and the less reliance there is on the L1, the faster she will become academically successful in English.

However, five different reviews of the research in this area have all arrived at the same conclusion: instructional approaches that utilize a child's L1 actually promote higher levels of achievement in English than English-only approaches (Goldenberg 2008; August and Shanahan 2006). This overwhelming consensus of the research requires us to reflect on how we can incorporate students' L1 in our own instruction to reap similar rewards of higher student achievement in English (García, Kleifgen, and Falchi 2008; Freeman and Freeman 2007). If you teach in a bilingual program, this L1 support is already in place. For mainstream and ESL teachers, there are specific ideas throughout this book on ways to utilize your students' L1 in the classroom.

Steps to Take with ELLs' Native Languages

1. Set Up Native Language Partners

One key way to take advantage of your students' L1 is to partner up each newcomer with an L1-speaking peer who has a higher proficiency level in English. This partner will be a linguistic and academic support for the beginning ELL as he figures out the new language of the classroom. This also provides ELLs a way to communicate their ideas fully in the L1 so they continue developing higher-order thinking skills and content knowledge. If there is no native language partner to match with a particular student's L1, try to find other ways to support her linguistically. See if there are any teachers, instructional assistants, or other students in the school who speak the student's L1 and could occasionally help her understand the core concepts she's learning at her grade level.

One year nearly a third of my class was made up of newcomers just beginning to learn English, and all of them were native Spanish speakers. So, I partnered each newcomer with a native Spanish speaker who also had a higher English proficiency. On the first day of school I prepared the class to do a collaborative activity and I reminded the students of how to include their newly arrived classmates by using both English and Spanish in the group discussion.

As each group began working, I noticed a trend throughout the room: Not a single group was making an effort to include the newcomers. They simply ignored them as they chattered away in English. Had I not explained my expectations clearly enough? I decided to briefly regroup the class. When I reiterated how to include *all* group members in academic conversations, one brave student raised her hand and said, "But Ms. Celic, last year we got in trouble if our teacher heard us speaking in Spanish." That comment opened the floodgates. All of a sudden hands were waving in the air as students wanted to share their experiences of being forbidden to use their native language. Their fear of speaking in their native language at school was so ingrained that it took several weeks to fully reassure them that there was an important role for their language in the classroom.

While my students' confession saddened me, it certainly wasn't the first time I had heard about this happening. Extremes in education are rarely beneficial for children. While there is no question we want ELLs to develop proficiency in English, it doesn't mean we have to swing to the other end of the pendulum by oppressing the use of their L1. The middle ground of utilizing the L1 as a vehicle to support the development of the L2 is what current research shows as best practice (García, Kleifgen, and Falchi 2008; Goldenberg 2008).

2. Find Native Language Resources

Begin looking for resources in your students' L1. Bilingual programs will already have books and materials in both the L1 and the L2, but mainstream and ESL teachers can also add L1 resources to the classroom. Remember that literacy skills and academic concepts learned in the L1 transfer to the L2 (Cummins 2000), and programs that make use of ELLs' native language in learning lead to higher academic achievement for those ELLs.

Country of Origin

The next piece of information I record on the whole-class profile is each ELL's country of origin. This can be found in an ELL's cumulative record or the Home Language Survey. If we know where our ELLs and their families are from, we can do a better job of including their cultural experiences and background knowledge in the classroom. When new learning begins from students' own experiences and knowledge, it makes the content they're learning more relevant and easier to comprehend (Freeman and Freeman 2002; Cummins 1989, Cary 2007; Mercado 2005; Moll et al. 1992).

When I started working as a bilingual teacher near Chicago, I planned a getting-to-know-you activity where the students could share information about their home countries with the class. On the first day of school I mounted a world map on the wall, and as each ELL shared where he was from, I stretched a strip of yarn from that location to a photo frame with his name on it. I was astounded to discover that nearly half of my ELLs were born near where I had grown up outside Chicago. Several other students were born in Texas and California. I had assumed that, as English language learners, my students would mostly be immigrants to the United States. However, research indicates that anywhere from 47 to 76 percent of all elementary school ELLs are born in the United States (Zehler et al. 2003; Capps et al. 2005; Batalova, Fix, and Murray 2007; Fix and Passel 2003). While everyone in my class that year spoke Spanish as his native language, the ELLs who were born in the United States certainly brought different cultural experiences, background knowledge, and identity issues to the classroom than their foreign-born classmates. By knowing this, I was better prepared throughout the year to tap into all of my ELLs' unique life experiences and help them put new learning into a meaningful context.

Steps to Take with ELLs' Countries of Origin

1. Gather Multicultural Resources

Begin learning more about the cultural backgrounds of your ELLs, and look for resources that are relevant to their cultural experiences (Freeman and Freeman 2001, 2007; Cary 2007). For the class in my example profile, I already had many books related to different Spanish-speaking cultures. However, it was the first time I had had any students from Nepal or India. Throughout the year I was able to find a number of nonfiction and fiction books about those cultures, a wonderful DVD series that tied into our social studies curriculum, and several magazine articles. The following websites can be a good place to start looking for multicultural literature. You can also save a copy of issues of periodicals like *Scholastic News* and *Time for Kids* when they have multicultural articles that might be useful in future years.

- Celebrating Cultural Diversity Through Children's Literature (www.multi culturalchildrenslit.com/): This website, containing resources for grades K–6, lets you search for children's literature based on a particular cultural background and genre. For each recommended book it provides a brief description, grade range, and a link to see information about purchasing the book.

- Database of Award-Winning Children's Literature (www.dawcl.com/search .asp): This database lets you search for award-winning multicultural literature based on the ethnicity or nationality of the characters, the language of the book, and other criteria such as age of students and genre.

2. Plan Getting-to-Know-You Activities

For the first days of school, plan activities that let ELLs begin to share information about their backgrounds and life experiences. The world map activity I described is one example. I also like to create a bar graph as a class that shows my students' countries of origin and read aloud books that help the students start talking about their backgrounds and experiences. Here are a few to try:

- *From Here to There* (Cuyler 1999): This is a simplistic picture book that shows where a girl and her family live, from small scale to large scale (home, street, neighborhood, city, state, country, continent, hemisphere, world). It's an excellent resource for students to think about where exactly they currently live and where they've lived before. You can help students each create their own version of the book, and have them orally share with the class what makes that home special to them. The book is available in both English and Spanish.

- *I Am of Two Places: Children's Poetry* (Carden and Cappellini 1997): This poetry collection is written by bilingual children aged eight to eleven, who share their experiences with speaking two languages and living in two different cultures. These bilingual poems can start a discussion about your students' own experiences with language and culture; encourage them to share what makes each of them unique and what they have in common.

- *The Color of Home* (Hoffman 2002): This picture book tells the story of a Somalian boy's first days of school in the United States after leaving his war-torn country. This book can help students think about what similar feelings or experiences they have had on the first day of school, as well as how this boy's experience is different from their own.

- *How Are You Peeling?* (Freymann and Elffers 2004): This book uses photographs of creatively carved fruits and vegetables to humorously depict the different feelings we have and how we express them with others. Students from all cultural backgrounds can relate to this book, and the clear visuals help ELLs at any proficiency level understand the text. It's an excellent resource for building classroom community during the first days of school.

3. Include Multicultural Perspectives in Everyday Instruction

The most powerful way to include diverse backgrounds and experiences in your classroom is through day-to-day instruction. Begin thinking about how any topic you teach could include other perspectives. For example, if you teach a unit on communities, have students compare and contrast their current community with other places they've lived. If you're teaching a math unit on addition, create number stories with the class that connect to familiar cultural experiences the students have had.

When I taught a unit on explorers, I broadened the United States focus to include the explorations of Latin American countries, where most of my ELLs' families were from that year. My ELLs knew quite a bit about how those countries were explored and settled, and tapping into that background knowledge helped them understand what we were learning about the exploration of the United States. During the unit my ELLs wrote letters from the perspectives of these different explorers, as well as from the perspectives of different indigenous groups, which we posted around a world map, as shown in Figure 2–4.

Knowing about our unit of study, my mother sent the class some books about explorers who had traveled to different parts of the world. Even though she also sent a number of high-interest series books for my ELLs, the real debate going on in the class was about who would have the new explorer books during independent reading. I finally had to set up a wait list and a one-day checkout limit so everyone would have a chance! Figure 2–5 shows a letter that Jason, a Level 4 ELL from Mexico, wrote to my mom thanking her for one of the books she sent about explorers. When I asked him why this particular book was his favorite of all the new books we had received, he said he liked knowing about things that happened all over the world and that he had learned new things about Hernán Cortés. This underscored for me that any unit of study could become more meaningful and engaging for my ELLs if I included different cultural perspectives.

English Proficiency Level

The next step in filling out the profile is to pinpoint each ELL's approximate proficiency level in English. This is a crucial piece of information. Once you know how your class is divided among the different English proficiency levels, you can tailor your instruction to help them all learn the grade-level curriculum.

What Is Language Proficiency?

Language proficiency is based on a student's ability to speak, listen, read, and write in the L2 for both *conversational* and *academic* purposes (Skutnabb-Kangas 1981; Cummins 2008, 1981). Conversational language is typically centered on concrete and familiar

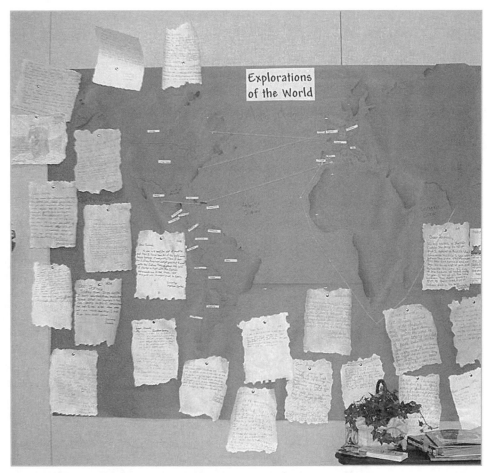

Figure 2–4 *A classroom display for our multicultural study of explorers*

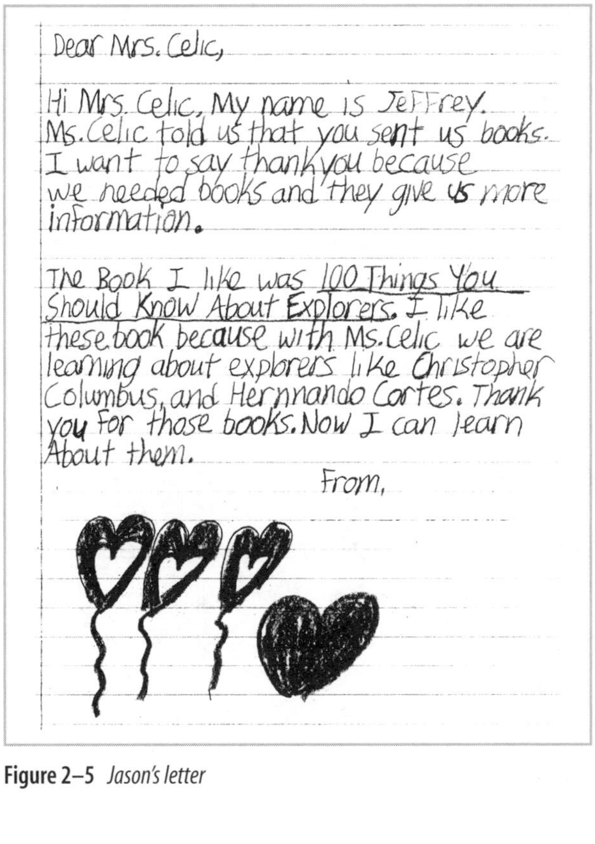

Dear Mrs. Celic,

Hi Mrs. Celic, My name is JeFFrey.
Ms. Celic told us that you sent us books.
I want to say thank you because
we needed books and they give us more
information.

The Book I like was 100 Things You
Should Know About Explorers. I like
these book because with Ms. Celic we are
learning about explorers like Christopher
Columbus, and Hernnando Cortes. Thank
you For those books. Now I can learn
About them.
                              From,

Figure 2–5 *Jason's letter*

experiences or events. It's also highly contextualized with gestures and other nonverbal cues, it uses common words that are frequently repeated, and it has more simplistic sentence structures.

Academic language, on the other hand, is the language ELLs need to understand and use to be successful with the grade-level curriculum. Academic language is typically used to discuss abstract and unfamiliar concepts, with minimal supports to clarify meaning. It uses more academic vocabulary and has more complex sentence structures.

It's important to understand that ELLs develop conversational and academic language simultaneously in the classroom. However, while ELLs can develop conversational language proficiency in as little as one to three years, academic language proficiency can take anywhere from *four to ten years* (Cummins 2008, 2003; Thomas and Collier 1997, 2002; Hakuta, Butler, and Witt 2000; Gándara 1999). Following are some examples of conversational language and academic language (Gibbons 1991; Scarcella 2003).

Conversational Language

- greeting someone
- chatting
- asking and answering everyday questions
- apologizing
- complaining
- making a request
- sharing a life event
- describing personal feelings

Academic Language

- comparing and contrasting
- describing cause and effect
- explaining
- defining
- giving examples
- justifying
- sequencing
- evaluating
- reporting
- predicting

How Is English Proficiency Divided into Levels?

TESOL has identified five distinct levels of English proficiency that students pass through as they develop their conversational and academic language skills:

- Level 1: starting
- Level 2: emerging
- Level 3: developing

- Level 4: expanding

- Level 5: bridging

Each of these English proficiency levels has certain characteristic features that let you know what kind of language ELLs are able to understand and use (Gottlieb et al. 2006). In Figure 2–6 I summarize these features, and in the last column I include the language structures, or grammatical aspects of the language, that Cappellini (2005) has identified as typically developing at each proficiency level. By looking across these features, you can determine approximately where each of your ELLs is at in her language development. Appendix B includes a reproducible version of Figure 2–6, which you can use as a general reference in your classroom. You can also use it as a rubric for individual ELLs to mark what characteristic features you notice about their language use and determine their overall level of English proficiency.

In mainstream classrooms, be on the lookout for students who have been transitioned from language programs, especially if they stopped receiving language services after only a few years. A quick transition after one to three years of language services is typical across the United States (García, Kleifgen, and Falchi 2008). These students typically have strong conversational skills that create the impression of nativelike English language proficiency. However, they haven't had enough time to fully develop their *academic* language proficiency in English. Since academic language demands in literacy and the content areas increase with each grade, these students will likely need extra support to strengthen their academic language skills in English in order to be successful with the grade-level curriculum.

How Is Language Proficiency Developed?

Through day-to-day communicative interactions ELLs can naturally develop conversational language because it's highly contextualized. However, ELLs need support to learn academic language (Freeman and Freeman, 2009). Teachers can make academic language more comprehensible for ELLs by using extra-linguistic supports such as gestures, pictures, media, realia, manipulatives, and graphic organizers, and by building on ELLs' background knowledge. This is known as providing *comprehensible input* (Krashen 1985).

Teachers also need to explicitly teach ELLs the key academic vocabulary words and grammatical structures necessary for each learning activity. Currently this kind of explicit academic language instruction isn't happening in many classrooms, even though it greatly influences how successful ELLs will be in school (Scarcella 2003). Regardless of where your ELLs are at in their English development, you can weave academic language instruction into your literacy and content-area instruction. This will help your ELLs develop the language skills they need to meet grade-level standards. Chapter 5 outlines how to teach academic language, with examples to guide you.

Steps to Take with ELLs' English Proficiency Levels

1. Get a General Idea of Your ELLs' English Proficiency Levels

Before the school year begins, look through results from formal assessments of English, which are administered on a yearly basis at the state level. This data may be recorded in your ELLs' cumulative records or printed out by the school. While the results aren't timely since the test was probably administered in the spring of the prior school year, they still indicate an approximate English proficiency level for each of your ELLs. With

	Characteristic Features of Speaking and Writing	Conversational Vocabulary	Academic Vocabulary	Language Structures Used When Speaking and Writing
Level 1 Starting	Often silent; responds nonverbally through gestures, pointing, nodding, yes-or-no answers, and drawing. May speak in single words, simple two-word phrases, or memorized chunks of text. May answer yes-or-no and either-or questions. Writing in the L2 may involve labeling with letters or sounds, labeling basic vocabulary, or filling in simple form sentences.	Learning common high-frequency words and everyday vocabulary in the school setting to express basic concrete needs.	Learning basic content-specific vocabulary, but may not be speaking or writing this vocabulary just yet.	Uses common nouns: *dog, boy, book* Uses regular plurals: *dogs, boys, books* Uses basic prepositions: *in, on, at* Uses *verb to be: I am happy.* Uses basic sentence structure (SVO): *I am a girl. I play soccer.* Uses basic commands: *Look! Help!*
Level 2 Emerging	Speaks and writes in phrases or short sentences. Makes basic errors that often interfere with communication.	Developing conversational language to communicate simple and routine experiences.	Beginning to use some content-specific and general academic vocabulary and expressions, but lacking a range of vocabulary beyond the basic.	Uses subject pronouns: *I, you, he, she, it, we, they* Uses statements: *there is/are, here is/are* Uses present tense Makes negative statements: *That is not my paper.* Uses present progressive tense: *We are going to the party.* Uses prepositional phrases: *in the book, on the bed* Uses basic adjectives: *big* instead of *huge, enormous* Uses coordinating conjunctions: *and, or, but*
Level 3 Developing	Speaks and writes in expanded sentences. Makes grammatical errors that may interfere with communication, but maintains much of the meaning.	Has a foundation for conversational language to communicate familiar matters that are regularly encountered.	Increasingly using content-specific and general academic vocabulary and expressions.	Uses possessive pronouns: *mine, yours, his, hers, ours, theirs* Uses habitual present tense: *He goes to Mexico every summer.* Uses past tense: *I played with my friend.* Uses subject-verb agreement: *She likes science.* Uses adjectives correctly: *the beautiful red flowers* Uses more coordinating conjunctions: *so, yet* Uses subordinating conjunctions: *because, when, before, after* Uses basic contractions: *I'm, it's, can't, didn't* Uses comparatives: *This magnet is stronger than the other one.* Asks questions in future tenses: *Will you go to the museum? or Are you going to go to the museum?*
Level 4 Expanding	Speaks and writes using a variety of sentence lengths of varying complexity. Makes minimal grammatical errors that do not interfere with the overall meaning.	Has a strong command of conversational language to communicate both concrete and abstract situations. Can apply language to new situations.	Using a wider range of content-specific and general academic vocabulary and expressions.	Uses reflexive pronouns: *myself, yourself, himself, herself, itself, ourselves, themselves* Uses abstract nouns: *democracy, freedom, trust* Uses irregular past tense: *I found the book and I bought it.* Uses gerunds: *Voting is a responsibility citizens have.* Uses superlatives: *Which planet is the largest in our galaxy?* Uses adverbs: *quickly, carefully, well (instead of good)* Uses synonyms and antonyms Use more coordinating and correlative conjunctions: *however, therefore, either ... or* Asks question in past tense: *Where did the colonists settle?*
Level 5 Bridging	Speaks and writes extensively using a variety of sentence lengths of varying complexity. Speaking and writing approach comparability to English-proficient peers.	Near English-proficient command of conversational language, communicating in a wide range of situations and understanding implicit meaning.	Nearing English-proficient command of content-specific and general academic vocabulary and expressions.	Uses perfect tenses: *has been, had been, will have been* Uses conditional perfect tense: *If I had checked my answer, I would have gotten it correct.* Uses auxiliary verbs and contractions: *could/couldn't, would/wouldn't, should/shouldn't* Uses a wider range of adverbs: *already, still, often* Uses relative pronouns: *who, whom, whose, which, that* Uses more subordinating conjunctions: *although, whenever, until, whereas, even though* Uses the passive voice: *The seed was planted in the garden.* Uses metaphors and similes

Figure 2–6 *What to expect from ELLs at each proficiency level (Source: Gottlieb et al., 2006; Cappellini, 2005)*

this information, you can seat ELLs strategically in groups to mix different proficiency levels, as described in Chapter 1. I also like to take a look at how my ELLs are spread among the different L2 proficiency levels. Do I have a lot of ELLs at any particular level? Chapters 4–6 give practical suggestions for ways to differentiate instruction based on your ELLs' English proficiency levels.

2. Determine Amount of Time ELLs Have Been Learning English

Find out how long each of your ELLs has been learning English. That puts her proficiency level in context, and you can be on the lookout for any discrepancies that indicate a student isn't progressing as expected. This information is often in an ELL's cumulative record where it shows when he began his schooling in the United States and what type of language services he received each year. Keep in mind that an ELL's proficiency in English will depend on the amount of time he's been learning it as well as the type of language program he's been in. For example, some bilingual programs begin with a greater percentage of instructional time in the L1 to help ELLs build a strong foundation of literacy and cognitive skills in their native language and then gradually add in more instructional time in English.

3. Assess Your ELLs' Current English Proficiency Levels

Once the school year begins you can start assessing your ELLs' current proficiency in English. You may find that their levels are different than what you initially recorded on the profile. The best way to assess your ELLs' language proficiency is by paying attention to how they use the language authentically during classroom activities (Cary 2007; Cappellini 2005). For example, how do your ELLs use English when retelling a story, writing a narrative, comparing and contrasting different shapes in math, or describing the life cycle of a butterfly? When you assess your ELLs' literacy or content-area skills in class, you can assess their English proficiency at the same time.

To assess my ELLs' language use when they speak and write, I use a language structures checklist (Figure 2–7) that looks at the grammatical features ELLs typically develop at each English proficiency level, as listed in Figure 2–6 (Cappellini 2005). Whenever I interact with my ELLs in the classroom, I take note of the language structures they're able to use accurately when speaking and writing and which ones they're still developing. See Appendix B for a reproducible version of this checklist.

For example, when I sit down for a reading conference with an ELL, I take out the Language Structures checklist *and* my reading conference form to record what that ELL is doing with reading and language use. This can be a bit of a balancing act, since I'm paying attention to both her language use and her reading ability. However, with a little practice it becomes much more automatic. Without realizing it, I find myself thinking, "Ah! María just used the present progressive tense perfectly," or "OK, Jorge is still learning some of the irregular past tense verbs. I'll need to help him with that." Sometimes I get so engrossed in the conversation I'm having with an ELL about reading that I forget to take note of how he's using the language. But having the checklist in front of me helps me remember to do both things whenever possible. Once I see what level of language structures an ELL is currently using, I have a better idea of her current English proficiency level. I compare this with the other features of each level of English proficiency in Figure 2–6 to get a more complete picture of the level that represents that student.

Keep in mind that the more familiar you are with the language structures on the checklist, the less mental effort it takes to record your ELLs' language use. From just one

	Language Structures																			
Level 1	Common nouns (*boy, dog, school, bathroom*)																			
	Regular plurals (*boys, dogs, pencils, books*)																			
	Basic prepositions (*in, on, at, to*)																			
	Verb *to be* (*I am happy.*)																			
	Basic sentence structure (SVO) (*I play soccer.*)																			
Level 2	Subject pronouns (*I, you, he, she, it, we, they*)																			
	Statements (*There is/are, Here is/are*)																			
	Present tense																			
	Negative statements (*That is not my paper.*)																			
	Present progressive tense (*I am going to school*)																			
	Prepositional phrases (*in the book, on the bed*)																			
	Basic adjectives (*big* instead of *huge*)																			
	Coordinating conjunctions (*and, or, but*)																			
Level 3	Possessive pronouns (*mine, yours, his, hers, ours, theirs*)																			
	Habitual present tense (*He goes every summer.*)																			
	Regular past tense (*I played with my friend.*)																			
	Subject-verb agreement (*She likes science.*)																			
	Uses adjectives correctly (*the beautiful red flowers*)																			
	More conjunctions (*so, yet, because, when, before, after*)																			
	Basic contractions (*I'm, it's, can't, didn't*)																			
	Comparatives (*better than, faster than*)																			
	Asks questions in future tense (*Will you help me?*)																			
Level 4	Reflexive pronouns (*myself, yourself, himself, herself*)																			
	Abstract nouns (*trust, freedom, happiness*)																			
	Irregular past tense (*found, brought, went, saw, were*)																			
	Gerunds (*Going to the park is fun.*)																			
	Superlatives (*the best, the fastest, the most difficult*)																			
	Adverbs (*quickly, carefully, well*)																			
	Synonyms and antonyms																			
	Advanced conjunctions (*however, therefore, either … or*)																			
	Asks questions in past tense (*Where did you go?*)																			
Level 5	Present perfect (*I have learned a lot.*)																			
	Past perfect (*I had lived in Mexico.*)																			
	Future perfect (*I will have been here for four years.*)																			
	Conditional perfect (*If I had tried, I would have won.*)																			
	Auxiliary verb contractions (*couldn't, wouldn't, shouldn't*)																			
	Wider range of adverbs (*already, still, often*)																			
	Relative pronouns (*who, whom, whose, which, that*)																			
	Advanced conjunctions (*although, whenever, whereas*)																			
	Passive voice (*The houses were built quickly*)																			
	Uses metaphors and similes																			
	Overall Proficiency Level:																			
	Key: blank square = structure not evident; D = developing structure; S = secure structure																			

Figure 2–7 *Language structures checklist (Source: Adapted from Cappellini, 2005)*

conversation with an ELL you probably won't get all the information you need about his ability to use all of these language structures. Little by little as you have more conversations with your ELLs and read more of their writing, you'll get a more complete picture of their English levels. That's why it's important to always have the checklist with you: you're able to take note of things you hear and see throughout the instructional day, without the pressure of trying to record it all at once.

I like to use Figure 2–7 as a whole-class checklist. I write my ELLs' names across the top (I make two copies to fit my entire class), and I keep it in the front pocket of an assessment binder that goes with me whenever I'm meeting with students. The benefit of having a checklist for the whole class is that you can compare your ELLs' needs without having to flip through a stack of individual assessments. By glancing across the whole-class checklist, you may find that your beginners all need help with basic sentence structure, or that you have a large group of ELLs who aren't using the past tense correctly, or that many of your ELLs need to learn how to use adjectives correctly. I organize my ELLs' names across the top of the checklist based on their approximate English proficiency levels so that the list of names goes from beginning ELLs to more advanced ELLs. This helps me see if there are similar needs among ELLs with a similar proficiency level. If you prefer, you can also use the Language Structures checklist for individual ELLs to track their progress over time. Instead of putting the names in the spaces at the top, you would write the different dates you met with a particular ELL throughout the year. With the insight you gain from this checklist, you can begin thinking about which grammatical aspects of the language you'll need to focus on in literacy activities and content-area instruction, which is detailed in Chapter 5.

Record-keeping systems are very personal for each teacher, and we all have our preferences about what works best for us. The system I describe here for making notations on the checklist is one way I've found to be effective. If an ELL isn't showing any signs of using a particular structure (or if I just haven't heard or seen her use it yet), I leave the square blank. If she's starting to use a structure when speaking or writing, but isn't using it accurately just yet, I write *D* for developing. And if she's using a structure accurately when speaking or writing, I write *S* for secure (Cappellini 2005). If a language structure is developing, I write the letter *D* in the upper left corner of the square, leaving space in the lower right corner to indicate later on when it becomes a secure part of the ELL's language use.

Since language learning is a fluid process, rarely will an ELL only use the language structures up to a single level. More often, they span several levels with the language structures they're securely using and developing. Look for the highest level where an ELL has some secure structures as well as some developing structures. This will give you an idea of his current L2 proficiency level. The checklist also helps you spot any gaps in knowledge (Cappellini 2005). For example, you may have an ELL who's at a Level 4 but still makes mistakes with subject-verb agreement, typically developed at Level 3 ("He *go* to school in New York."). I'm often surprised at some of the gaps I find when I listen to my ELLs speak or when I read their writing. These gaps can happen for a number of reasons. An ELL may have never picked up on a particular language structure, or she may have heard it used incorrectly and used that as a model. It's important to identify gaps and then fill them in by helping ELLs correctly use those language structures in literacy and content-area studies.

Assessing English Proficiency: A Student Example

Edwin is one of the ELLs on my example profile. He was labeled as an advanced language learner (Level 5) on the most recent state test of English as a second language, but I was curious to find out if that was an accurate reflection of his current speaking and writing abilities. On the first day of school I had all of my students write a narrative describing one special moment from the summer. I didn't assist or guide the students in any way as they wrote their narrative, since I wanted to know what they were able to produce on their own. Figure 2–8 shows Edwin's initial writing sample. This provided me with a baseline for the *quality* of Edwin's writing as well as his *ability to use English*.

From Edwin's writing I was able to learn quite a bit about his abilities as a writer and as an English language learner. As teachers we tend to quickly spot the areas for improvement, but it's equally important to identify what the student already knows about writing and using English. I start here by identifying Edwin's strengths and then thinking about some of the main areas he needed to develop.

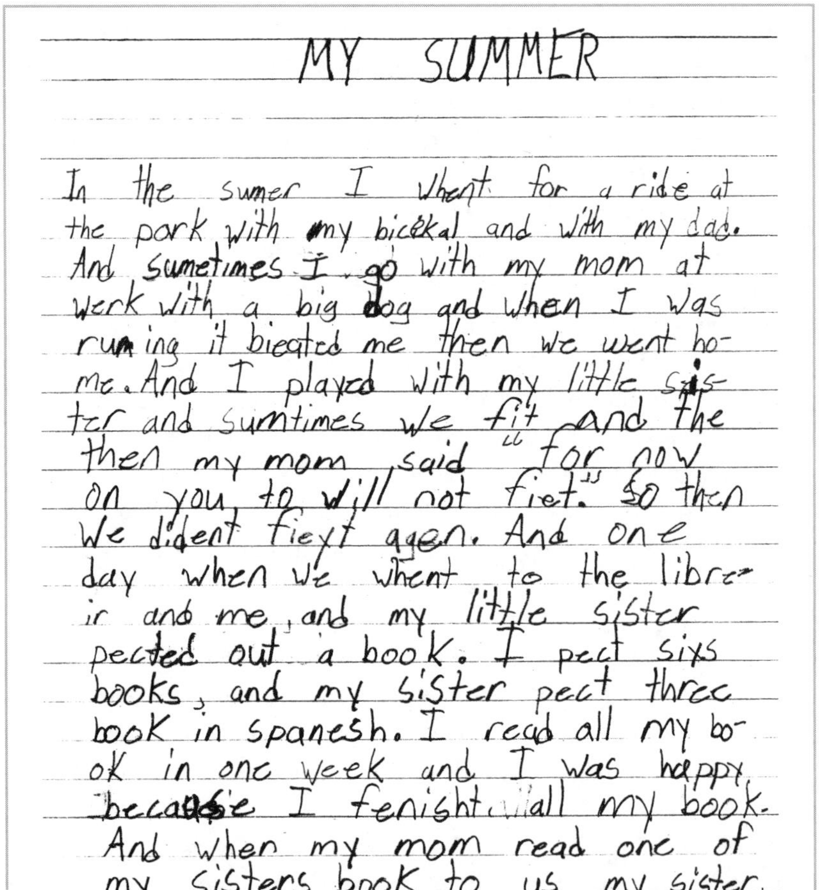
MY SUMMER

In the sumer I whent for a ride at
the park with my bicekal and with my dad.
And sumetimes I go with my mom at
werk with a big dog and when I Was
ruming it bieated me then we went home. And I played with my little sister and sumtimes we fit and the
then my mom said "for now
on you to will not fiet." So then
We dident fieyt agen. And one
day when we whent to the libre-
ir and me, and my little sister
pected out a book. I pect sixs
books, and my sister pect three
book in spanesh. I read all my book in one week and I was happy
because I fenisht all my book.
And when my mom read one of
my sisters book to us my sister,
my mom, and me was happey

Figure 2–8 *Edwin's initial writing sample*

Transcription: *In the summer I went for a ride at the park with my bicycle and with my dad. And sometimes I go with my mom at work with a big dog and when I was running it [bit] me. Then we went home. And I played with my little sister and sometimes we [fought] and the then my mom said, "For now on you two will not fight." So then we didn't fight again. And one day when we went to the library and me and my little sister picked out a book. I picked six books, and my sister picked three books in Spanish. I read all my books in one week and I was happy because I finished all my books. And when my mom read one of my sister's books to us my sister, my mom, and me was happy.*

Quality of Edwin's Writing

Strengths

- He's able to tell stories about his own life.

- He's able to elaborate his experience of going to the library with some additional sentences.

- He knows how to use dialogue as a way to elaborate a narrative. When his mother tells the siblings not to fight, you can almost hear her scolding them.

- He uses capitalization and end punctuation with some regularity.

Areas to Develop

- His narrative jumps from one event to the next, lacking focus and sufficient elaboration.

- His narrative is not organized with a beginning, middle, and end.

- He needs support to develop his spelling skills, particularly with the past tense suffix *-ed*, short vowel sounds, and high-frequency words like *went, again, two,* and *some*.

- He also needs support to expand his word choice, in particular to use a greater variety of transition words.

Secure Language Structures in Edwin's Writing

Level 1

- common nouns (*park, dad, dog, book, sister*)

- basic prepositions (*in, at, out*)

- verb *to be*

- basic sentence structure

Level 2

- subject pronouns (*I, you, it, we*)

- present tense

- negative statements (*you will not fight*)

- basic adjectives (*little, big*)

- conjunctions (*and*)

Level 3

- past tense (*played, pected, fenisht*); although some are misspelled, he's using the past tense

- conjunctions (*because, so*)

- basic contractions (*didn't*)

Developing Language Structures in Edwin's Writing

Level 1

- regular plurals (*book*)

Level 2

- prepositional phrases: *in the sumer* is correct, but *a ride at the park* and *go at work* are not

Level 3

- uses adjectives correctly: wrote *sixs books* instead of *six books*

Level 4

- irregular past tense: (*was* and *whent* are correct, although *went* is misspelled, but *bieated [bit]* and *fit [fought]* are incorrect); doesn't use *were* in last sentence

Putting It All Together

I put this information about Edwin's language use into the Language Structures checklist, which you can see in Figure 2–9 on page 47. Just from this one writing sample, it appeared that Edwin was able to use most language structures securely up to Level 3 in English. His writing also matched the characteristic features of Level 3 writers outlined in Figure 2–6. He wrote in expanded sentences that provided greater detail, yet his common grammatical errors at times made it difficult to understand what he had written. Interestingly, he showed some gaps in language use, such as using plural nouns (a Level 1 structure) and using prepositional phrases accurately.

Since this was just one snapshot of Edwin's language use, it was certainly not a complete picture of his abilities, and therefore it was too soon to determine an overall English proficiency level. During the weeks that followed I listened to Edwin in different academic situations and collected more of his writing. What I found was that Edwin was starting to develop some of the Level 4 structures, but he was mainly using the Level 3 (and earlier) structures. At this point Edwin had a Level 3 proficiency level in English but was beginning to transition to Level 4.

Taking note of Edwin's language use during those first weeks of school helped me pinpoint what areas I could focus on to support his language development. It also showed me that his speaking and writing skills in English were not as advanced as the standardized test of English proficiency had indicated. But I now had the information I needed to know exactly what aspects of the language I could teach Edwin to continue developing his English proficiency. I also knew what areas Edwin needed help in to develop as a writer.

Academic History in the L1 and L2

The rest of the profile is dedicated to recording information about your ELLs' academic performance in literacy and the content areas, because ultimately your responsibility is to ensure that your ELLs meet state standards in each of these areas. It's better to know right away which students appear to have struggled in prior years with reading, writing, or math so you can assess them quickly and start differentiating instruction if necessary.

Your ELLs may have three different types of academic background (Freeman and Freeman 2007; Olsen and Jaramillo 1999). The difference between them becomes quickly apparent in the classroom. The types of ELLs you have in your classroom will influence what kinds of support they need to be academically successful.

	Language Structures	Sulekh	Brando	Angélica	Diana	José	James	Samuel	Fernando	Conrad	Tamasi	Ramón	David	Julia	Edwin	Jesús
Level 1	Common nouns (*boy, dog, school, bathroom*)														S	
	Regular plurals (*boy<u>s</u>, dog<u>s</u>, pencil<u>s</u>, book<u>s</u>*)														D/	
	Basic prepositions (*in, on, at, to*)														S	
	Verb *to be* (*I am happy.*)														S	
	Basic sentence structure (SVO) (*I play soccer.*)														S	
Level 2	Subject pronouns (*I, you, he, she, it, we, they*)														S	
	Statements (*There is/are, Here is/are*)															
	Present tense														S	
	Negative statements (*That is not my paper.*)														S	
	Present progressive tense (*I <u>am going</u> to school*)															
	Prepositional phrases (*in the book, on the bed*)														D/	
	Basic adjectives (*big instead of huge*)														S	
	Coordinating conjunctions (*and, or, but*)														S	
Level 3	Possessive pronouns (*mine, yours, his, hers, ours, theirs*)															
	Habitual present tense (*He <u>goes</u> every summer.*)															
	Regular past tense (*I play<u>ed</u> with my friend.*)														S	
	Subject-verb agreement (*She <u>likes</u> science.*)															
	Uses adjectives correctly (*the <u>beautiful</u> <u>red</u> flowers*)														D/	
	More conjunctions (*so, yet, because, when, before, after*)														S	
	Basic contractions (*I'm, it's, can't, didn't*)														S	
	Comparatives (*better than, faster than*)															
	Asks questions in future tense (*Will you help me?*)															
Level 4	Reflexive pronouns (*myself, yourself, himself, herself*)															
	Abstract nouns (*trust, freedom, happiness*)															
	Irregular past tense (*found, brought, went, saw, were*)														D/	
	Gerunds (*<u>Going</u> to the park is fun.*)															
	Superlatives (*the best, the fastest, the most difficult*)															
	Adverbs (*quickly, carefully, well*)															
	Synonyms and antonyms															
	Advanced conjunctions (*however, therefore, either … or*)															
	Asks questions in past tense (*Where did you go?*)															
Level 5	Present perfect (*I <u>have learned</u> a lot.*)															
	Past perfect (*I <u>had lived</u> in Mexico.*)															
	Future perfect (*I <u>will have been</u> here for four years.*)															
	Conditional perfect (*If I <u>had tried</u>, I <u>would have</u> won.*)															
	Auxiliary verb contractions (*couldn't, wouldn't, shouldn't*)															
	Wider range of adverbs (*already, still, often*)															
	Relative pronouns (*who, whom, whose, which, that*)															
	Advanced conjunctions (*although, whenever, whereas*)															
	Passive voice (*The houses <u>were built</u> quickly*)															
	Uses metaphors and similes															
	Overall Proficiency Level:															

Key: blank square = structure not evident; D = developing structure; S = secure structure

Figure 2–9 *Edwin's language use*

47

ELLs with Adequate Formal Schooling

ELLs with *adequate formal schooling* have developed grade-level cognitive skills, abilities, and knowledge, which they can apply to everything they're learning and doing in the L2. These students may have received the adequate formal schooling in their home countries and/or in the United States.

One example of an ELL with adequate formal schooling is Mayra, who was a second-grade student of mine from Mexico. Mayra had attended kindergarten in Mexico and had been studying in a bilingual program in the United States since first grade. From her schooling in Mexico and the United States she had developed a strong foundation of literacy skills in Spanish as well as English. Mayra's reading and writing skills improved rapidly throughout second grade in both languages, and she was also doing grade-level work in the content areas. The combination of adequate formal schooling in Mexico and the United States helped Mayra experience academic success in English.

Another example of this type of ELL is Eliana, a fourth-grade student who had just arrived in the United States. Before that, Eliana had studied at a school in Ecuador, and she was able to read and write at grade level in Spanish. She also had strong math and science skills. As Eliana began developing her knowledge of English vocabulary, spelling, and language structures, she was able to transfer everything she knew about reading and writing in Spanish to her reading and writing in English. Eliana's strong literacy skills in her native language made her transition to academic work in English much easier than students who arrive with below grade-level literacy skills.

ELLs with Limited Formal Schooling

ELLs with *limited or interrupted formal schooling* are below grade level in literacy and math in their native language and therefore lack the skills and knowledge to apply to their learning in English. These students need significantly more support in school since they need to learn the new language and at the same time strengthen their academic skills to catch up to their peers.

I've worked with a number of ELLs in this situation. One example is Adán, who moved to the United States from Mexico and was placed in my fifth-grade bilingual class based on his age. However, Adán had grown up in a very rural area, and he admitted to me that he had attended school only some of the time. As a result, Adán's reading and writing skills in Spanish were extremely low. Because he did not have grade-level literacy skills in Spanish, he faced a much greater challenge in learning how to read and write in English. In addition to the differentiated instruction I provided for him in class, I immediately recommended Adán for intervention services in literacy and math to help him build the foundation of skills he needed.

ELLs Who Are Long-Term English Language Learners

Long-term English language learners are students who have been studying English for at least five years but still haven't demonstrated full proficiency in the language. They may have strong conversational skills but haven't developed the academic language they need to understand the decontextualized, abstract, and technical language common in the upper grades.

For example, Graciela was a sixth grader in my bilingual program. She had been attending the school since kindergarten, and she sounded completely fluent in English with no noticeable accent. In fact, many teachers questioned why she was still classified as an ELL. However, when it came to understanding the academic language in her textbooks, Graciela really struggled. This lack of reading comprehension affected her academic performance in every content area. Graciela needed explicit academic language instruction to help her understand the complex texts of her grade level so she could be successful in reading, writing, and the content areas.

As you read the following sections on launching assessment and instruction in reading, writing, and math, keep in mind the three types of ELLs described here. This can help you understand why your ELLs are showing certain academic strengths or difficulties in literacy and the content areas.

Reading in the L1 and L2

It's important to quickly get to know your ELLs' needs in reading so you can launch appropriate reading instruction for them. I do this within the structure of a reading workshop, but you could certainly apply these ideas for assessment and instruction to other reading programs. The reading workshop begins with the class gathering for a *minilesson* where you teach students something specific about reading, such as a print strategy for decoding text or a reading comprehension strategy that you want them to use in their own reading (Calkins 2001). You can model the strategy using a *read-aloud* or *shared reading* text that the class is already familiar with, and you give the students an opportunity to practice the strategy with you multiple times (Miller 2002). Then the students try out this strategy, along with all the other strategies they've learned, in their *independent reading* (Calkins 2001; Taberski 2000). While students are reading independently, you can assess them individually in conferences, which I describe in this section. Once your initial reading assessments are done, you can use this time to begin meeting with *guided reading groups*. The reading workshop ends with students having a chance to read with a partner and share what they did as readers with the whole class. Chapter 3 shows how the reading workshop fits into a complete daily schedule and mentions resources that detail the ins and outs of implementing a reading workshop.

When you launch your reading workshop in the first weeks of school, your top priority is to help students learn what they're expected to do during the workshop so that they're productively working and learning during this time. Without this management in place, it's impossible to begin the important task of assessing your ELLs to get to know their strengths and needs as readers. With this in mind, I provide some suggestions for ways to assess your ELLs that also get the reading workshop off to a smooth start.

Steps to Take with ELLs in Reading

1. Check Previous Reading Assessments

Grades 1–6 teachers can look through ELLs' portfolios from the previous school year, if available, to see how they performed on reading assessments. Some schools summarize the data from these reading assessments and provide it to teachers in a separate document. What are your ELLs' reading levels in English and their native languages? How well do your ELLs know the letter names, the sounds letters make, and high-frequency words in English and their native languages? How does their reading ability compare with what's expected at your grade level? Depending on your grade, these reading assessments could include the following:

- Formal reading assessments from the district or state level

- Running records: This informal assessment tracks students' reading behavior as they read a text. You take note of what types of miscues (errors) the students make while reading, as well as their ability to comprehend the text on a literal and inferential level (Clay 2006). This gives you data about the needs each student has in the areas of decoding, fluency, and comprehension. The goal is to determine a student's *instructional reading level*. Running records can be done with any leveled text, but there are also programs that have all the materials prepared for you, such as the DRA and QRI (see below).

- Developmental Reading Assessment (DRA): This informal assessment program has leveled texts teachers can use for conducting running records and tracking reading behaviors. The DRA is available in English as well as Spanish.

- Qualitative Reading Inventory (QRI): This is another informal assessment program that has leveled texts to conduct running records and track reading behaviors. There are also additional features, such as leveled word lists to determine decoding ability.

- Concepts About Print assessment: This checks a child's awareness of how books work, including knowing that print carries meaning, how to hold a book, how to turn the pages, and the directionality of text from left to right, among other concepts (Clay 2000). The assessment is used in the primary grades until students show mastery of these concepts. However, ELLs who have limited formal education in the L1 may arrive in the upper grades without this awareness of how books work.

- Letter names assessment: The teacher has students read uppercase and/or lowercase letter names from a list and checks to see how many they can correctly identify. This assessment is used in primary grades until students master the letter names, but it can also be used with older ELLs to track their learning of letter names in English.

- Letter-sound correlation assessment: The teacher shows students a list of letters and has them say the sound each letter makes. This is another primary-grade assessment that can also be used with older ELLs to track their understanding of the sounds letters make in English.

- High-frequency words assessment: This assessment tests a student's ability to read the words that are most commonly used in texts. This primary-grade assessment can be useful with older ELLs, but remember that even if ELLs can correctly read a word, it doesn't guarantee they understand the *meaning* of the word.

After seeing your ELLs' previous reading performance on these assessments, you may have concerns about particular students. You can highlight their reading results on the profile and make those ELLs a priority for assessment in the first days of school. For example, on my profile I saw that Miguel had tested at an advanced L2 proficiency level, but based on his most recent running record assessment, he was reading at Fountas and Pinnell Level J (beginning second-grade level) after four years as an ELL. Vicente, Joana, and Gracia were in a similar situation. They had also tested at an advanced L2 proficiency level but were reading at Fountas and Pinnell Level K after four years as ELLs. These four ELLs should have had a reading level closer to grade level based on their advanced L2 proficiency, so I wanted to find out what was holding them back as readers. Another concern for me was Fernando and Conrad, the students who had tested at a beginning L2 proficiency level and were still reading at Level A after two years as English language learners. I wanted to know why they seemingly weren't progressing with English or with reading. Did they lack reading skills in Spanish? Did they have limited formal education? On my profile I marked these six students as my top priority for assessment in reading for the first days of school.

2. Create Personal Book Bags

One way to get your reading program and student assessment off to a smooth and productive start is to put together a book bag for each ELL to use during independent reading time starting the first day of school. If you have your ELLs' reading levels from the year before, you can put books at those levels in a bag for each of them, along with some other nonleveled books you think they would find interesting. On the first day of school when you're ready to launch your independent reading time, explain to the students that you've chosen some books especially for each of them that you think they'll enjoy. Let them know that in the future they'll be choosing their own books, but that for the first week of school you wanted to share some of your favorite books with them.

The benefits of preparing these book bags are numerous:

- The students are motivated about having books that you chose just for them.

- You've ensured that each ELL is productively reading books close to her current reading level in the L1 and/or L2 from day one.

- It's easier to manage independent reading time when ELLs have books they can read because they're more engaged.

- It helps you assess their reading levels through quick checks (see next section).

If possible, include books in your ELLs' native languages, particularly for newcomers. I also like to give ELLs in the early stages of English proficiency an individual tape recorder with several simple books on tape in English so they can begin hearing the sounds of the language and following along with the picture books. This combination of books in the native language and books on tape in English helps beginning ELLs stay focused during independent reading. They also benefit from reading with a partner during this time.

If you don't have the time to make personal book bags, you can instead set up baskets of books to place at each group of desks during independent reading. The baskets should have a range of levels that reflect what your ELLs can read in the L1 and/or L2. Then, as soon as you start assessing their current reading levels, they can choose books from the library to place in their book bags.

3. Begin with Quick-Check Reading Assessments

During the first days of school your main priority with the reading workshop is for the class to understand what it is expected to do during this learning time. It can be difficult to enforce the management of independent reading if you're sitting off on the side of the room for extended periods of time assessing each student's reading level. To have more of a physical presence during independent reading on the first days of school, while still assessing your students, I suggest doing quick-check reading assessments. This helps you quickly match all your students to appropriate books during the first week of school (Calkins 2001).

To do this, I circulate around the room, reminding students as needed about the expectations for independent reading, and then I briefly sit next to one of my ELLs. I ask my ELL about the book she's reading and have her read aloud part of the text to me. While she's reading aloud, I listen for how well she's decoding the text and how fluent her reading is. After she finishes reading, I ask her a few comprehension questions to see how well she understood the text. Her ability to decode the text, read it with fluency, and comprehend it gives me an idea of whether the level is easy, just right, or challenging for her. If it seems too easy I help her get books at a higher level, and if it seems too challenging I suggest other books for her to try at a lower level. If you've made personal book bags for your students, you already know that the books they have reflect their reading levels from the previous year. So this quick assessment lets you know right away if your ELLs lost ground over the summer, maintained their reading level, or improved. If I feel an ELL's level is higher or lower than where he tested in the previous school year, I put an up or down arrow next to his reading level on the profile. While this is just a ballpark idea of each ELL's reading level, it gives you a good idea of what level you should start testing each ELL at once you begin the more thorough reading assessments.

Keep in mind that for a reading level to be an *independent* reading level, students need to be able to

- decode the text with at least 95 percent accuracy,
- comprehend the text at a literal and an inferential level, and
- read the text with fluency (Fountas and Pinnell 2006).

Many ELLs can decode a text well but aren't able to comprehend the text, particularly at the inferential level. If this is the case, it's *not* their independent reading level, no matter how great they sound when reading it aloud. All three aspects of reading must be in place for a level to be considered an independent reading level.

Remember that when you listen to ELLs during these quick checks you can also take note of their ability to use English. Have the Language Structures checklist with you as you circulate around the classroom and meet with ELLs. You don't have to do an exhaustive assessment of all the language structures each ELL is using; simply jot down any observations that stand out to you about her language use each time you listen to her speak. Over the course of the first weeks of school this will give you a more complete picture of each ELL's language proficiency level and what aspects of the language you can teach her. The trick is to keep the Language Structures checklist handy during these meaningful academic interactions with your ELLs.

4. Conduct Informal Reading Assessments

Once your independent reading time is running smoothly, you can begin more thoroughly assessing your students' reading abilities with whatever assessments your school uses to track student progress. If you gathered information about your ELLs' reading levels from the previous school year and did a quick check of their ability to read books at those levels, then you should already have a good idea of their current levels. This will help you know at which reading level to start testing each ELL, which is a real time-saver.

The benefit of conducting these reading assessments is that they give you highly detailed information about exactly what each ELL needs help with in the areas of decoding, comprehension, and fluency. This will become the basis for what you teach them in whole-class minilessons, in guided reading groups, and in individual conferences (Fountas and Pinnell 2006). These more in-depth reading assessments are also a great time to take note of ELLs' language use on the Language Structures checklist.

It's time-consuming to test students' reading abilities in one language, but bilingual teachers have the extra job of testing each ELL in two languages. This process can drag on for weeks as teachers do their best to assess students during any spare moments they can find. The whole point of assessing ELLs in reading is to inform instruction; if you aren't finding out the information until the second month of school, you've already lost valuable instructional time. Consider talking with your school administration about providing someone to cover your class for part of the day so you can get all the assessments done at once.

5. Form Guided Reading Groups

As you get an idea of your ELLs' current reading levels, you can start forming guided reading groups. With guided reading you meet with a small group of students who are at a similar reading level, give them each a copy of a text at their instructional level (a level that is slightly more difficult than what they're able to read independently), and then strategically support them so they can successfully read the text on their own (Fountas and Pinnell 1996, 2000). Chapter 6 provides examples of what a guided reading group can look like with ELLs at different reading levels and L2 proficiency levels. I've found guided reading to be one of the best ways to help ELLs progress to a higher reading level, so the sooner I can get it started, the better. This would be applicable to second through sixth grade, and possibly first grade as well if your school has a kindergarten program that focuses on getting students into leveled books during the second half of the year. The whole-class profile helps you see all the reading levels in your class so you can form groups accordingly. These groups will change throughout the year as your ELLs' needs evolve.

Writing in the L1 and L2

As with the reading workshop, your main priority when launching the writing workshop is to help students learn the routines of what they're expected to do during this time. Your other main focus is to get to know the quality of your ELLs' writing and their ability to write in the L2 so you can help them improve in each area. A writing workshop follows a similar structure as the reading workshop. It begins with a *minilesson* that teaches the class something about the craft of writing and allows students a chance to practice this aspect of writing with you. Students then have time to try this on their own in *independent writing*. During independent writing you can have *writing conferences* with individual students to help them improve their writing or meet with a small group of students who have a similar writing need. At the end of the workshop there's time for students to share what they've worked on (Davis and Hill 2003). Following are some specific ways to assess your ELLs' writing and language use during writing workshop in the first weeks of school.

Steps to Take with ELLs in Writing

1. Look at Your ELLs' Writing from the Previous Year

Before the year starts, if you have samples of your ELLs' writing from the previous school year, take a look at what they were able to create. How does the quality of their writing compare with what's expected at your grade level, based on the standards for writing used at your school? How does their language use compare with the L2 proficiency levels in Figure 2–6?

2. Collect Initial Writing Samples

I strongly suggest getting an initial writing sample from your ELLs on the first day of school during the writing workshop, such as what I did with Edwin. This sample will give you a baseline understanding of your ELLs' current writing ability, both for the quality of their writing (genre, focus, organization, elaboration, word choice, voice, conventions) and their ability to use the L1 and/or L2 (spelling, language structures, vocabulary). In bilingual programs you'll want to get an initial writing sample in both languages.

For the initial writing sample you can have ELLs at any grade level write a story about a particular moment from the summer—a "small moment" narrative (Calkins et al. 2003, 2006). Resist the temptation to help ELLs as they're writing because this will alter the results. When you collect these writing samples, you can analyze them as I did with Edwin's narrative. Look first at the strengths each ELL shows as a writer, and then determine areas in which he can improve. Using the Language Structures checklist, mark any structures you see your ELLs using securely, as well as ones they're developing an ability to use. Then you can help your ELLs with the areas they need to develop during whole-class minilessons or when you begin meeting with individual ELLs in writing conferences, as discussed in Chapter 5. As the school year progresses and your ELLs create more pieces of writing, you can see how both the quality of their writing and their language use are evolving.

3. Include a Letter Writing Activity

A letter writing activity has become one of my favorite ways to start the new school year because it lets me get to know my ELLs' writing and language use while also learning about them as people. On the first day of school I share a letter with the students that I've written on chart paper, revealing information about myself and modeling the type of writing I'm hoping they'll produce when they write their own letters. Then I ask my ELLs to write me a letter, in whatever language is most comfortable for them, telling me about themselves. I've found that ELLs from second to sixth grade love this activity, especially after hearing me read the letter I wrote to them.

Figure 2–10 contains one such letter I received from Samuel, a Level 1 ELL from Colombia who was a newcomer to our school at the end of the previous school year. He wrote the letter in Spanish, although interestingly he incorporated the English greeting that I had modeled in my own letter.

Samuel's letter told me about some of his interests, which I hoped to learn more about. His writing also gave me insight into his Spanish literacy skills. I saw that although Samuel had a base of literacy skills in Spanish, in this example of his work his writing skills seemed to be significantly below grade level. This let me know that Samuel would probably need more support in developing his English literacy skills because he wouldn't be able to rely on as much transfer of literacy skills from the L1 to the L2.

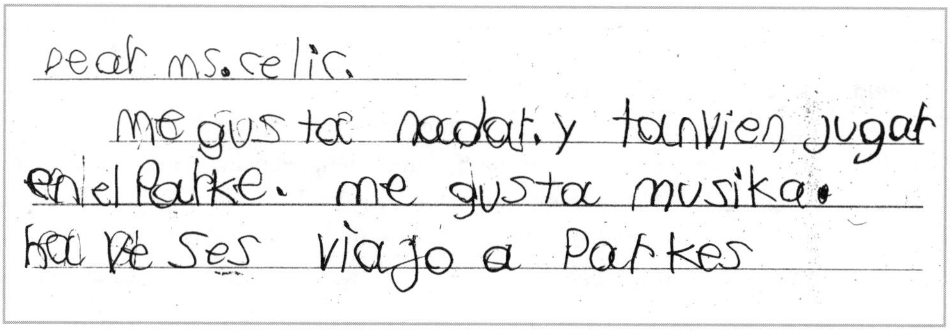
Dear ms.celic.
me gus ta nadar. y tanvien jugar
en el Parke. me gusta musika.
Ka Ve Ses viajo a Parkes

Figure 2–10 *Samuel's letter from the first day of school*
Translation: *Dear Ms. Celic, I like to swim. And also play in the park. I like music. Sometimes I travel to parks.*
[There is no closing.]

4. Administer a Developmental Spelling Assessment

Finally, for ELLs in grades 1–6, a spelling assessment lets you measure their phonetic development in the L2. This information will help you plan whole-group and small-group instruction that targets their phonetic needs. One source for this type of spelling assessment is *Words Their Way for English Learners* (Bear et al. 2007). It has assessments for primary and upper grades in English, Spanish, Chinese, and Korean as well as sequences of lessons for yearlong instruction. Bilingual teachers should administer this type of assessment in the L1 and the L2.

Math in the L1 and L2

Many people assume that math is a universal language and therefore easy for ELLs. In fact, success for ELLs in math is highly tied to language and literacy (Coggins et al. 2007). ELLs need to understand and use academic mathematical language, have the reading skills to understand directions and problems, and have the writing skills to compose responses about how they solved a math problem. As you're getting to know your ELLs' strengths and needs in math, consider if any of their difficulties are related to their development of language and literacy skills in the L2.

Steps to Take with ELLs in Math

1. Determine Your ELLs' Previous Math Performance

Before the school year begins, look at your ELLs' report card grades in math, samples of class work, and the results from standardized math tests, if applicable. Are they performing at grade level? Were they tested in the L1 or the L2? If it was in the L2, how might that have affected their ability to demonstrate their math content knowledge? Highlight on the profile the ELLs you have concerns about so you can watch their progress in class closely.

2. Assess Your ELLs' Knowledge of Previous Concepts

If your ELLs have gaps in their mathematical knowledge, you want to find out right away. This is particularly important for ELLs who have limited formal education. At the beginning of the school year, consider giving your ELLs an informal assessment that covers key concepts from previous years. You can create something yourself or simply get an end-of-the-year cumulative assessment from the previous grade's math curriculum. Some curricular programs have these materials in Spanish as well as English. This can help you accurately assess any beginning ELLs who speak Spanish. For ELLs with an intermediate proficiency in the L2, I often provide copies of the assessment in both languages. That way they can use their mathematical language and literacy skills from both the L1 *and* the L2 to help them understand the problems. For ELLs who don't speak Spanish, try finding a native language speaker in the school who can help translate. It's worth the extra effort to get the best understanding of your ELLs' capabilities.

3. Make a Plan for ELLs with Limited Formal Education

If you have any ELLs with limited formal education, they will likely be significantly behind in math. Keeping the curriculum challenging and having high expectations for ELLs with limited formal education helps them make academic improvements (Freeman and Freeman 2001). Have them participate with the rest of the class in grade-level math work, but also provide them with small-group instruction to develop the concepts and skills they're missing. See if your school has specialists who can provide small-group intervention to further target these ELLs' needs in a personalized setting.

The Big Picture of the First Week of School

Having read about these ways that you can get to know your English language learners, it's helpful to see how it all fits together. Figure 2–11 on page 57 shows an overview of what you can do before the school year begins and during the first week of school to research your ELLs and assess their linguistic and academic abilities. Figure 2–12 on page 58 summarizes the information discussed in this chapter.

Communicating with Families

Throughout this chapter I've described ways to get to know ELLs by reviewing their school records and then assessing their linguistic and academic abilities once the school year has started. The missing piece that's vital to understanding your English language learners is communicating with their families. What you learn from ELLs' families will give you great insight into their backgrounds, personal interests, and academic experiences. Some teachers go to students' homes before the school year begins to get to know their students in the home environment. There are also many ways to reach out to your ELLs' families during the first weeks of school.

- Send home a welcome letter introducing yourself and telling the family a little about your classroom. If possible, have the letter translated into your ELLs' native language.

- Along with the welcome letter, send home a Family Survey (see Appendix C) to find out more information about your ELLs and to encourage family involvement in school. Not all families will complete the survey, but my experience has been that the majority do, and it's an excellent way to learn about your ELLs.

Before School Begins	Day 1	Day 2	Day 3	Day 4
☐ Look through ELLs' records to see L1 and countries of origin. ☐ Look through ELLs' records to see L2 proficiency test scores. ☐ Look through ELLs' portfolios to see previous reading, writing, and math performance. ☐ Talk to former teachers if possible. ☐ Fill in the whole-class profile as completely as possible based on this information. ☐ Begin to gather culturally relevant resources and books in your ELLs' native languages. ☐ Set up seating arrangements based on ELLs' L2 proficiency. ☐ Prepare the Language Structures checklist with your ELLs' names. ☐ Prepare a book bag for each ELL with appropriately leveled books in the L1 and/or L2.	☐ Use getting-to-know-you activities that help ELLs share their backgrounds and experiences. ☐ Use read-alouds that build community and connect to ELLs. ☐ Launch the reading workshop. ☐ Give ELLs their personalized book bags for independent reading time. ☐ Begin quick-check reading assessments, starting with the ELLs you marked as a priority. ☐ Launch the writing workshop. ☐ Collect an initial writing sample from each ELL. ☐ Do a letter writing activity.	☐ Continue using read-alouds that build community and connect to ELLs. ☐ Continue quick-check reading assessments. ☐ Begin having writing conferences with ELLs to learn more about their writing ability and language use, starting with the ELLs you marked as a priority. ☐ Administer an assessment of math concepts that your ELLs should have learned previously.	☐ Continue using read-alouds that build community and connect to ELLs. ☐ Continue quick-check reading assessments. ☐ Continue writing conferences. ☐ Administer a developmental spelling assessment to the class. ☐ As you start math lessons, pay close attention to ELLs who struggled with math in previous years and to your newcomers.	☐ Continue using read-alouds that build community and connect to ELLs. ☐ Continue quick-check reading assessments, or begin informal reading assessments with individual ELLs if your independent reading time is running smoothly. ☐ Continue writing conferences. ☐ Continue watching your ELLs closely during math time to identify individual needs.

Figure 2–11 *Planning for the first days of school*

Find Out Each ELL's:	So You Can More Effectively:	Using:
Native language	• Partner each newcomer with a native language peer, if possible. • Provide academic support in students' L1. • Gather resources in students' L1.	• Home Language Survey
Country of origin	• Connect learning to ELLs' cultural experiences and knowledge. • Gather culturally relevant resources.	• Data in cumulative records
L2 proficiency level	• Plan what supports to use in instruction so all your ELLs can understand and participate in lessons and activities. • Group ELLs with *different* L2 proficiencies for group work and partner work.	• Standardized L2 tests • Other formal assessments such as LAS-Oral and LAS- Reading/Writing (Language Assessment Scale) • Language Structures checklist • Language use when speaking for academic purposes • Language use in writing samples
Number of years learning the L2	• Put ELLs' L2 proficiency levels in context and pinpoint any discrepancies; do their L2 levels reflect the amount of time they've been learning the language?	• Cumulative records
Level of literacy in the L1 and/or L2	• Determine ELLs' strengths and needs with reading (decoding, fluency, and comprehension). • Determine ELLs' strengths and needs with writing (quality of writing, vocabulary, spelling, language structures). • Pinpoint areas of particular concern that may require special interventions. • Plan appropriate whole-class, small-group, and individual instruction to meet your ELLs' literacy needs. • Determine if a difficulty in literacy is related to learning the L2, or if the student has also experienced difficulty with literacy in the L1.	• Informal reading assessments (running records, DRA, QRI, concepts about print, letter names, sound identification, high-frequency words) • Writing samples • Spelling assessments • Standardized language arts tests
Content-area abilities in the L1 and/or L2	• Determine ELLs' strengths and needs with computation, math concepts, and problem solving. • Determine if a difficulty in math is related to learning the L2, or if the student has also experienced difficulty with math in the L1. • Take note of strengths and weaknesses with science and social studies concepts.	• Class work • Performance on in-class assessments • Standardized tests of math, science, and social studies

Figure 2–12 *Gathering information about your ELLs*

- For the families you see before or after school, take the time to initiate an informal conversation with them about their children. If you don't speak a family's native language, don't let this deter you. Find someone who can translate (perhaps your student or a member of the school community). .

- For families you don't see at school, call them during the first weeks just to introduce yourself and talk a little about their children. This can be intimidating when you don't speak the family's native language, but it is possible to do with a translator from the school.

- If you have a particular concern about certain ELLs, invite their families to meet with you at school. By meeting early on in the first month of school, you can get to know the family and the student better and keep the conversation positive by focusing on what you hope to do to help their child during the year. This is also a good time to mention ways the family can support what you're doing in the classroom. Every year there are a handful of ELLs whom I have concerns about, and every meeting I've had with families in this way has been an incredibly positive experience. Families have expressed that they appreciate seeing so early on how sincerely I want to help their children be successful. They've also mentioned that the positive approach encouraged their children to make an effort to improve.

Establishing communication in any of these ways lets families see your interest in helping their children learn, shows your ELLs that there's a strong relationship between the home and school, and helps you discuss with families ways they can be involved in their children's education. It also gives you insight into the students' background that can shed light on their performance in school.

Final Thoughts

We teach at a time when instruction has become increasingly data driven, and at times it feels like this focus on cold, hard numbers has taken some of the heart out of teaching. But I've never felt that using my whole-class profile has reduced my ELLs to just a list of numbers. It simply gives me a way to stay organized with everything I'm learning about my ELLs' backgrounds, language abilities, and academic abilities. In previous years, much of that information got lost in the craziness of the first weeks of school, and it took longer for me to really get to know each child. By taking these steps to get to know your ELLs, you're prepared to address their specific academic and linguistic needs through purposeful instruction after just a few days of school. That leaves a lot more time to help ELLs meet the goals you've set for them.

Reflecting on the Keys to Success

Raise the Bar

- Am I planning to teach my ELLs the *same* curriculum that other students in the grade will be learning, without watering it down?

- Do I assess my ELLs in reading, writing, and math to see how their current level compares with what is expected of the grade level?

Differentiate Instruction

- Do I learn about my ELLs' academic abilities and needs before school and through initial assessments?
- Do I plan differentiated instruction based on that information?
  - leveled books for independent reading
  - guided reading groups
  - individual reading conferences that target specific needs each ELL has in decoding, comprehension, or fluency
  - individual writing conferences that target areas each ELL needs to develop in the quality of her writing and her language use
  - small-group instruction in math
- Am I assessing my ELLs' L2 proficiency levels to see what language structures I'll need to teach them through literacy and the content areas?

Connect Learning to Students

- Do I learn about my ELLs' cultural backgrounds and make them a part of my instruction?
- Have I found resources that my ELLs can relate to culturally?

Use Students' Native Languages to Support Learning

- Do I know what my students' native languages are?
- Do I set up native language partnerships to support ELLs who are beginning to learn the L2?
- Do I have books and other resources in my students' native languages?

Involve Families

- Do I reach out to families during the first days and weeks of school through notes home, phone calls, or in-person conversations?
- Do I focus my communications on the positive aspects of learning about their children and discussing how we can support the children's development together?

References for Further Reading

Assessing English Language Learners

Cappellini, Mary. 2005. *Balancing Reading and Language Learning: A Resource for Teaching English Language Learners, K–5*. Portland, ME: Stenhouse.

Gottlieb, Margo. 2006. *Assessing English Language Learners: Bridges from Language Proficiency to Academic Achievement*. Thousand Oaks, CA: Corwin.

Reading Assessment

Calkins, Lucy, and the Teachers College Reading and Writing Project, Columbia University. 2002. *A Field Guide to the Classroom Library: Volumes A–G.* 7 vols. Portsmouth, NH: Heinemann.

Clay, Marie M. 2000. *Concepts About Print: What Have Children Learned About the Way We Print Language?* Portsmouth, NH: Heinemann.

———. 2006. *Running Records for Classroom Teachers.* Portsmouth, NH: Heinemann.

Fountas, Irene C., and Gay Su Pinnell. 2006. *Leveled Books K–8: Matching Texts to Readers for Effective Teaching.* Portsmouth, NH: Heinemann.

Launching a Reading Workshop

Collins, Kathy. 2004. *Growing Readers: Units of Study in the Primary Classroom.* Portland, ME: Stenhouse.

Fountas, Irene C., and Gay Su Pinnell. 2000. *Guiding Readers and Writers, Grades 3–6: Teaching Comprehension, Genre, and Content Literacy.* Portsmouth, NH: Heinemann.

Taberski, Sharon. 2000. *On Solid Ground: Strategies for Teaching Reading K–3.* Portsmouth, NH: Heinemann.

Writing Assessment

Anderson, Carl. 2005. *Assessing Writers.* Portsmouth, NH: Heinemann.

Samway, Katharine Davies. 2006. *When English Language Learners Write: Connecting Research to Practice, K–8.* Portsmouth, NH: Heinemann.

Launching a Writing Workshop

Calkins, Lucy, and the Teachers College Reading and Writing Project. 2003. *Units of Study for Primary Writing: A Yearlong Curriculum.* 9 vols., 1 CD-ROM. Portsmouth, NH: Heinemann.

———. 2006. *Units of Study for Teaching Writing, Grades 3–5.* 7 vols., 1 CD-ROM. Portsmouth, NH: Heinemann.

Davis, Judy, and Sharon Hill. 2003. *The No-Nonsense Guide to Teaching Writing: Strategies, Structures, Solutions.* Portsmouth, NH: Heinemann.

Math Instruction with English Language Learners

Coggins, Debra, Drew Kravin, Grace Dávila Coates, and Maria Dreux Carroll. 2007. *English Language Learners in the Mathematics Classroom.* Thousand Oaks, CA: Corwin.

CHAPTER 3

Classroom Management with English Language Learners

*B*efore the school year began with the group of ELLs I described in Chapter 2, I knew I was going to have to really buckle down with my classroom management. Aside from the information I had gathered about their linguistic, academic, and cultural backgrounds, I also knew the reputation this particular group had for its serious behavior problems during previous years. I was worried about how much learning we would be able to accomplish with constant interruptions. Even though I always establish a predictable schedule and routines with my ELLs and set up clear rules and accountability for their behavior, I knew that this year I would have to be even more consistent if I wanted my ELLs to have a productive year.

The first few weeks of school were totally frustrating; I felt like I was wasting too much time enforcing class rules and reviewing the routines of our daily schedule. But I kept at it, and near the end of that first month of school, things finally started to click. I began to notice how smoothly our day was flowing from one part of the schedule to the next, and I realized with great relief that I wasn't stopping nearly as often to address behavior issues. The best part was that my ELLs were becoming incredibly productive with their academic work. The consistency of the classroom management was starting to pay off.

Right around this time I had three newcomers join the class. It was one of those moments where I felt my stomach sink because I knew it would be difficult to manage my original group of ELLs and support the three newcomers in adjusting to all the intricacies of our *classroom routines. I was hoping I could depend on the rest of my ELLs to help bring these newcomers into the fold of our classroom community, even though they themselves had just started following the rules and routines. Hoping for the best, I scrambled to get three more desks. I did a little rearranging to seat two of the newcomers next to partners who spoke Spanish. The other newcomer, Lian, was from Taiwan and I didn't have any other students who spoke Mandarin. I imagined that without being able to communicate in her native language, Lian would have a more difficult time adjusting to our routines.*

When the newcomers got settled in, it was time for the writing workshop. As the students started working on their narratives, I saw Lian's partner, Isabel, go to the writing center and get Lian some paper with a picture box at the top and lines underneath. Isabel showed Lian her own writing from her writing folder and then gestured how Lian should draw her own story and write about it. The two girls sat down to work, as did the other newcomers, whose partners had also prepared them with the materials they needed and explained in Spanish what they should do. By the time I made my way over to Lian's group, I saw that she had already drawn a detailed picture of herself in the classroom and had started writing on the lines below the picture box in her native language. I later took Lian's writing to another student in the school who was literate in Mandarin, and I found out that Lian had written a narrative about coming to her new classroom and feeling happy there.

I marveled at how responsibly my class modeled the classroom culture throughout the day and how quickly Lian and the other newcomers were picking up on the class routines. My ELLs knew exactly what routines to model to the newcomers, and they even knew how students with different L2 proficiency levels could participate in each instructional activity. Lian's narrative showed that she was feeling comfortable in her new learning environment, something extremely important for English language learners. Although Lian and the other newcomers would need a lot of support to get fully acclimated to our classroom, having a predictable environment certainly helped smooth the transition for them. As September came to a close, I realized how much I was looking forward to the remaining eight months I had to work with this group of students, which now included my newcomers—a far cry from the apprehension I had felt during those first weeks.

No matter how nicely you've set up your classroom or how many great learning activities you've planned for the first weeks of school, without strong classroom management in place, students can't get the most out of their learning. This is particularly true for ELLs. The way you develop a daily schedule, routines, rules, accountability, and homework procedures with ELLs will affect how well they understand what's expected of them and how productive they'll be.

In this chapter I describe

- the benefits of classroom management for ELLs
- setting up a daily schedule that works for ELLs
- practicing classroom routines
- establishing class rules
- developing a system for accountability
- structuring homework procedures with ELLs

Benefits of Classroom Management for ELLs

Making the Most of Your Time

When you plan for and implement consistent classroom management, you ultimately spend less time explaining routine procedures or putting out fires sparked by inappropriate behavior. This results in having more time for teaching (Shalaway 2005). Maximizing instructional time is critical because there's a lot to accomplish during the school day and seemingly never enough minutes to fit it all in. Not only are you teaching your ELLs the content for their grade, but you're also helping them learn all the conversational and academic language that goes along with it. The more time ELLs have for practicing language and content, the more success they'll experience.

Providing a Predictable Environment

Another benefit of developing strong classroom management is that it creates an anxiety-free environment where ELLs know exactly what to expect (Krashen 1982). They know what things they need to do in the morning to get ready for learning. They know how the day flows and how they're expected to work independently or collaboratively in each subject area. They know when and where they need to copy down homework and how to take home the appropriate materials. When a student is just beginning to learn another language, not knowing how a classroom works or how she needs to act within that classroom is incredibly stressful. If every day brings a different routine and expectations, it creates a great unknown. This, combined with the great unknown of the language that surrounds her, causes high levels of tension. When we provide a predictable environment through consistent routines, rules, and daily schedule, we alleviate that stress and help focus ELLs' mental energies on their learning.

Learning the Classroom Culture

Your ELLs may come from many different countries, each with their own cultural understanding of what's expected at school and how things work in a classroom. By clearly modeling what to do during each part of the day, and by providing ELLs with ample opportunities to practice during the first weeks of school, you'll help them understand what the expectations are in their new classroom and new culture. For example, many ELLs are used to a model of education where they work only independently at school, so the concept of collaborative work is new to them. They need clear models for how you expect them to work with a partner or a group for different activities, and they need time to feel comfortable participating in this kind of learning structure. Another cultural difference I've encountered is that some ELLs are accustomed to sharing an idea or answer only when called upon by the teacher. It can take a while for them to feel comfortable raising their hands during a class discussion. I make an effort to call on these students so they actively participate, and I also encourage them little by little to raise their hands when I know they have something to share. Being sensitive to the cultural adjustments your newcomers are going through is the first step, and then you can use the predictability of your classroom management to help them understand any new expectations.

Setting Up a Daily Schedule

When you think about your daily schedule for the school year, keep in mind that ELLs function best when there's consistency. A predictable structure eases anxiety for students and increases their ability to be productive in the classroom (Bickart, Jablon, and Dodge 1999). If ELLs know exactly how the day is going to flow from one subject to the next, they can become an active part of the classroom regardless of their language proficiency level (Goldenberg 2008). They don't need to rely on verbal explanations from you to understand what's happening next or to know what they're expected to do. ELLs can be prepared to take out the appropriate materials for the next subject, be in the appropriate part of the room, and complete learning activities in an appropriate way. Think about how you can make your daily schedule as consistent as possible throughout the week. There are always factors out of your control that affect the consistency of your schedule, such as when you have special subjects like art and physical education, or when other teachers come into your classroom to support particular students. Take all of these variables into account, and design a weekly schedule that's as predictable as possible. Then think through what you want your ELLs to do within each part of the daily schedule.

- How should your ELLs transition from one instructional activity to the next?

- Where should they go in the room?

- What are they expected to do? Are the learning activities different for ELLs at different proficiency levels?

- What materials will they need? Are the necessary materials different for ELLs at different proficiency levels?

The more you've thought through these details, the more clearly you can model for ELLs what you expect them to do. This helps them understand how the classroom functions and enables them to work more productively.

To display the daily schedule in the classroom, I like to laminate index cards that have the names of each instructional component and an accompanying picture. For example, on the "Reading Workshop" index card, I put a picture of students reading books independently. That way my beginning ELLs can use the visuals to understand what's going to happen during each part of the school day. I also include cards for the specials for the day like music, art, and physical education. I put a magnet on the back of each index card and stick the cards to a board in the front of the room where my students can easily see them. Next to each component I have another index card with the time frame written down and shown with clock faces. This helps my ELLs know what to expect at each time throughout the day.

Every morning I arrange the instructional components on the board based on that day's schedule, and I write a short sentence next to each one explaining what we'll specifically be doing. At the beginning of the school day, I briefly walk the class through the schedule, letting the students know what we'll be learning. If there are any changes to the normal schedule, I point them out so my ELLs can anticipate them.

Adjusting a Daily Schedule for ELLs

There's no right way to sequence the different literacy and content-area components throughout the instructional day. How you choose to consistently arrange them will depend entirely on the expectations of your school and any schedule constraints you have (Shalaway 2005). However, there are several considerations I keep in mind when planning a daily schedule for ELLs.

- I plan a solid one-hour block of time for math. This provides the much-needed time to develop academic language for math along with the new math concepts. I also try to teach math in the morning. Math can be a very challenging subject for ELLs because they're learning new math concepts and academic language at the same time. I find that it's easier for ELLs to focus on this difficult, yet fundamental, subject in the morning.

- I dedicate the afternoon to content-area studies, although social studies and science concepts are also integrated with morning literacy components whenever possible. In the upper grades, I dedicate more than a full hour to science or social studies each day since the curricula for these subject areas become increasingly demanding. This gives ELLs time to strengthen their understanding of the content-area concepts and to develop the necessary academic language skills. Within that time, I plan for a variety of reading and writing activities to support language, literacy, and content development. Chapter 4 describes in detail how to integrate content areas with literacy in the primary and upper grades.

- I plan for the read-aloud to be either before or after lunch. This is a nice transition for ELLs, and it puts the read-aloud close to science or social studies time, which is beneficial because it often connects with these content areas.

- Interactive writing is a common primary-grade literacy component that is very beneficial for ELLs at *any* grade level in helping them develop the connection between oral language and written language in English. I include interactive writing at the end of the day in both the primary and upper grades to help ELLs summarize their content-area learning while also developing their writing skills in the L2.

Sample Daily Schedules

Figures 3–1 and 3–2 on pages 68 and 69 provide a primary- and an upper-grade example of one way you can include all the literacy and content-area components in a daily schedule. The sample schedules allot time for routines such as the morning routine, transitioning to lunch, and an end-of-the-day routine. In the next sections I give a brief description of each literacy component in the daily schedule to provide a common understanding for the remaining chapters of the book. Then I explain in detail how to establish routines, which are an essential part of the daily schedule for ELLs.

Literacy Components in a Daily Schedule

If you're unfamiliar with balanced literacy, the different components included in the daily schedules can seem overwhelming. These literacy components are designed to allow for a gradual release of responsibility from teacher-directed instruction to student independence (Pearson and Gallagher 1983; Freeman and Freeman 2006). The goal is to help ELLs become independent with their reading and writing skills, applying and

8:30–9:00	• Morning routine—5 min. Students unpack their bags and turn in homework and notes. • Morning meeting—10 min. Share the daily schedule. Complete math routines. • Shared reading—15 min.
9:00–9:50	Reading workshop • Minilesson with a familiar read-aloud or shared reading—10 min. • Independent reading and partner reading—35 min. Have conferences with individual ELLs—about 5 min. each and/or Meet with ELLs in guided reading groups—about 10–15 min. each. • Share (with a reading partner or whole class)—5 min.
9:50–10:10	Word study • Activities to develop language structures • Small-group or whole-class work on phonemic awareness and spelling skills 5-min. stretching break
10:15–11:05	Writing workshop • Minilesson: modeling writing and shared writing—10 min. • Independent writing—30 min. Have conferences with individual ELLs—about 5 min. each and/or Meet with small groups of ELLs—about 10 min. each. • Share (with a writing partner or whole class)—10 min. Can include a quick edit and a language minilesson based on observations.
11:05–12:05	Math • Math lesson: model and practice the math concept and academic language • Collaborative and/or independent practice • Regroup to review math concept and academic language 5-min. transition to lunch
12:10–1:00	Lunch and recess 5-min. transition to classroom
1:05–1:25	Read-aloud with language development
1:25–2:00	Social studies or science • Can include a content-area shared reading, read-aloud, or shared writing. • Can include vocabulary development activities and hands-on activities.
2:00–2:15	Content-based interactive writing
2:15–2:45	Specials (art, music, physical education)
2:45–3:00	End-of-the-day-routine • Prepare materials for homework, pack bags, dismissal.

Figure 3–1 *Sample primary-grade schedule*

8:30–8:40	• Morning routine—5 min. Students unpack their bags, turn in homework and notes, complete class jobs. • Morning meeting—5 min. Share the daily schedule. Complete math routines.
8:40–9:30	Reading workshop • Minilesson with a familiar read-aloud or shared reading—10 min. • Independent reading and partner reading—35 min. Have conferences with individual ELLs—about 5 min. each and/or Meet with ELLs in guided reading groups—about 10–15 min. each. • Share (with a reading partner or whole class)—5 min.
9:30–10:20	Writing workshop • Minilesson: modeling writing and shared writing—10 min. • Independent writing—30 min. Have conferences with individual ELLs—about 5 min. each and/or Meet with small groups of ELLs—about 10 min. each. • Share (with a writing partner or whole class)—10 min. Can include a quick edit and a language minilesson based on observations. 5-min. stretching break
10:25–10:45	Word study • Activities to develop language structures • Small-group or whole-class work on spelling skills
10:45–11:45	Math • Math lesson: model and practice the math concept and academic language • Collaborative and/or independent practice • Regroup to review math concept and academic language
11:45–12:05	Read-aloud with language development 5-min. transition to lunch
12:10–1:00	Lunch and recess 5-min. transition to classroom
1:05–2:00	Social studies or science • Can include a content-area shared reading, read-aloud, and/or shared writing. • Can include vocabulary development activities and hands-on activities.
2:00–2:15	Content-based interactive writing
2:15–2:45	Specials (art, music, physical education)
2:45–3:00	End-of-the-day-routine • Prepare materials for homework, pack bags, dismissal.

Figure 3–2 *Sample upper-grade schedule*

reinforcing what they've learned with support from you. Chapters 4–6 give detailed examples of each of these literacy components in action with ELLs.

Read-Alouds → Shared Reading → Guided Reading → Independent Reading

More teacher support   *More student independence*

Modeled Writing → Shared Writing → Interactive Writing → Independent Writing

More teacher support   *More student independence*

Read-Alouds

Read-alouds are a time for students to listen to you read a text that is more challenging than what they could read independently. As you read aloud, you can occasionally pause to do think-alouds, which verbalize for the class the thoughts that are going through your mind about the text. These think-alouds open a window into the mind of a good reader, helping students see how readers naturally use a variety of reading comprehension strategies to help them understand a text.

These reading comprehension strategies include the following (Keene and Zimmermann 2009; Harvey and Goudvis 2000):

- making predictions
- making connections
- monitoring and revising comprehension
- visualizing
- inferring
- determining importance
- questioning
- synthesizing

In addition to doing think-alouds, you can also provide moments during a read-aloud for students to "turn and talk" to their partner to practice these reading strategies (Collins 2004). This is particularly helpful for ELLs as a way to develop their speaking skills. Practicing reading comprehension strategies in this supportive environment prepares students to ultimately use them in their independent reading. Read-alouds are also a vital way for ELLs to hear the language modeled in a fluent way, be exposed to a wealth of new vocabulary and language structures in context, and develop their listening comprehension skills (Cappellini 2005). Read-alouds with ELLs should incorporate some time for language development before, during, and after the reading.

Shared Reading

Shared reading was developed by Don Holdaway (1979) as a way for teachers to read a text *with* students, thinking together about what it means by using reading comprehension strategies. In order for the class to read a text with you, it has to be large enough for everyone to see. You can use big books, copy a text on chart paper, or use an overhead projector to display a text. Whereas with read-alouds the teacher is doing all of the reading, shared reading makes it a collaborative process with students. In the primary grades this allows you to help students learn concepts about print, such as how to handle a book, the directionality of text, and one-to-one correspondence with words. It also helps ELLs at any grade level see how they can combine different print strategies to read the words in the text.

Print strategies include the following (Collins 2004; Cappellini 2005):

- using graphophonic cues (matching sounds to letters)
- using syntactic cues (using what they know about the structure of sentences to read words)
- using meaning cues (determining if what they are reading makes sense)
- breaking a word into chunks
- looking for familiar parts within a word
- self-correcting
- rereading and looking back
- reading ahead

The first exposure to a shared reading text typically focuses on helping students understand the text using a variety of print strategies and reading comprehension strategies. Additional readings of the text help students build fluency, reinforce new words they've learned, or reinforce new sounds they've learned. Later you can use the shared reading text during word study to help ELLs examine how the language is used, including phonetic features, word patterns, high-frequency words, and language structures.

Reading Workshop

The goal of the reading workshop is to help move students toward independence with their reading. You've been reading *to* them with read-alouds and reading *with* them with shared reading. The reading workshop is a time for students to independently use all the print strategies and reading comprehension strategies they've seen and practiced (Calkins 2001; Collins 2004; Taberski 2000; Miller 2002). Of course, as students try this out on their own, you're by their side to support them with reading conferences and guided reading groups.

Minilesson

The reading workshop begins with a minilesson where you use a familiar read-aloud or shared reading text to model a particular reading strategy. Students have an opportunity to practice this strategy with you several times, and then you have them go to their reading spots to try using this reading strategy on their own during independent reading.

Independent Reading

During independent reading each student reads the books he's chosen for the week, which are a combination of leveled books at his independent reading level and nonleveled books of interest. This supports ELLs who have a wide range of reading levels by giving them time to read texts that are appropriate for their L2 proficiency levels and reading ability.

ELLs may be reading their leveled and nonleveled books on their own, listening to texts on tape, or reading with a partner. While they're doing this reading work, you can meet with students in reading conferences or support small groups of students with guided reading. Reading conferences are a time to sit next to different students, listen to them read, talk with them briefly about the text, and determine what you can teach them to help them as readers (Taberski 2000; Calkins 2001). Is there a particular print strategy they're not currently using? Is there a reading comprehension strategy you could help them use? During a reading conference you help students put that strategy into practice right then while you're sitting side by side. You can take notes on a reading conference form about what you taught each ELL about reading *and* about language. See Appendix D for a sample reading conference form that I use with ELLs, which has space for recording information about both of these areas. You can also take note of the language you observed each ELL using on the Language Structures checklist (Figure 2–7).

Guided Reading

In both the primary and the upper grades, guided reading is a way to gather together a small group of students who are reading at a similar level, giving them the support they need to be able to read a text that is slightly more difficult than what they can read independently (Fountas and Pinnell 1996, 2000; Routman 2000). This is referred to as the students' *instructional level*. In a guided reading group session you're not reading *to* the students or *with* the students, but rather preparing them so they can read a book that's at their instructional level *on their own*. To do this, you begin by briefly introducing the book to the small group, discussing what the readers think it might be about, talking about important language that appears in the book, and helping them make connections to what they already know about the topic. This gives your ELLs a context for understanding the text and a preview of the key vocabulary they'll be encountering. After the introduction, students stay where they're seated on the rug or at the table and begin to read the text independently.

While students are reading to themselves, you can listen to each one quietly read aloud part of the text to you, monitoring his decoding, fluency, and reading comprehension. If a student is struggling to read or understand a particular part, you can guide him to figure it out and then have him continue to read. When students have finished reading the text, regroup them and lead a brief discussion about what they've read, using the key language introduced at the beginning. At this point you can talk to the whole group about a particular decoding or reading comprehension strategy, based on observations of what your students struggled with when reading the book on their own. With ELLs you may also want to point out a particular aspect of the language they had difficulty reading, such as certain sounds, high-frequency words, or language structures.

Writing Workshop

Just as in reading, with writing there is a gradual release of responsibility to the students to support them with the strategies and skills they'll need to write independently (Davis and Hill 2003; Routman 2000; Calkins 1994). This begins with a minilesson where you model writing *to* students and have students practice it *with* you, perhaps using shared writing. The writing workshop continues by having students work *on their own* in independent writing.

Minilesson: Modeled Writing

In a writing workshop minilesson you first model a particular aspect of the writing process to students so they specifically see what a writer does to create a written text. By thinking aloud while you model your writing, you help students understand what goes through a writer's mind to compose a text. This kind of modeling will, of course, look very different for a kindergartner than for a sixth grader. Depending on where your class is in the writing process, you may be modeling how to gather ideas, draft, revise, edit, or publish writing.

Minilesson: Shared Writing

During the minilesson you then have students practice the same aspect of the writing process that you just modeled, often through shared writing. With shared writing you write your students' ideas on chart paper or the board so they can all see it. Your students are involved in the writing process because they're generating the ideas, but you're the one physically writing down the text. While you write the text, you can think aloud whatever you want your students to be thinking as they write independently, such as how to write letters that match the sounds in the words, how to use certain high-frequency words, or how to punctuate the text. However, the main focus of the shared writing is on helping students see how they can communicate an idea effectively through writing.

For ELLs, shared writing is a wonderful way to share ideas orally, hear the language, and then see how that language connects to the written text. The vocabulary and language structures from a shared writing text can also become a model for ELLs' own writing.

Independent Writing

During independent writing students have an extended period of time to work on their own writing, based on what was modeled and practiced in the minilesson (Graves 1994). While the class is doing this writing work, you can meet with individual students in writing conferences or support small groups of students with shared writing or interactive writing. Writing conferences are a time to sit next to different students, talk with them about what they're doing with their writing, and determine what you can teach them to help them as writers. Do they need help writing in that particular genre? Do they need support in focusing their writing, elaborating certain parts, or organizing their ideas in the text? Do they need you to help them brainstorm language related to their topic? You can take notes on a writing conference form about what you taught each ELL about writing *and* about her language use. See Appendix D for a sample writing conference form I use with ELLs, which has space for recording information about both of these areas. You can also record the language you observed each ELL using on the Language Structures checklist (Figure 2–7 on page 42).

Interactive Writing

Similar to shared writing, interactive writing is another supportive structure that allows you to write *with* students (McCarrier, Pinnell, and Fountas 2000). The main difference is that with interactive writing, instead of you writing the entire text, your students physically write certain parts of the text on chart paper or on the board. This is referred to as *sharing the pen*. Once the class has determined the content of what it wants to write, you can write some parts of the text and have different students come up to write other parts. Students could help with writing certain letters, high-frequency words, vocabulary words, or adding appropriate punctuation and spacing, depending upon what writing skills you want to focus on with the class. Interactive writing is very supportive for ELLs because regardless of their L2 proficiency level, they can each contribute something to the text. ELLs with beginning proficiency levels can help add certain letters they've learned already, basic high-frequency words they've practiced in class, or familiar aspects of punctuation. ELLs with higher proficiency levels can add more difficult high-frequency words, vocabulary words, or more difficult letter combinations. You can do interactive writing with the whole class, with a small group of ELLs, or even with individual ELLs during a writing conference to help them put their ideas into writing.

I've adapted interactive writing to the upper grades by having ELLs share the pen in a slightly different way. I have upper-grade ELLs determine what the text will say, but then they *all* participate by writing the text in their notebooks as I write it on chart paper or on the board. Instead of having upper-grade ELLs physically come up to the chart paper to write certain letters or words, I simply have them share their contributions orally and I write them down. This keeps the activity fast paced enough for older students, yet it's still interactive since they're all contributing and writing the text in their notebooks.

Word Study

Word study is a part of the day when students explicitly study the language used for reading and writing (Bear et al. 2007). The goal is to help ELLs develop phonemic awareness, spelling skills, and language structures in the L2. With ELLs, you're already weaving a lot of this language development throughout each part of the day as you teach them the language needed for different content-area and literacy activities. Even so, it's beneficial for ELLs to have a specific time of the day set aside for word study where they can explicitly examine how the L2 works. Some days of the week can be used to implement a spelling program your school uses. On other days you can examine certain language structures that you want to focus on, based on the needs you've determined from the Language Structures checklist (Figure 2–7).

Practicing Classroom Routines

Once you fit these different instructional components into a consistent daily schedule, you can help ELLs learn the routines they'll need to follow throughout the school day. Shalaway (2005) describes routines as the backbone of classroom life, creating a predictable environment that allows for more teaching and learning. For ELLs to learn the routines of the classroom, it's important to clearly model what you would like them to do, provide opportunities for them to practice the routine, and reinforce it whenever necessary so that every part of the school day runs smoothly (Dragan 2005). Some routines help students to know what to do during lessons, collaborative work, and independent work time. Other routines help with transition times such as entering the classroom in the morning, going to and from the rug, lining up for lunch, going to the bathroom, switching from one subject to the next, and packing up at the end of the day (Shalaway 2005; Wong and Wong 1998). The following examples illustrate how to model and practice routines in a class with ELLs by using consistent and clear language as well as gestures and visual aids (Goldenberg 2008; Freeman and Freeman 2002). While I outline just a few routines, you can use the same scaffolds when teaching any classroom routine.

The Morning Routine for the First Day of School

The morning routine is the first thing I teach my class on the first day of school because it sets the tone that the classroom is a respectful place where I expect students to be productive and not waste any learning time. When the students are lined up in the hallway outside the door, I welcome them to their new classroom and say something like this:

"When you come into your new classroom [pointing to the door], there are four things I want you to do. First [holding up one finger]: Enter the room quietly [placing a finger over my mouth in the "sh" symbol]. Second [holding up two fingers]: Find the desk with your name on it [holding up an extra name plate and pointing to the name]. Third [holding up three fingers]: Put your backpack on the floor next to your desk. Don't open it [acting out placing backpack on floor]. Fourth [holding up four fingers]: There's an activity on your desk. Please begin completing it for me [holding up an extra copy of activity and acting out filling it in]. So, let's review [holding up fingers consecutively]: Enter quietly, find your desk, put your backpack on the floor, and start the activity. OK? Let's see if these first four students can follow the steps."

I let those students in first and then let in more students when I see that they're following the routine. If they're not doing what I expect, I calmly ask them to return to the hallway to try it again. I remind them of the four steps and let them back in the room. Don't be afraid to repeat the routine numerous times until it's exactly the way you expect it to be. It's the first impression students have for what's appropriate in the classroom, so it pays to devote extra time to this. After a few days you should be able to let the whole class enter at once, instead of a few students at a time.

Having an activity on the desks for students to complete as soon as they come in on the first day of school sends ELLs a clear message that this classroom is a place where learning happens. I have sharpened pencils at each group of desks so students don't need to unpack the supplies in their backpacks just yet. I circulate as ELLs complete the activity, helping those who I know are newcomers or have a lower L2 proficiency level, based on the information I have recorded on my whole-class profile (see Chapter 2). Later I have students unpack their bags, but I wait to organize their school supplies until the following day.

Modeling How to Organize Supplies

Waiting to organize school supplies until at least the second day of school is advisable because not all ELLs come with the requested supplies on the first day, or even the first week. This is particularly true for newcomers whose families may not know what they need to send with their children. Have extra copies of the supply list available to send home with ELLs on the first day and stress the importance of them bringing in the supplies. If possible, have the supply list translated for families who don't speak English. It's very common for new ELLs to arrive throughout the first few weeks of school, so keep extra copies of all the letters and forms you're sending home so you can give new ELLs the same information. To accommodate students who don't have their supplies for a number of days, have several extra notebooks, folders, pencils, scissors, and glue sticks available that they can borrow until they bring their own. You might also have ELLs whose families simply aren't financially able to purchase the required supplies. Speak with your administration about any students in this situation because schools often have extra supplies that can be used to help these families.

On the first days of school, structure activities that don't require students to use their own notebooks or folders. Once you decide to organize supplies with the class, you'll need a system for helping your ELLs correctly label their supplies. If you're teaching in the primary grades, or if you have a large number of beginning ELLs, you can print off labels with the names of the notebooks and folders. That way your ELLs need only to stick the labels on their supplies without worrying about the lengthy process of trying to copy words in a completely unfamiliar language. Having preprinted labels also makes it easier to quickly organize supplies with ELLs who arrive after the first day of school. In the upper grades you could post the list of notebook and folder names on the board, and, if you don't have too many beginning ELLs, you can assist them individually in the process of labeling their supplies.

Once supplies are labeled, explicitly model for ELLs where each notebook and folder needs to go in the classroom. Have them put things away step-by-step with you. In the following days, as ELLs need to add papers to specific folders or use specific notebooks, make sure to model exactly which ones they should be using. Circulate around the classroom to check that your ELLs have taken out the correct materials. As soon as your ELLs learn the routine of what materials they use during each part of the day, this will no longer be necessary.

The Morning Routine for the Rest of the Year

On the second day of school, present the morning routine that you intend to use for the rest of the year, again acting out the specific steps you want your ELLs to follow. The steps in the routine will depend on how you plan to start your instructional day. Figure 3–3 shows an example of a morning routine I used one year. Next to each step I included a visual to help my beginning ELLs remember what they needed to do. The morning routine always ends with a learning activity you want your class to get started on. For example, this could be solving a problem of the day in math or reading a book independently.

Using Music with the Morning Routine

There are always some students who struggle to complete the morning routine on time. They may get distracted by the excitement of seeing their friends again or lost in the details of unpacking their things. To solve this problem, I like to use music. As soon as the class enters the room, I turn on a song that lasts about four minutes. ELLs learn that by the time the song ends, they need to be beginning the learning activity part of the routine, whatever that may be for your grade and classroom.

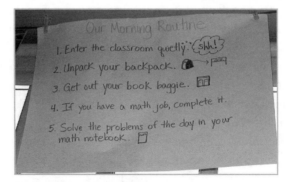

Figure 3–3 *A morning routine chart*

Using music is also a great way to connect with other cultures. I like to use songs from other countries during the morning routine. One way to do this is to ask ELLs to bring in music they have at home that's in their native languages. Remind ELLs that it has to be something low-key enough to play in the background. Preview the music before you play it to make sure it has an appropriate length and tone. To take matters into your own hands, try doing a search online or at a music store for international music. It's a meaningful way to make your classroom representative of all your students.

If you have ELLs who still struggle to complete the routine on time, help them for a few days. This is often the case with newcomers who are still unfamiliar with the materials. Physically show them how to unpack their bags efficiently, and indicate what they need to have on their desks. You can also ask an ELL's partner to help with the routine until the student feels more comfortable with it.

Routine for Transitioning to and from the Rug

Students will be coming and going to the rug multiple times a day for the reading minilesson, the writing minilesson, read-alouds, class meetings, and possibly content-area lessons, shared reading, and interactive writing. Therefore, it helps to have a routine in place that provides for a quick transition.

The first step is to teach students what they will always need to bring with them to the rug for each time of day. For example, if you want students to have their reading notebook and a pencil with them for every reading minilesson, this needs to become part of the routine. If there's ever a day when they need to bring different materials, you can let them know before they come to the rug by clearly holding up whatever material they'll need. Showing ELLs the things to bring instead of just saying it helps them adapt to the change in routine.

To teach ELLs how to come to the rug for a reading minilesson, you might say something like: "Every time we come to the rug [motioning from the desk area to the rug area], we want to make sure we do it quickly [circling hands in a "hurry up" motion] and quietly [making a "sh" motion]. The longer it takes, the less time we have for learning. So, today when you come to the rug I would like you to do these four things. First [holding up one finger]: Bring your reading notebook and a pencil [holding them up for the class to see]. You'll always bring these things with you for reading lessons. Second [holding up two fingers]: Push your chair in quietly [physically demonstrating]. Third [holding up three fingers]: Quietly walk over to the rug area [physically demonstrating]. Fourth [holding up four fingers]: Sit anywhere on the rug for now [physically demonstrating]. Later you'll have a specific spot on the rug. So, let's review [holding up fingers consecutively]: Bring your reading notebook and pencil, push your chair in, quietly walk over, and sit on the rug. OK? Let's try it. Let's see how well Group 3 can follow those steps."

Just like with the morning routine, I have a small group of students try this routine first. If students don't follow this routine exactly the way you would like, then calmly ask them to return to their desks so they can try it again (Wong and Wong 1998). Let them know what they need to change, modeling so the whole class can understand. Continue in this way, allowing more groups to come until everyone is seated on the rug. When students leave the rug after the lesson, have them follow a similar routine, letting them know where to go and what they should begin doing.

Establishing Class Rules

Having a consistent schedule with predictable routines is effective only if there are rules that govern how students act in the classroom. Some schools struggle more with student behavior than others, and some classes within a school can be more of a behavioral challenge, as was the case with the class I described at the beginning of this chapter. No matter what the dynamics are with your class, *all* students benefit from having clearly established rules. Just as ELLs need clearly modeled routines so they know what to do throughout the school day, they also need clearly modeled rules to understand their role in the classroom.

If we develop rules collaboratively with ELLs, model what the rules mean, and then consistently hold them accountable to the rules, we create a learning environment that's respectful and productive. Before the school year begins, decide what four or five rules you feel will be important for your classroom to run smoothly and jot them down. Some examples of rules include

- Respect each other.
- Work without disturbing others.
- Listen carefully and follow instructions.
- Raise your hand to share an idea with the class.
- Complete work on time.

The rules you choose can be as general or as specific as you feel necessary. When your class collaboratively brainstorms rules on the first day of school, it will inevitably come up with ideas that are similar to the ones you determined ahead of time. You can then summarize students' ideas in a way that parallels your original list (Wong and Wong 1998; Bickart, Jablon, and Dodge 1999).

Scaffolding Language for the Class Rules

Consider how you can create class rules in a way that includes your ELLs so everyone contributes to building the classroom community. One way to do this is to model the type of language ELLs can use to share an idea they have about a class rule. If your ELLs have a structure for the language needed to discuss class rules, it increases their listening comprehension and makes them more comfortable participating. You can write a structure such as "I think we should _____" on the board, and then model using it to share an idea you have for a class rule. This doesn't mean every ELL is developmentally ready to use this type of language structure when speaking; it's simply a way to scaffold the discussion so that the language ELLs are hearing other students use is more familiar.

Once your ELLs are familiar with this language structure and with what they're expected to do, you can have the class work collaboratively in groups to think of class rules. ELLs will be more likely to orally share an idea with a small group than with the whole class, particularly on the first day of school. If you've seated ELLs strategically to mix L2 proficiencies and have provided native language partners for beginning ELLs, then every ELL will have linguistic support for sharing ideas (Freeman and Freeman 2007; Gibbons 1991). While the groups are talking, circulate to each group and listen to its ideas. Take your whole-class profile with you to remember what approximate proficiency level each ELL is at in English (see Chapter 2). If you notice that ELLs with lower proficiency levels aren't participating, model for the group how to help them contribute. For example, you can ask Level 1 ELLs a yes-or-no question to see if they agree with a rule that another student has shared, and you can encourage Level 2 ELLs to share a short phrase or sentence such as "No hitting." When you consistently model how to include ELLs at different proficiency levels in class discussions, students incorporate those same interactions in their collaborative work with ELLs. Finding ways to encourage all ELLs to participate also sends the message that their ideas are an important contribution to the classroom, regardless of how grammatically correct their speech is (Cappellini 2005).

After ELLs have brainstormed with their collaborative groups, you can have them share with the whole class. Record their ideas on the board, changing the sentence structure to "We should . . ." and sketching a picture to illustrate the concept. From this list you can combine ideas as necessary to form an official list of class rules that parallels what you previously determined to be the important rules for your class to have.

Tapping into ELLs' Background Knowledge

When I have my class brainstorm rules, I often use the analogy that our class is like a team. ELLs from different cultural backgrounds can all relate to the idea of sports teams, and they understand that for players to be a part of a team they need to follow the rules of their sport. I bring in photographs of athletes from different cultural backgrounds that I find on the Internet, trying to include famous players and popular sports from my ELLs' countries of origin if possible. I have the class tell me a few rules that those sports players need to follow. I then explain that our class is also a team, and that just like sports players we must follow certain rules so we can learn in our classroom. This gives students a context for thinking of rules that would be appropriate for our class.

One year when I did this activity I knew I had two students from Bangladesh and one student from India in my class, so I found some images of cricket players, since it's a very popular sport in those countries. When I displayed the images of the sports players on the first day of school, one of my students from Bangladesh, Rajib, was the first to raise his hand to share an idea. It turned out that his uncle was a famous cricket player, and even though he had a Level 2 English proficiency, his connection to the sport motivated him to share quite detailed ideas about the rules cricket players follow when they're part of a team.

In the days that followed, Rajib brought in photos of his uncle and cricket memorabilia to share with the class. This simple connection to my ELLs' cultures made the activity much more meaningful for them. It also made Rajib an instant class expert on cricket and sports in general. Instead of his classmates viewing him as a student who wasn't proficient in English, they viewed him as a knowledgeable peer they could learn a lot from. As you develop a respectful classroom community during the first weeks of school, it's important to place a strong emphasis on how much you and the students can learn from each other and, in particular, from the ELLs in your class. By providing opportunities for ELLs to share their native languages, cultures, and knowledge of specific topics, you build up their status as experts and create a more respectful learning environment (Kottler, Kottler, and Street 2008).

Acting Out the Rules

Once you've collaboratively determined a list of class rules, it's helpful to act them out as a whole group (Dragan 2005). This works well in primary as well as upper grades. Role-playing helps ELLs visualize the rules, clarifies the rules for all students, and builds community. Model this role-playing for the class by acting out one of the rules and having the class guess which rule it is. You can also act out something students shouldn't do and have the class guess which rule you've broken. After this modeling, assign one rule to each group and have it come up with ways to act out examples of following that rule. Once the rest of the class has guessed the rule, you can reinforce the language structure of "In our classroom, we should . . ." as well as the negative form, "In our classroom, we shouldn't . . ." For example, "In our classroom, we should raise our hands," and "In our classroom, we shouldn't call out."

Displaying the Rules

Writing the class rules on a chart that you post in the classroom provides a visual reminder of the agreed upon rules. Some teachers like to have students sign the chart to show that the rules represent the whole class (Miller 2002). You may want to set aside a certain part of the classroom to display everything related to classroom management, including the daily schedule, the class rules chart, and any charts related to routines. This way you can easily refer to them when reinforcing students' behavior in the classroom.

In bilingual programs, consider creating the rules in one language on the first day of school and then reviewing the rules when you switch to the second language, whether it's later in the day or the next day. That way you can display a class rules chart in each language, giving importance to both. If you're teaching in a side-by-side bilingual program, it's helpful if you and your teaching partner establish similar rules and routines to create consistency between the two classrooms.

Developing a System for Accountability

While making a list of rules is important, it's crucial to discuss with students how they will be held accountable for following the rules (Wong and Wong 1998). When you have a simple, consistent system in place that holds students accountable for their behavior, then you can focus your time and energy on instruction. Remember that your main goal with classroom management is to minimize any time lost from the day so that there's more time for ELLs to develop their linguistic and academic abilities.

Individual Accountability

One behavior system I've found to be successful with ELLs is a stoplight, shown in action in Figure 3–4 (Chang 2004). Since a stoplight is a highly recognizable symbol, it's easy for everyone, including beginning ELLs, to understand the meaning of having his name on green, yellow, or red. I write each student's name on a clothespin, which is clipped to the green section of the stoplight at the beginning of each day. When I first explain the stoplight to my ELLs, I relate it to soccer, which is a common ground for a large part of the world. I explain how soccer players get a yellow card when they don't follow the rules of the game or work together as a team. If they continue to ignore the

Figure 3–4 *A visual system for behavior management*

rules, then players get a red card and aren't allowed to play anymore. This is something most ELLs can relate to easily, and it makes the system more meaningful.

For this or any system to work, you have to be consistent with enforcing it. My students know that if they follow the class rules, they'll stay on green. If they do something that goes against one of our rules, I give them a verbal warning. If I have to say something again to certain students, I put their names on yellow. If the students' behavior improves later on, I recognize the positive change they've made and I move their names back to green. Use your own judgment as to what you feel students need to do to move back. If, however, the poor behavior continues, I put their names on red. When this happens, there needs to be an established series of consequences, such as sending a note home, calling their families, meeting with their families, or talking with the principal, depending on the severity of what happened. Even when a student is on red, she has a chance to improve her behavior and move back to yellow or green, although I typically let the family know that there was an issue that their child was able to resolve. You can keep track of which students are on which color at the end of each day by using a class list on a clipboard or in a record book.

In Figure 3–4 you can see that several students are on red. That particular day they got into a fight during recess time, which violated our most basic rule of respecting each other. Students should know that if they're physical with another person they will immediately be placed on red. It's important for everyone's safety that this be nonnegotiable.

If you consistently enforce a system for accountability, your ELLs will understand exactly what is expected of them in the classroom. However, if they see that in some instances certain behavior is allowed and in other instances it's not, then you send a mixed message about how the classroom works.

Accountability with Collaborative Work

Aside from having a system for individual students' behavior, I like to have something in place to encourage accountability within groups. Collaborative group work is very beneficial for ELLs, but only if the groups are working together in a respectful and productive way. One way to encourage this kind of group work is to post an incentive chart for each group. When I see a group doing a great job following a particular routine, helping each other, or working collaboratively, I add a sticker on their chart. If certain groups are having a difficult time working together, or if they're having a hard time working with a particular student, I try to recognize smaller steps they're taking toward positive collaborative work. When groups complete a row of stickers they have access to certain privileges we've previously determined as a class. I find that as the year progresses I use these group stickers less often because students are naturally working together and are intrinsically motivated to support each other in their learning.

Accountability with the Whole Class

Having a system in place to recognize how the whole class has positively contributed to following the rules is also effective. One way I do this is by creating a compliment chain. I cut strips of construction paper and start a paper chain that I affix to the ceiling. When the class gets a compliment from another adult in the school, I add a paper link to the chain. Once the school community knew about this system, the staff members made an effort to compliment the class whenever they observed good behavior. For example, one year my class had a particularly difficult time adjusting to the routine of independent reading. The principal knew that we were working on this, and he also knew about our compliment chain. When he walked into my classroom one morning and saw how focused all of my ELLs were on their reading, he made sure to compliment them. That positive recognition, made visual by adding a link to our chain, reinforced my students' good behavior. Every time the chain reached the floor, we decided as a class how the students would like to celebrate their accomplishments.

Modeling Expectations with ELLs

If a newcomer displays inappropriate behavior, it could very well be a culture clash. In other words, what he's accustomed to doing in schools in his home country may be different from what he's expected to do at his new school. While you have to hold the same expectations of behavior for all students, it's important to show newcomers what they need to do in the classroom. One year I had a student from China who wasn't used to sitting on a rug during lessons. While the other students sat up quietly with their legs crossed, he wanted to lay down on the rug and roll around. I calmly told him no while moving my finger in a way that expressed this. Then I gently helped him sit up and showed him how the other students were sitting. By the second day he had learned the protocol for sitting on the rug and followed the other classroom routines as well.

It's imperative that other students don't make fun of newcomers who are learning a new classroom culture. Talk with students about how difficult it is to move to another country and start all over in a new school. If other students have made a similar move at some point, have them describe what it was like for them. Many ELLs aren't too far removed from going through the same newcomer experience, and they can candidly express what they felt at the time and how others treated them. Developing empathy for what others are experiencing is crucial for students to accept and respect each other (Kottler, Kottler, and Street 2008). This kind of empathy can lead to students being more willing to help ELLs because they have a better idea of how challenging it is to be in their situation.

Structuring Homework Procedures

A lot of frustration can arise over the topic of homework. There can be any number of issues, such as students not copying it down correctly, not taking home the appropriate materials, not being accountable to anyone at home for doing their work, or not completing the homework. With ELLs you may encounter even more problems, such as not understanding the assignments, not knowing what materials to use, or families feeling they can't help in another language. While it would certainly be easier to not assign ELLs any homework, there's a reason why we use it in the first place. It's a way to extend the school day by practicing what they were learning in class and to prepare for continued learning the next day (Hill and Flynn 2006; Goldenberg 2008; Marzano et al. 2001). This is a far too important piece of the learning process, especially for ELLs, to discard it or settle for it being less than ideal. While it may be impossible to eliminate every homework issue with every ELL, there are certainly ways to increase the effectiveness of homework for ELLs.

Appropriate Homework for ELLs

The following examples of appropriate versus inappropriate homework assignments in different subject areas are by no means the only types of homework you can assign. They're simply examples of typical types of homework you can use with ELLs with varying L2 proficiencies. Whenever you're determining if a potential homework assignment is appropriate for your ELLs, think about the linguistic demands it will place on them and how ELLs with different proficiency levels will be able to complete it. When ELLs take home the assignment, will they be able to understand what they need to do? Will they be able to complete some or all of the assignment given their L2 proficiency? It's easy to fall into the trap of thinking that beginning ELLs can't complete academically rigorous assignments or that they don't need to do homework like the rest of the class. These examples show that there are ways to hold all ELLs accountable for homework.

Reading: Ineffective Homework for ELLs

- *ELLs take home a grade-level basal reader and write answers to questions about the text or fill in graphic organizers about the text.* Homework in reading is meant to help ELLs improve their reading level. Research shows that reading at a frustration level will not help students improve as readers (Fountas and Pinnell 2006; Calkins 2001). Since most ELLs are not yet at grade level in their L2 reading, this assignment would be at a frustration level for them. It wouldn't contribute to improving their reading comprehension, fluency, or decoding skills.

Reading: Effective Homework for ELLs

- *ELLs take home books that are at their independent reading level (based on running record assessments) and familiar shared reading texts. They respond to the text in a variety of ways in their reading notebook and record their reading in a reading log.* Every ELL at every proficiency level can be successful with this assignment. And the time spent reading these books at their independent level will help them advance to reading texts at progressively higher levels. With a reading log you can see if ELLs are increasing the amount of pages they can read during a specified time and track the types of books they're reading. During reading minilessons you can model for your ELLs different ways they can respond to a text. Once your ELLs are familiar with creating responses to text in class, they can do it at home as well. Some responses can be purely pictoral, such as drawing what they visualized when reading different parts of the text or drawing a sequence of pictures of the important parts of the text. Other responses you model for your ELLs can use graphic organizers to help them express their thinking about the text in writing (see Appendix G).

- *ELLs take home books that are at their independent reading level in their native language as well as English.* This will always be the case in bilingual programs where the goal is for all students to develop literacy skills in both languages. However, students in ESL programs can also benefit from this practice (Freeman and Freeman 2007; García, Kleifgen, and Falchi 2008; Thomas and Collier 2002). Reading texts in both the L1 and the L2 allows ELLs to continue developing as readers and thinkers at a more advanced level with native language texts while reading more basic texts in English. This is particularly important in the upper grades for newcomers. Many of these ELLs were likely reading grade-level texts in their native language, and now all of a sudden they're back to reading lower-level texts in English. They need to continue challenging their reading skills with native language texts while also developing literacy in English. An added bonus is that by reading in two languages, they're developing biliteracy skills, a powerful asset for students to have in today's world.

Writing: Ineffective Homework for ELLs

- *ELLs have to respond to a writing prompt, such as a journal entry topic, an essay topic, or a story starter.* Choice is a key element in writing for ELLs. When ELLs are able to choose what they write about, the quality and quantity of their writing improves (Chen and Mora-Flores 2006). ELLs need a context to understand what they're going to be writing about. If you give ELLs a writing prompt without any context or preparation, most won't be able to complete the assignment well. ELLs also need the related vocabulary and language structures to be able to compose a text. If the prompt isn't an extension of something they've already been learning about in class, then ELLs may lack the background knowledge and language they need to create the text. Prompts have the potential to be effective if they're used as part of an integrated content-area unit of study where ELLs have had many opportunities to understand the content and learn the key vocabulary related to the prompt.

Writing: Effective Homework for ELLs

- *ELLs continue work from the writing workshop at home. Depending on the grade and the classroom focus, this might be gathering ideas in their writing notebook, drafting one of those ideas, or revising a draft.* This homework is effective for ELLs because it's simply an extension of what they're already doing in the classroom during writing workshop. This gives ELLs additional time to develop their writing skills and their writing stamina. ELLs can use the same supports from the classroom to help them write in English at home, such as a bilingual picture dictionary, model shared writing texts, model interactive writing texts, model guided reading texts, and a personal high-frequency word list.

- *ELLs continue work from the writing workshop in their native language as well as in English.* Just as with reading, ELLs in bilingual programs will always have opportunities to write in both languages because the goal is for all students to be biliterate. Again, students in ESL programs can also benefit from this practice (Freeman and Freeman 2007; Samway 2006; Faltis and Hudelson 1998). It allows ELLs to develop more advanced writing skills in their native language while they're writing more simplistic texts in English. This is particularly important for newcomers. Instead of halting their writing development, you can promote native language writing while helping them learn how to write in English.

Math: Ineffective Homework for ELLs

- *Assigning homework without explaining how to complete the activities.* It's not enough to tell ELLs that they'll be completing certain pages in a certain math book for homework. Many ELLs don't have an adult at home who can read English at a high enough level to comprehend an academic math text. The instructions ELLs receive at school are often their main support for being able to complete a homework assignment.

- *Assigning homework that addresses math topics you haven't taught yet in class.* Sometimes a math series includes homework activities that have little to do with the concepts ELLs have been studying in class. This is highly confusing for ELLs, who rely heavily on a familiar context. Look over the homework activities carefully before assigning them to make sure they're relevant.

- *Assigning homework that contains a large amount of unfamiliar language.* Many math problems are about a topic that has unfamiliar vocabulary for ELLs. For example, there may be an entire page of multiplication and division story problems that have to do with places and wildlife in Africa. Be aware that if you don't preteach this vocabulary, many ELLs will struggle to comprehend and solve the story problems.

Math: Effective Homework for ELLs

- *Preview the homework assignments with your class.* It pays to take just a moment at the end of math time to show ELLs the activities they'll be completing for homework. You can point out the different types of problems and refer to similar problems on the board or on math charts so ELLs visually connect the learning in class with the work they'll need to do at home.

- *Choose homework activities that clearly build upon class work, and provide resources ELLs can take home for reference.* When homework and class work go hand in hand, there's a greater probability that ELLs will complete the activities successfully (Hill and Flynn 2006). As another support, some math series have a reference book ELLs can take home with examples of problems. Make an effort to educate families on how they can use these examples to help with their children's homework.

- *Include homework activities that are less language dependent as well as activities that are more language dependent.* Assigning a variety of math activities throughout the week ensures that your ELLs will be able to complete at least some of the problems successfully. Remind ELLs and their families that you expect them to make their best effort based on what they understand and that you will always review homework the following day.

- *Use math materials in the L1 as well as in the L2 for homework assignments.* Bilingual programs typically have math materials in both languages. In ESL programs, consider providing ELLs with a math homework workbook in the L1 and the L2 to increase their comprehension and their families' ability to help with the homework.

Science and Social Studies: Ineffective Homework for ELLs

- *Assigning ELLs a section of a chapter to read and having them answer the accompanying comprehension questions.* This is a common assignment in upper-grade classrooms. As mentioned in the reading section, most ELLs aren't at grade level yet in reading, and many content-area textbooks are at a reading level that's even higher than grade level. As a result, this is a very frustrating task to give ELLs. If you assign this kind of reading before ELLs learn the content in class, it's even more difficult because ELLs lack a context to orient them while reading (Rea and Mercuri 2006).

- *Assigning vocabulary activities without first teaching the meaning of the words in class.* A list of vocabulary words without a context holds little meaning for ELLs. Avoid assigning vocabulary activities unless ELLs have already learned the concept during an integrated unit of study and have had a chance to practice the vocabulary words in context in class.

- *Assigning a content-area project without modeling the end product or explaining the steps to complete the project.* Projects can be a great way for ELLs to delve into a particular content-area topic. They also encourage whole-family involvement in the learning process. However, if you don't model your expectations, many ELLs won't be able to visualize what they need to do to complete the project.

Science and Social Studies: Effective Homework for ELLs

- *Assign activities that are an extension of the learning that already took place in the classroom.* There's nothing wrong with having ELLs use their science or social studies textbook as one type of resource to help them complete a homework assignment. Make sure you've already studied the material in class as part of an integrated unit of study, including many uses of nonlinguistic representations such as images, realia, DVDs, picture books, graphic organizers, and hands-on activities (Hill and Flynn 2006). Then design assignments that involve having ELLs use a familiar graphic organizer to record key information about the concepts. See Appendix G for ways to use graphic organizers with ELLs.

- *Give ELLs vocabulary activities to complete at home with words they've already learned during your integrated content-area studies.* Once ELLs have learned vocabulary words in context through classroom activities, there are a number of ways you can have them continue practicing the words at home. Chapter 5 describes vocabulary activities that work well with ELLs, including beginning ELLs. Another option is to use vocabulary activities related to the content-area version of the Oxford Picture Dictionaries. This content-area version is a great resource for ELLs to practice vocabulary related to different math, science, and social studies topics.

- *Assign meaningful projects with visual examples of how you expect them to be completed.* Choose projects that tie in closely with what ELLs have been studying in an integrated unit. During a discussion of the project, show the class examples of what the finished product could look like, and model the steps students will need to follow to complete the project successfully. Be mindful that some ELLs may not have materials at home to complete the project. Be willing to offer support by helping them gather the materials they'll need.

Word Study: Ineffective Homework for ELLs

- *Assigning the same list of spelling words to all students to practice at home for a test at the end of the week.* This is the way many teachers are used to teaching spelling. I tried implementing it with my ELLs multiple times but finally had to admit that it really wasn't a beneficial practice for them. A Level 1 ELL is at a completely different stage of development in spelling than a Level 3 or 5 ELL. For example, while one group may need to work on short vowels, another group may need to study long vowel patterns, and a third group may be ready to study words with prefixes and suffixes (Bear et al. 2007).

- *Assigning pages from a grammar book for all students to complete.* ELLs benefit from an explicit study of how the L1 and L2 work. However, this is most helpful when language structures are studied in a meaningful context. Chapter 5 has examples of ways to teach language structures explicitly, yet contextually.

Word Study: Effective Homework for ELLs

- *Assign spelling words to groups of students based on your assessment of their developmental spelling ability.* Instead of assigning all ELLs the same words, you can assess their developmental spelling level (in the L1 and the L2 for bilingual programs) and then create small groups based on their needs. The *Words Their Way with English Learners* program (Bear et al. 2007) works well with K–6 students for administering an initial assessment. It also details how to manage small-group spelling instruction with ELLs, provides a sequence of lessons for each week, and suggests types of homework that can be assigned daily with this type of program.

- *Assign contextualized activities to practice language structures.* After teaching language structures through a meaningful context, you can provide ELLs with different assignments to complete at home. For example, you can give the class a cloze passage where you've deleted certain language structures that you've been studying in class. It's helpful to cover a combination of some easier structures and some more complex ones so that ELLs at different proficiency levels are able to determine at least some of the missing words or word parts. Chapter 5 shows how you can use cloze passages with ELLs. You can also give your ELLs a complete text to read and have them underline or color certain language structures that you've been studying in class. Another option is to have your ELLs do a language search at home in the books they're reading, in their writing, or in other environmental print to find examples of a particular language structure. This search can be different for ELLs at different proficiency levels. For example, beginning ELLs may search for examples of plural nouns while intermediate and advanced ELLs search for examples of regular and irregular past-tense verbs, depending on whatever structures you've been studying in class.

Copying Down Homework in the Upper Grades

If you have ELLs copy down the day's homework, keep in mind that this can be challenging for newcomers. I remember when I first realized this. I had given my students about five minutes to copy down the assignments and pack up their bags. By the end of that time almost everyone was finished, except for my newcomers. They were diligently trying to copy the homework letter by letter, but they weren't even halfway through. And they had no idea what materials they needed to take home. This was a much-needed reminder for me of the challenges beginners face. Copying written words in an unfamiliar language takes an incredibly long time because your eye doesn't recognize any of the words. They're simply strings of letters, and your efforts go toward trying to copy each letter in the right order and putting spaces in the correct spots. What a process!

There are several ways to get around this issue with newcomers:

- Have the homework printed out for them ahead of time, and while everyone else is copying the homework, begin showing newcomers the key words that correspond to certain materials they'll need. For example, for one of our recurring math assignments, I explicitly point to the words *Study Links* on the homework list, and then I take out the *Study Links* book so my newcomers can see the connection.

- If you have only one or two newcomers, jot the homework down yourself in their notebooks and then help them gather the necessary materials.

- As ELLs become more comfortable writing in the L2, have them begin copying the homework earlier. You can also ask beginning ELLs' partners to make sure they're packing up the appropriate materials.

Previewing Homework

Knowing what materials to take home is far easier for newcomers if you've shown them what their homework will be throughout the day (Hill and Flynn 2006). For example, at the end of a social studies lesson, you may hold up the vocabulary activity they'll be taking home and give an example of how they should complete it. Other materials will quickly become a routine for newcomers because they'll be taking them home every day, such as their book bag with independent reading books and reading log, a picture dictionary to help with writing, or the materials for practicing spelling words.

Consistency with Homework Assignments

English language learners also benefit from having homework consistently written in the same place every day. If there are certain assignments you always have, such as reading for a particular amount of time at home, recording the reading in a reading log, completing a reading response, completing a page from a math book, or working with vocabulary words, then put those assignments in the same order on the list of homework every day and use the same language every time to describe the assignments. For example, if you write, "Do a reading response," one day and write, "Create a response to your reading," another day, ELLs could think these mean two different things.

Final Thoughts

While it takes some organization and time at the beginning of the year to get these elements of classroom management in place, your ELLs will benefit academically, linguistically, and emotionally throughout the rest of the year. You will have created an environment where you can take advantage of every minute to help your ELLs learn language and content. I can only imagine how unproductive the school year would have been for the class I described at the beginning of the chapter if I had not implemented this kind of consistent classroom management. Instead, I was able to take advantage of eight solid months of instruction during which my ELLs were motivated, respectful, and focused on learning. This class ended up becoming one of the most special groups of ELLs I've worked with, in large part because I knew how dramatically they had changed and how this had opened the door for them to reach their potential.

Reflecting on the Keys to Success

Raise the Bar

- Do I set up a daily schedule that includes all of the literacy and content-area components necessary to teach the grade-level curriculum?

- Do I plan homework assignments for all of my ELLs that connect to the grade-level content?

Differentiate Instruction

- Is my daily schedule displayed in a visual way so that ELLs know what to expect during the school day?

- Do I model routines in a visual way so that all of my ELLs understand what they're expected to do in the classroom?

- Do I model for ELLs the routines of how to do independent, collaborative, and whole-group work for each instructional component?

- Do I think about how ELLs with different proficiency levels will complete relevant homework assignments?

Connect Learning to Students

- Do I find ways to include ELLs' cultures and experiences to give them an expert status in the classroom?
- Do I consider common cultural understandings when setting up class rules and systems for accountability?

Use Students' Native Languages to Support Learning

- Do I use native language partnerships to support newcomers in learning the routines of the classroom?
- Do I use native language partnerships as a support for ELLs during collaborative group activities, such as establishing class rules?

Be Consistent

- Is my daily schedule as consistent as possible each day of the week so ELLs know what they're expected to do? Would my ELLs be able to support a newcomer in following the daily schedule?
- Are my daily routines consistently used during transition times and during each instructional component? Would my ELLs be able to support a newcomer in following these routines?
- Do I consistently use the same words or phrases when signaling for transitions?
- Do I consistently enforce class rules through a clear accountability system?
- Do ELLs know what types of homework they will have on a regular basis throughout the week and what materials they need to take home?
- Do I consistently use the same words or phrases when assigning homework?

References for Further Reading

Read-Alouds

Trelease, Jim. 2006. *The Read-Aloud Handbook.* New York: Penguin Group.

Shared Reading in Primary and Upper Grades

Allen, Janet. 2002. *On the Same Page: Shared Reading Beyond the Primary Grades.* Portland, ME: Stenhouse.

Parkes, Brenda. 2000. *Read It Again! Revisiting Shared Reading.* Portland, ME: Stenhouse.

Reading Workshop Minilessons, Conferences, and Guided Reading Groups

Calkins, Lucy. 2001. *The Art of Teaching Reading.* New York: Longman.

Fountas, Irene C., and Gay Su Pinnell. 1996. *Guided Reading: Good First Teaching for All Children.* Portsmouth, NH: Heinemann. [primary grades]

———. 2000. *Guiding Readers and Writers: Teaching Comprehension, Genre, and Content Literacy.* Portsmouth, NH: Heinemann. [upper grades]

Information About Teaching Reading Strategies

Harvey, Stephanie, and Anne Goudvis. 2000. *Strategies That Work.* Portland, ME: Stenhouse.

Keene, Ellin Oliver, and Susan Zimmermann. 2009. *Mosaic of Thought.* 2d ed. Portsmouth, NH: Heinemann.

Miller, Debbie. 2002. *Reading with Meaning: Teaching Comprehension in the Primary Grades.* Portland, ME: Stenhouse.

Writing Workshop

Calkins, Lucy. 1994. *The Art of Teaching Writing.* Portsmouth, NH: Heinemann.

Davis, Judy, and Sharon Hill. 2003. *The No-Nonsense Guide to Teaching Writing: Strategies, Structures, Solutions.* Portsmouth, NH: Heinemann.

Interactive Writing

McCarrier, Andrea, Gay Su Pinnell, and Irene C. Fountas. 2000. *Interactive Writing: How Language and Literacy Come Together, K–2.* Portsmouth, NH: Heinemann.

Developing Routines and Rules

Shalaway, Linda. 2005. *Learning to Teach . . . Not Just for Beginners: The Essential Guide for All Teachers.* 3d ed. New York: Scholastic Professional Books.

Wong, Harry K., and Rosemary T. Wong. 1998. *How to Be an Effective Teacher: The First Days of School.* Mountain View, CA: Harry K. Wong.

Homework with ELLs

Hill, Jane, and Kathleen M. Flynn. 2006. *Classroom Instruction That Works with English Language Learners.* Alexandria, VA: Association for Supervision and Curriculum Development.

CHAPTER 4

Integrating Literacy and Content-Area Instruction

*I*t was a Friday afternoon in early November, and all the fourth-grade classes were gathered in the auditorium to hear two Native Americans discuss how they combined their cultural traditions with modern-day life in New York City. The students were captivated, and at the end of the program the presenters allowed time for questions. I wondered if my students would get up the courage to participate in front of such a large group. They were all English language learners with a wide range of proficiencies in the language. But they had a wealth of knowledge about the topic because I had integrated our study of Native Americans with reading, writing, science, word work, and math for the past month. My ELLs had repeatedly used the academic language related to Native Americans and they had had many opportunities to deepen their understanding of the social studies concepts. Even so, I wasn't sure it would be enough to make them feel comfortable sharing questions with the group.

I soon realized I should never have doubted their capabilities! When the presenters asked for volunteers, the majority of my ELLs started waving their hands in the air, hoping they would be called upon. I was so proud when student after student asked relevant questions about the topic using specific vocabulary we had studied. And the questions weren't just from my more proficient ELLs. With the help of other students, even some of my beginning ELLs posed questions to the presenters. My principal was standing next to me in the auditorium and he commented on how impressive it was to see that kind of participation. I invited him to the celebration we were having the next day to share the students' culminating projects and their published expository writing about Native Americans. After seeing the students' work, my principal said he never would have imagined that this group of ELLs could have achieved such a high level of academic success.

My English language learners' ability to use the L2 to read, write, listen, and talk about Native Americans certainly wasn't accidental; it was the result of finding ways to weave together the literacy components and content-area studies I was expected to teach my fourth graders. Instead of teaching reading, writing, social studies, science, math, and word study as completely isolated subjects within the school day, I planned how those areas could be integrated as much as possible.

When I first began teaching I followed the more traditional type of instruction my fellow grade-level teachers were implementing. Every subject was isolated from the others, and we rarely made connections between them. But when my bilingual students weren't meeting content and literacy standards in English or in Spanish, I was forced to take a step back and objectively examine my teaching. Why weren't my long hours of lesson planning and preparation paying off in student performance? Why weren't my ELLs retaining the content and language we were learning? I realized it had to do in part with the disjointed way my instructional day was organized. I couldn't expect my ELLs to deeply understand a particular concept when we studied it only during one part of the day, and I certainly couldn't expect them to retain the academic language when I provided so few opportunities for them to use it.

I began researching integrated (thematic) instruction, and I liked how teachers could combine literacy and content-area work throughout the school day. The research consistently showed that this was an instructional approach that benefited ELLs (Freeman and Freeman 2007). Even so, I was hesitant to start implementing it in my classroom. The thematic units I read about in the professional literature used so many resources that my school didn't have available. I also knew I had to stay on track with the curricular requirements my district had, and I wasn't sure how thematic instruction would fit into that scope and sequence. So, I experimented with how I could take the concept of thematic instruction and make it work with my curricular requirements, limited resources, and limited planning time. What I found was that this type of instruction doesn't have to be an all-or-nothing approach; there are many simple ways to integrate literacy and content-area instruction throughout the school day that address these common concerns.

In this chapter I describe

- how integrated instruction benefits ELLs

- practical ways to integrate the content areas with balanced literacy components

- examples of integrated instruction in action

Benefits of Integrated Instruction with ELLs

Over the years, research has consistently shown that integrated, thematic instruction is beneficial for English language learners in a number of ways.

It Increases ELLs' Content-Area Knowledge

When you integrate instruction throughout the school day, everything ELLs are reading, writing, hearing, and talking about relates to familiar content-area topics. They're able to use the content and language they've already learned about a topic to understand new content and language related to that topic (Gibbons 2002). Since the curriculum makes more sense to them, it's easier for ELLs to focus on what they're learning and to stay engaged. Freeman and Freeman (2001, 2007) explain that this increased engagement results in ELLs developing greater content-area knowledge. When I moved temporarily to Brazil and became a beginning Portuguese language learner, I realized that I had forgotten just how mentally exhausting it is to be immersed in an unfamiliar language *and* try to learn new information in that language. I had a renewed appreciation for what my beginning ELLs went through as new arrivals, and I related to the wiped-out look they typically had on their faces by the afternoon. This helped me remember just how important it is to use integrated instruction in the classroom so ELLs are better able to make sense of the new language around them and can learn the grade-level content so they don't fall behind academically. It's inevitable that beginning ELLs will go through a tiring transition period as they adjust to learning content in a new language, but by integrating instruction, we can make the adjustment smoother for them and help them keep up academically with their peers.

It Increases ELLs' Reading and Writing Skills

When you integrate content-area studies with literacy activities, ELLs are reading texts about a familiar topic with familiar language. Current research shows that when ELLs have this kind of contextual support it improves their reading comprehension (Goldenberg 2008). The research also shows that as ELLs learn more about a particular topic, they can read increasingly difficult texts because they have greater background knowledge and vocabulary to support their reading comprehension (Goldenberg 2008).

When I started reading in Portuguese, my comprehension depended completely on my background knowledge and vocabulary for the topic. For example, since I love talking about education, I made sure I learned all the related vocabulary right away, and whenever I read magazine articles about education, my comprehension was very strong. However, I'd then turn the page and encounter a different article about an unfamiliar topic that I couldn't understand for the life of me. Without contextual support and the necessary vocabulary in Portuguese, I was at a loss. The same is true for our ELLs; the more we integrate instruction, the more opportunities ELLs have to develop a strong context for reading content-area texts and for learning all the key language they'll need to understand them.

Integrated instruction also affects ELLs' writing ability. When you help ELLs make connections between the language of the texts they're reading and the language they're using in their own writing, ELLs become more aware of how they can use this language to express their ideas in writing (Samway 2006). The more we enrich ELLs' vocabulary and use of language structures through integrated instruction, the greater their ability to use that language when writing.

It Increases ELLs' Academic Language Skills

In order for ELLs to learn new language, such as vocabulary words, phrases, or language structures, they need to hear it, read it, write it, and speak it multiple times in meaningful contexts (Freeman and Freeman 2001, 2007). With integrated instruction, important academic language is repeated naturally in the different content-area and literacy activities throughout the day and throughout a unit of study, giving ELLs the opportunity to learn *through* the language. Research shows that having this meaningful context supports the language learning process (Gibbons 2002). Also, ELLs are more engaged because the language used for learning is familiar and more comprehensible, which results in greater language development (Freeman and Freeman 2001, 2007).

As I was learning Portuguese I took language classes where, in a two-hour block of time, we jumped around from one topic to the next, each with its own set of vocabulary and language structures to remember. Sometimes we reviewed the language in later classes, but normally we were off to the next topic in the language book. I vividly remember one class when my instructor asked me to read a passage, and when I questioned what one of the words meant she looked at me in exasperation and said, "Você já aprendeu essa palavra!" ["You learned that word already!"] She then proceeded to flip through the book until she came to a page several units back where I had "learned" the word one time. As I thought more about this frustrating language experience, I realized that I'd also been guilty of the same exasperation with my ELLs. At times I had wondered how it was possible that they didn't remember a particular vocabulary word we had previously learned, but of course, upon reflection, I knew that I must not have provided enough ways for them to hear, speak, read, and write the language. Integrated instruction helps us make sure we're creating an environment where that repetition of language is a part of each school day.

Planning the Big Picture for Yearlong Integrated Instruction

Knowing how beneficial integrated instruction is, let's look at how to get started in making it a part of the school day. The rule of thumb I keep in mind when designing an integrated unit is that it should combine literacy and content-area studies while following the curricula required of the grade level. By the end of the school year, my ELLs should have been exposed to all of the learning objectives for their grade level in each subject area. It can be tempting to create an integrated unit that spends a lot of time focusing on just one particular subject area but leaves little time to teach the full scope and sequence of the other parts of the curricula. This cheats ELLs out of access to grade-level learning and sets the stage for them to fall behind their peers in knowledge and skills. However, this doesn't mean that I necessarily teach everything in the same order. Whenever possible, I rearrange certain literacy or content-area units so I can match up units that will complement each other.

To do this, I start by looking at the scope and sequence I'm required to teach for each subject area throughout the year, which is based on state standards and includes specific learning objectives. What will my ELLs need to learn this year in reading, writing, math, science, and social studies? If you're new to a particular grade or new to teaching, you're probably in survival mode just trying to get through each day. But it's important to know the big picture of where you're going with instruction so you can make better decisions about how to teach each unit. I spread out the curricular guides I have for each subject area and look at the individual units I'm expected to teach over the course of the year.

- I first focus on the content-area curricula. Are any of the topics in social studies, science, and math related in some way? If so, do I have the flexibility to rearrange the time of year when we study those topics so they can be taught at the same time?

- I then look at the units for reading and writing throughout the year. Would certain units pair up well with certain content-area topics? If so, do I have the flexibility to rearrange when I teach those units so they coincide with the related content-area studies?

Figures 4–1 and 4–2 (pages 98 and 99) show a possible yearlong curricular framework for first grade and for fourth grade based on the units of study adopted by New York City. I've highlighted in bold the units I rearranged to greater facilitate integrated instruction. As you can see, some subjects, such as math and social studies, have a set sequence of topics that can't be changed because the concepts build upon each other from month to month. But I was able to make some alterations to the order of the reading, writing, and science units.

Adapting a Curricular Framework for First Grade

In first grade, the alterations I made had to do with certain reading and writing units. I kept most of the writing units in the order recommended in the curriculum, but I specified how they would be integrated with content-area studies. For example, in January ELLs could write letters to people in the community, in February and March ELLs could write how-to books and all-about books related to what they were learning about animals, and in April ELLs could read and write poetry about topics related to the seasons, the community, and animals.

I decided to move the reading unit that would have students read texts focused on one topic, which was originally scheduled for May, to March. This way, during reading workshop ELLs could read texts centered on the topic of different animals of interest, and then they could use what they learned about those animals to write all-about books in writing workshop.

I switched the reading with fluency unit from March to April so that it would coincide with the study of poetry. Poetry is an excellent way to focus on reading fluency, and after reading poems in the reading workshop ELLs would have many models for their own writing of poetry. While the poems could be about many different topics, including poems relating to the community and animals would create a greater content-area connection.

After rearranging these different units in the spring, it left character study and realistic fiction in May, which would support each other beautifully to help ELLs transfer elements from their fictional reading to their fictional writing.

For the month of June I decided to wrap up the year with a full focus on content-area reading and writing, integrating literacy completely with the study of life cycles in the science curriculum. ELLs could use all of the nonfiction reading strategies they had learned throughout the year to read books on the life cycles of different animals, and in writing they could create diagrams and written explanations of the life cycle process.

Adapting a Curricular Framework for Fourth Grade

In fourth grade, the alterations I made were again with certain reading and writing units, plus one of the science units. Figure 4–2 also indicates when fourth-grade classrooms in New York City prepare for standardized tests in certain subject areas, which affects the curricular focus at different times of the year.

In September and October I liked how the social studies and science units overlapped with each other. There were many conceptual connections between geography,

	Reading	Writing	Social Studies	Science	Math
Sept	Launch independent reading— readers build good habits	Launch independent writing— narratives	Families are important	Changes in weather and seasons (ongoing throughout the year)	Establishing routines: counting, number line, tallies, calendar, using a thermometer
Oct	Using print strategies to support conventional reading	Small moments: writing personal narratives		Properties of matter: solids, liquids, and gases	Everyday use of numbers: number grids, clocks, money (pennies and nickels), number stories
Nov	Using patterns in books to read with accuracy, fluency, and comprehension	Using writing conventions to make writing more understandable	Families, now and long ago		Visual patterns, number patterns, and counting (adding and subtracting; dimes, nickels, pennies)
Dec	Growing ideas about books: reading comprehension	Authors as mentors: using writing techniques from other authors			Measurement (inches, feet; telling time to quarter hour) and basic facts
Jan	Using word power and print strategies to read more challenging books	Writing for different purposes: letter writing **(to people in the community)**	Families in communities: shaped by diverse people, places, and events		Place value (tens and ones; greater than, less than, equal to), number stories, and basic facts
Feb	Nonfiction reading strategies	Nonfiction explanatory writing: how-to books **(connected to animals)**		Animal diversity: comparing physical structures and characteristics and their functions	Developing fact power: addition and subtraction facts
Mar	**Reading, thinking, and talking about texts on the same topic (books about animals)**	Nonfiction informational writing: all-about books **(connected to animals)**			Geometry and attributes: three-dimensional shapes and symmetry
Apr	**Reading with fluency**	Poetry **(linked to the community, seasons, and/or animals)**	The community: workers and jobs, needs and wants, rules and laws		Money (dollars, place value to hundreds, making change) and fractions (equal shares)
May	**Character study**	Realistic fiction		Animal life cycles and life spans	Place value (add and subtract two-digit numbers) and fractions (compare parts of a whole)
June	**Content-area reading: life cycles**	**Content-area writing: describing a life cycle**			End-of-the-year review and assessments

Note: The reading and writing units are based on the Teachers College Reading and Writing Project units of study for the primary grades. The social studies and science units are based on the curriculum developed by New York City, and the math units are from the Everyday Mathematics program adopted by New York City.

Figure 4–1 *Yearlong curricular framework for first grade*

	Reading	Writing	Social Studies	Science	Math
Sept	Launch independent reading (fiction and nonfiction)	Launch independent writing—narratives	Geography	Animals and plants in their environment	Naming and constructing geometric figures
Oct	Character study (fiction)	Improving quality of narrative writing	Native Americans	↓	Place value, data
		Informational essays 1. **Native Americans** 2. **Other topic of choice**			Multiplication and division
Nov	Nonfiction reading strategies: social studies		Three worlds meet: Europe, the Americas, and Africa	**Properties of water**	Number sentences
					Decimals
Dec	Reading short texts (fiction and nonfiction), *review of reading skills for state testing*	Writing for reading, *review of writing skills for state testing*	Colonial life		Big numbers, extended multiplication, estimation, rounding
Jan	*English language arts testing*	*English language arts testing*	The Revolutionary War	Electricity and magnetism	Division, frames, angles
	Genre study: mystery book clubs	Writing realistic fiction			
Feb	**Genre study: biography book clubs**	**Persuasive writing: letters to community and governmental leaders**	The new nation: foundation for government and culture	↓	Fractions and their uses, probability, *review of math concepts for state testing*
Mar	Nonfiction reading strategies: science	**Expository writing: feature articles (science)**	X	Review of science concepts for state testing	*State math testing*
					Perimeter and area
Apr	Social issue book clubs: inference and interpretation (fiction)	Poetry	Industrial growth and immigration	*State science testing*	Fractions, decimals, and percents; reflection and symmetry
May	Reading about communities around the world: integrating reading strategies (fiction and nonfiction)	**Writing memoirs**		Interactions of air, water, and land	Three-dimensional shapes; weight, volume, capacity
			Local and state government		
June	**Content-area reading: integrating reading strategies (nonfiction)**	**Content-area writing projects: government**		↓	End-of-the-year review and assessments

Note: The reading and writing units are based on the Teachers College Reading and Writing Project units of study for the upper grades. The social studies and science units are based on the curriculum developed by New York City, and the math units are from the Everyday Mathematics program adopted by New York City.

Figure 4–2 *Yearlong curricular framework for fourth grade*

plants and animals in their environment, and Native Americans. I decided to switch the properties of water unit in science to November and December, because I knew I could make meaningful connections between how European explorers and African slaves traveled by boat to the Americas and our study of water, which included sinking and floating (Why were their boats able to float? What makes something sink?), the water cycle (How did the water cycle affect explorers and slaves during sea travel?), and states of matter from ice to water to gas (How did changes in states of matter affect sea travel?).

In the writing workshop, I pushed up the unit on expository writing by a week to give ELLs more time to write informational essays about Native Americans as well as expository writing on another topic of choice.

I moved the study of persuasive letter writing to February so that ELLs could write letters to different community and government leaders, which connected with the social studies focus on government. I also chose biographies as a genre study because many biographies are about people in government and inventors, a connection to both the social studies unit and the science unit.

In March I wanted the majority of the school day to revolve around science as the class prepared to take the state science test. There was already a nonfiction reading unit on science scheduled for March, and I decided to teach the expository unit on feature articles during this month as well so ELLs could write feature articles based on what they were reading about the different science topics.

At the end of the year I moved the memoir writing unit from June to May to have it coincide with the social studies unit on immigration. For the month of June I decided to include a unit on content-area reading and writing so ELLs could dedicate a substantial amount of time to projects related to government, an abstract concept that can be very difficult for ELLs to understand.

Planning an Integrated Unit for ELLs

Once you've organized your curriculum in a way that allows for the most compatibility between subject areas, you can begin planning specific ways that you'll integrate content-area studies and balanced literacy components during a particular unit. You can begin by trying out a few of the approaches for integrating instruction, including others as you feel more comfortable with this type of planning. During some units of study you may be integrating just a few aspects of literacy and the content areas, while at other times of the year you may be able to develop a highly integrated unit that pulls together all the components of instruction. Any steps you take to integrate literacy and content-area instruction will help your ELLs experience greater academic and linguistic success in the classroom. Figure 4–3 shows how you can conceptualize and plan for this integration.

1. Begin by thinking about what conceptual connections you can make between social studies, science, and math in a particular unit for ELLs. To do this you'll need to have your curricular guides at hand to know what specific content objectives you need to teach ELLs in each content area during this period of time. See if any of those content objectives relate to each other and how you could use language and concepts from one content area during the study of another.

Connections between the content arreas:

Language focus:

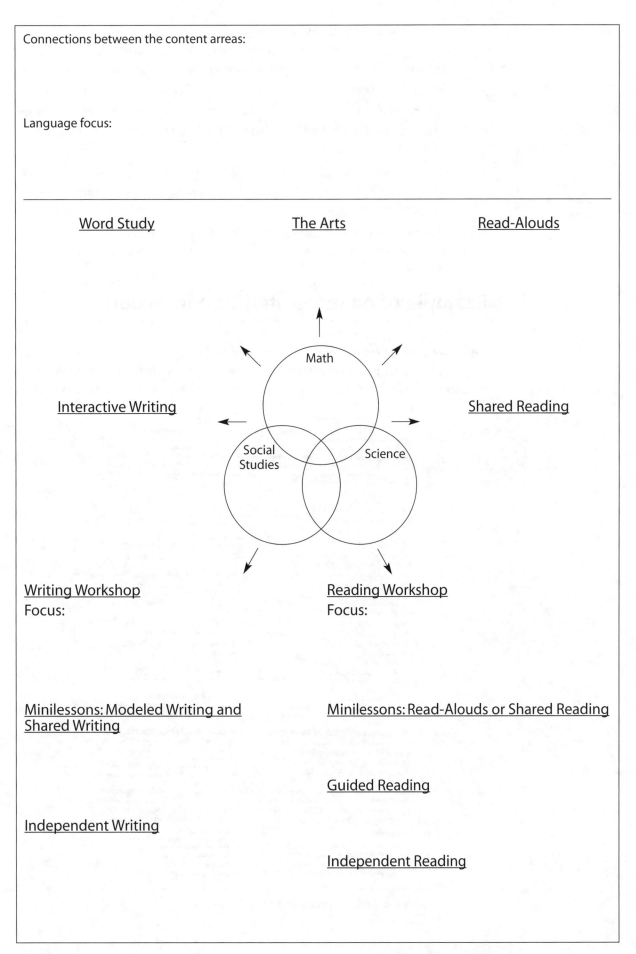

Word Study   The Arts   Read-Alouds

Interactive Writing   Shared Reading

Math

Social Studies   Science

Writing Workshop
Focus:

Reading Workshop
Focus:

Minilessons: Modeled Writing and
Shared Writing

Minilessons: Read-Alouds or Shared Reading

Guided Reading

Independent Writing

Independent Reading

Figure 4–3 *Planning an integrated instruction*   © 2009 by Christina M. Celic from *English Language Learners Day by Day*. Portsmouth, NH: Heinemann.

2. Next, think about ways you can integrate those content areas with the different balanced literacy components. Again, have your curricular guides for reading and writing nearby so you know what content objectives you have in literacy during this period of time.

   ▪ Think about how ELLs could learn content-area concepts and language through reading: read-alouds, shared reading texts, guided reading books, books for independent reading.

   ▪ Think about how ELLs could learn content-area concepts and language through writing: modeled writing, shared writing, interactive writing, and independent writing.

The more connections you make, the more opportunities your ELLs have to develop content-area knowledge, literacy skills, and language skills in English.

Example of an Integrated Unit in Action

Figure 4–4 shows an example of how I planned for integrated instruction during October and November based on what I had to teach in the fourth-grade curriculum. On the planning framework I first jotted down my ideas for ways to make connections

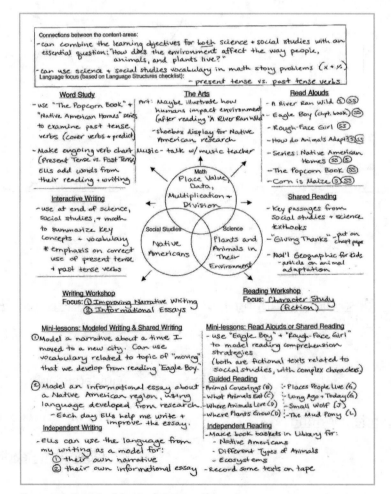

Figure 4–4 *Example of planning for integrated instruction*

between social studies, science, and math. Then I recorded the ideas I had for how I could integrate those content areas with literacy.

During this time period I was expected to teach a unit on Native Americans in social studies and continue our science study of plants and animals in their environment. This was a part of the year when there were many conceptual connections between the social studies and science topics. Since there was such a great overlap, I was able to use the same essential question to guide our learning for the two content areas: How does the environment affect the way people, animals, and plants live? When social studies and science topics don't have a conceptual connection, I use separate essential questions to guide our study of each subject area. There weren't any obvious connections to the math concepts we were studying at the time. However, I made an effort to use social studies and science vocabulary in our multiplication and division number stories. This gave ELLs another way to hear the content-area vocabulary, and it made the story problems more comprehensible because ELLs were familiar with the language. For example, I used story problems such as this one in our math lessons:

> There were 12 men from an Eastern Woodlands tribe who were building longhouses for their families. If each man worked on the longhouses for 18 hours during the week, how many hours did they work in all?

Based on our literacy curriculum, I was required to teach a reading unit on character study, which involved helping my students use a variety of reading comprehension strategies to understand and analyze the characters in their leveled fictional books. To parallel this focus on fictional reading, the writing curriculum had a unit on improving the quality of narrative writing, which was an extension of the narrative writing students did in September. In the last week of October we transitioned to expository writing, which I integrated with our study of Native Americans.

I include this particular time of year as an example because even though there were many connections between science and social studies, determining how to integrate these content areas with fictional reading and narrative writing wasn't as straightforward. In the remainder of the chapter I describe what learning activities I planned for this unit in social studies and science, and I explain how I integrated those content areas with each balanced literacy component.

Social Studies

In social studies we researched different Native American groups across what is now the United States to learn about how their ways of life depended greatly upon their environment. A grade-level field trip to the American Museum of Natural History helped my ELLs visualize everything they were learning about Native Americans. Throughout the unit of study we compared these Native American groups with indigenous groups that students were familiar with, such as the Aztecs, Mayas, and Incas, to build on my ELLs' background knowledge and make the learning relevant to them.

I often began the social studies block with a shared reading that had to do with Native Americans to help my ELLs continually deepen their content-area knowledge about the topic and build related vocabulary. Whenever we learned new vocabulary words, I added them to our social studies word wall. Chapter 5 describes how to teach ELLs new content-specific vocabulary.

I then provided time for my ELLs to work on a collaborative group activity. Some days this involved different vocabulary development activities, and other days they worked in small groups to research how a Native American group of their choice lived in a particular region, using a variety of nonfiction texts and websites. They recorded and organized all of their research findings in their social studies notebook and later compiled the key information in a graphic organizer web using the Kidspiration computer program. Figure 4–5 shows the web created collaboratively between Julia, a Level 3 ELL from the Dominican Republic, and Angélica, a Level 1 ELL from Colombia who was starting to transition to a Level 2 proficiency. They were both researching the Navajo Native Americans, and by working together on their web, Julia was able to support Angélica's language development, and they both were able to share complex ideas about the topic in Spanish. Their Kidspiration web became the basis for their informational essays in the writing workshop.

At the end of our social studies block we would regroup and discuss what they had been working on, using academic vocabulary to reinforce the key concepts they were learning. I would then use interactive writing to help my ELLs write a brief summary of what they had learned, record questions they had, fill in a graphic organizer, or explain key vocabulary. My ELLs always recorded these interactive writing texts in their social studies notebooks. Since the texts were short, most of my ELLs were able to copy them without a problem. For beginning ELLs and ELLs with limited literacy skills, I had their partner help them record the interactive writing text in their notebooks if necessary. Years when I had a number of ELLs in this situation, I would later type up the text and give it to each ELL to cut and paste into her notebook.

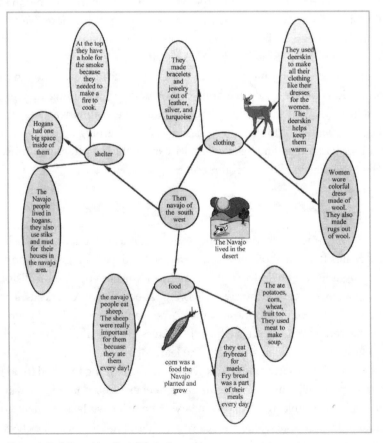

Figure 4–5 *Julia and Angélica's Kidspiration web*

As a culminating project, each ELL created a shoe box display of the Native American region he had researched, including details that showed how the Native Americans used natural resources from their environment for their food, clothing, and shelter. Each student complemented this display with his informational essay from the writing workshop that explained how Native Americans used the natural resources in their environment.

Science

In science we looked at how different plants and animals adapt their way of life to survive in a particular environment, just as the Native Americans did. We also learned about how humans change their environment and how this human activity can affect organisms in both beneficial and harmful ways. We compared how Native Americans changed their environment with what people do today.

As with social studies, I typically began the science block with a shared reading that had to do with these science topics to help my ELLs deepen their content-area knowledge and build related vocabulary. This vocabulary also went onto the science word wall as a reference and resource for vocabulary-building activities.

I then had my ELLs use the rest of the time to work collaboratively on an activity that would put their content-area knowledge and vocabulary to use. We often integrated art as a way to illustrate the science concepts they were learning, and we added labels or short texts to the drawings.

I would end the science time by reviewing key vocabulary and concepts with my ELLs, and using that discussion, we would compose a short interactive writing text about what they had learned that day. My ELLs kept records of these texts in their science notebooks in the same way as in social studies.

To accompany the culminating activity for Native Americans, I had my ELLs explain several ways Native Americans changed their environment and how each change was respectful of the animals and plants in that environment. I modeled for them how they could either write about these changes or, for beginning ELLs, draw a picture of each change and its effect on organisms in that environment.

Read-Alouds

One way you can integrate the content areas with literacy is through the read-alouds you choose. There are many wonderful nonfiction and fiction trade books that relate to different content-area topics. You can use read-alouds to activate your ELLs' background knowledge about the content-area topic and make connections from that knowledge to the new information found in the book. Discussion before reading aloud the book can help ELLs share the vocabulary they already know about the topic, and then as you read the book you can help them learn new vocabulary words connected to the science or social studies concepts. In Chapters 5 and 6 I give examples of how to read aloud a text with ELLs in a way that supports their vocabulary development and comprehension.

Of course, not all read-alouds have to integrate with social studies and science. There will certainly be times during the week when you read aloud a book that connects with a particular genre your class is studying in the reading workshop, such as mysteries, fairy tales, or realistic fiction. Or you may read aloud a book that you feel will help build classroom community, connect to your students' lives, or relate to an upcoming event. Through read-alouds we show students our love of reading, so it's important to include picture books and chapter books with a wide variety of genres and topics. That being said, I try to integrate as many of my fiction and nonfiction read-alouds as possible with science and social studies because I know that the familiar context will help my ELLs understand the text, and it will increase their content-area knowledge and academic vocabulary at the same time.

You don't have to have a vast number of read-aloud books related to your science and social studies topics. Finding just a few high-quality resources that clearly illustrate the concepts and expose ELLs to key vocabulary will be extremely beneficial for them. You can then get more mileage from each book by reusing it for different purposes. For example, after reading aloud a book, you can

- use it during a science or social studies lesson to reinforce content
- use it as a source for content-area vocabulary activities
- use a more challenging part of the text as a shared reading to help ELLs understand the content and language
- use it as a model during a reading or writing minilesson, if it connects with the genre you're studying
- record the book on tape and place it at the listening center for ELLs to listen to and read along with during independent reading
- use a part of the text during word study to examine the use of certain language structures

For this integrated unit, I wanted to read aloud both fiction and nonfiction texts relating to the science and social studies concepts. I knew that if I could find a few fictional texts that connected with these concepts and that also had strong characters, then I would also be able to use those read-aloud books as models during my reading minilessons for our unit on character study.

Fictional Picture Book and Chapter Book Read-Alouds

- *Eagle Song* (Bruchac 1997): This chapter book with illustrations describes the experience of a modern-day Mohawk boy whose family moves away from its Native American reservation to live in Brooklyn. This book is an excellent way to compare the ways of life of Native Americans in the past with how Native Americans live today in the United States. Since the book deals with the problems the main character faces when trying to fit in at a new school in a new city, it's a terrific book for ELLs to relate to. Also, since the main character is complex and changes throughout the story, I could use this book during the reading minilessons as a model for how to analyze characters.
- *The Rough-Face Girl* (Martin 1998): This beautifully illustrated picture book is an Algonquin Cinderella story about a girl whose scarred face doesn't keep her from seeing the beauty in the natural world around her and the beauty inside her. My ELLs were able to use the illustrations and details from the text to discuss aspects of Native American life in the Northeast. The character development of the rough-face girl and her family members made this book another good model for character analysis in our reading workshop minilessons.

Nonfiction Read-Alouds

- *A River Ran Wild* (Cherry 2002): This picture book ties in with both social studies and science. It tells the true story of a river and how the river changed from the time when Native Americans lived by its shores, to when colonists settled there, to modern-day times when factories and other buildings polluted its waters and people decided they needed to save the river. The wonderfully detailed illustrations help ELLs understand the human effect on the environment and how it can be either beneficial or harmful.

- The Bridgestone Books: Native American Life series, including *Longhouses* (Gibson 2005a), *Plank Houses* (Gibson 2005b), *Teepees* (Preszler 2005a), and *Wickiups* (Preszler 2005b): This series has excellent photographs that clearly illustrate for ELLs the details about why different Native American regions developed different types of shelter and how they used the natural resources available in their environment to create their shelter. I modeled for ELLs that they didn't have to read a nonfiction book from start to finish; instead they could use the table of contents to read the parts that were most interesting to them. Using this strategy, I read aloud certain parts of each book in the series.

- *Food and Recipes of the Native Americans* (Erdosh 2001): This book was a visual resource for ELLs to learn about how Native Americans from five different regions used the natural resources in their environment to find and prepare food.

- *How Do Animals Adapt?* (Kalman 2000): This nonfiction science trade book has wonderful photographs and clear explanations of how and why animals adapt in different environments. I made connections with my ELLs between what Native Americans did to survive in different environments and what adaptations animals made in those environments. This book is also available in Spanish.

- *Animal Senses: How Animals See, Hear, Taste, Smell, and Feel* (Hickman 1998): This is another nonfiction science trade book that's a great visual resource for ELLs to learn about how different animals survive as a result of adaptations to their senses.

- *Corn Is Maize: The Gift of the Indians* (Aliki 1986): This picture book describes how corn was discovered and used by certain Native Americans, including relevant vocabulary for both science and social studies. We used this book to talk about how corn was a part of different food chains in different environments where Native Americans lived. This helped my ELLs review what they had learned in September about food chains and food webs and connect it to our current study of Native Americans.

Shared Reading

Another way I integrate content-area studies with literacy is through shared reading. As your ELLs are reading an enlarged shared reading text with you, using different print strategies and reading comprehension strategies to understand it, they're also exposed to the content-area concepts and language. In the primary grades, many shared readings can be connected to social studies, science, and math. A wealth of poems, songs, and big books relate to the content areas. You can also make your own shared reading texts by using a shared writing piece that you created with the class about a content-area topic. I've relied on this option many times when I didn't have reading materials about particular topics.

In the upper grades, shared reading isn't commonly used, but I've found that if I adapt it slightly it can support ELLs tremendously with reading. Shared reading in the upper grades has a different focus than in primary classrooms. Most, though not all, upper-grade ELLs already have a literacy base in their native language and/or in English, so shared reading sessions with the whole class are less about learning how to read and more about utilizing a variety of reading comprehension strategies to better understand the text. However, during the shared reading you can help upper-grade ELLs navigate any unfamiliar sounds or words in the L2 by using different print strategies (Cappellini 2005).

I like to use shared reading with upper-grade ELLs during the social studies or science block as a way to help them understand a challenging content-area text. We often revisit a particular shared reading text during word study to explicitly examine certain language structures that I want to teach my ELLs. There are a number of big books that discuss upper-grade science, social studies, and math concepts that can be used for shared reading. I also use important passages from our science or social studies textbooks for shared reading. Reading parts of the textbook with a supportive structure like shared reading ensures that all of my ELLs will be successful in understanding the content and at the same time develop the kind of reading skills necessary for future education. Other resources I use for shared reading are important pages from a content-area read-aloud that I put on an overhead transparency, articles from periodicals like *National Geographic for Kids* and *Scholastic News*, poems, and songs. During the integrated unit, I used the following shared readings:

- Excerpts from our social studies and science textbooks: I chose sections of the textbook that offered a good introduction to the topics of Native Americans and animal adaptations and that had excellent visuals and vocabulary labels. I read these sections with the class, helping my ELLs utilize a variety of reading comprehension strategies to understand the challenging text. We also made connections to their background knowledge to give them a context for the new learning. During these shared reading sessions, I modeled for my ELLs how they could outline main ideas and details from the text using a graphic organizer with boxes and bullets (see Appendix G). By practicing this skill with me, they were able to do the same kind of note taking as they researched a particular Native American region.

- Articles from *National Geographic for Kids*, saved from previous years: I used several short articles relating to animal adaptation and how humans affect the environment. I put them on overhead transparencies to read them with the whole class. We read the articles together, and I helped them use different reading comprehension strategies to understand the text and print strategies to figure out how to read any unfamiliar words.

- *Giving Thanks: A Native American Good Morning Message* (Swamp 2003): The short message of thanksgiving in this picture book reads like a poem and has beautiful illustrations that show how Native Americans lived in harmony with their environment. I first read aloud the book so my ELLs could see all the illustrations. I also had the text written on chart paper so we could then read it together to understand the language and concepts.

- Transparencies of a few important pages from some of the nonfiction read-alouds: I made transparencies of pages that I wanted to read again with the class. They were pages that really got to the heart of the science and social studies topics and presented the key vocabulary I wanted my ELLs to understand.

Reading Workshop

The reading workshop is a time for ELLs to take the reading strategies they've used with you during read-alouds and shared reading and try them on their own in independent reading. There are a number of ways to integrate the reading workshop with content-area studies.

Minilesson

The minilesson that begins each reading workshop typically uses a familiar read-aloud or shared reading text to teach ELLs how to use a specific reading strategy. I try to carefully choose my read-alouds and shared readings so that some of them connect with our science and social studies topics and also match whatever genre we're focusing on in reading and writing.

In many of the reading minilessons for my unit on character study, I modeled reading comprehension strategies with *Eagle Song* (Bruchac 1997) and *The Rough-Face Girl* (Martin 1998), two of the fictional books about Native Americans that I had previously used as read-alouds. This allowed me to use texts that my ELLs already understood for modeling reading strategies while we analyzed the characters in the books.

Figure 4–6 shows my classroom library after a minilesson using the read-aloud *The Rough-Face Girl*. In that day's lesson I had focused on how my ELLs could use the reading comprehension strategy *inferring* to determine character traits based on evidence from the text. To infer character traits, my ELLs would need to learn adjectives to describe both positive and negative character traits. In the pocket chart I displayed the adjectives we had initially brainstormed about character traits, along with a quick sketch to illustrate each one. Then, on the whiteboard I wrote down the language structures my ELLs would need to know to talk about their inferences. As I modeled this strategy during the reading minilesson and practiced it with my ELLs, we took adjectives from the pocket chart and used them to complete the language prompts for inferring. Since they already knew about the rough-face girl from our initial read-aloud, they had the background knowledge and language they needed to make the inferences. My goal

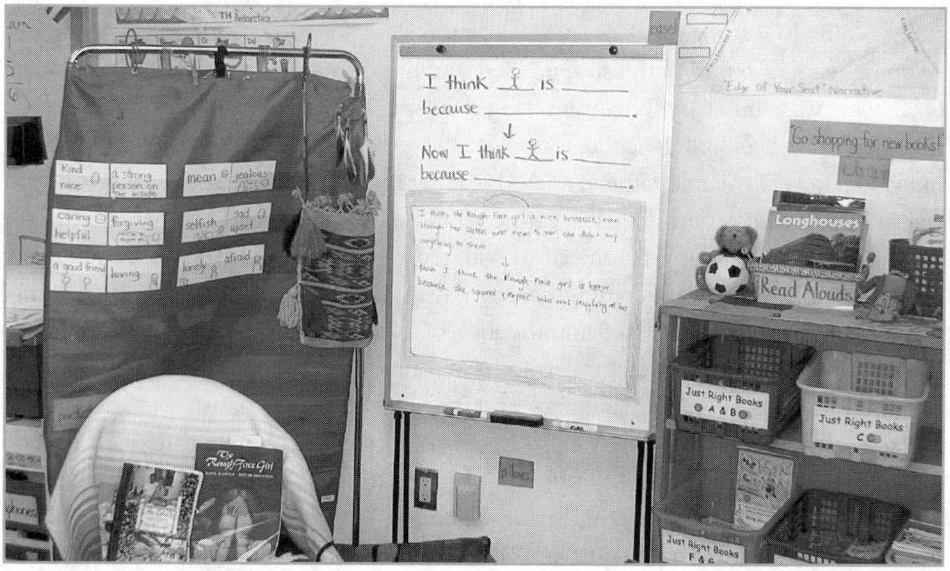

Figure 4–6 *Using a book about Native Americans for a reading minilesson*

with this lesson was for my ELLs to be able to make inferences about the characters in their own books when reading independently.

Independent Reading

After the reading workshop minilesson, my ELLs take their book bags and begin reading independently to put the reading strategies into practice with their own books. For every integrated unit, I have book baskets set up in the classroom library that relate to the content-area topics we're studying so ELLs can read them during this time. When my ELLs go shopping for new books each week, they always choose some books from the content-area baskets in addition to their leveled books. Reading books that connect with the science and social studies topics is very supportive for ELLs. They already have some background knowledge to understand the language and content in the texts, and it's one more way for them to read the academic language in a meaningful context.

If I don't have a lot of books to put in these content-area baskets for the topics we're studying, then several times a week I have students return their content-area books and take different ones to keep the titles rotating among the class. If necessary, I go to the school library and check out books related to the topic. Another option is to pool together books with other grade-level teachers and rotate the baskets between classrooms.

For this integrated unit, I set up several different book baskets in the classroom library that related to Native Americans, animals, and ecosystems. When my ELLs went shopping for new books each week, they put a few of these content-area books that interested them in their book bags, in addition to their fictional leveled books for our unit on character study.

During independent reading I also have some of my ELLs listen to books on tape. I record some of our content-area read-alouds and shared readings and have ELLs listen to them multiple times. Each time they reread the text with the audio support, they're solidifying their understanding of the content and improving their ability to read the language in the text. For this particular unit I recorded the read-alouds *The Rough-Face Girl* and *Animal Senses* (Hickman 1998) and the shared reading *Giving Thanks* (Swamp 2003). I already had *A River Ran Wild* (Cherry 2002) on tape. For my Levels 1 and 2 ELLs, I also recorded their guided reading books so they could continue listening to them and practicing the language during independent reading time.

Listening to recorded texts is especially supportive for beginning ELLs who are developing reading skills in English (Fu 2003). You may remember Fernando, from Chapter 2, who was still at the beginning stages of speaking and reading in English even though he had been at our school for nearly two years. I frequently set him up with an individual tape player and familiar shared reading texts that tied in with science and social studies. One day during this integrated unit he was at his reading spot on the floor against the wall, listening to one of the shared reading texts on tape and following along with his finger. I was sitting nearby having a reading conference with another student, but I couldn't help noticing the look of absolute concentration on Fernando's face as he was reading. I was thrilled to have found something that was engaging for him and that was building his literacy and language skills in English. But then, to my complete horror, a rather large bug happened to scurry by on the floor. Fernando looked up from his reading, stomped the bug with his shoe, and immediately went back to following the text with his finger! Of course I quickly came over to clean things up, but all the while Fernando just smiled at me and kept right on reading and following along with the audio support. Rereading a text about a familiar content-area topic with familiar language and with audio support was exactly what Fernando needed to focus on reading, no matter what distractions were going on around him!

Guided Reading

During independent reading time I typically meet with at least one guided reading group a day. Whenever possible, I choose multiple copies of texts that connect with our science or social studies topics. That way, my ELLs can use their growing background knowledge about the topic to support their comprehension of a text that's at their instructional level. It's also a great way to teach the group more academic language related to the topic (Cappellini 2005). They hear me use the language, they read it in the text, and they use the language when we discuss the text. This simultaneously supports literacy development, language development, and content-area knowledge.

Finding guided reading texts that are at students' instructional reading levels *and* tie in with a social studies or science concept can be challenging, depending upon the topic. If I can't find multiple copies of a leveled text that supports our content-area studies, then I at least make sure the text matches whatever genre we're focusing on in reading.

For this integrated unit, my ELLs were at a wide range of reading levels, including some as low as Level A. I knew that I wanted my guided reading books to relate to either the content-area topics or our character study unit, and ideally some would connect with both. I began by seeing what multiple-copy texts I already had available in my classroom. I found six copies of *Small Wolf* (Benchley 1994), a Level J fictional book that describes what happens to a Native American boy when he makes a surprising discovery in the island of Manhattan, where he lives. I also found six copies of *The Mud Pony: A Traditional Skidi Pawnee Tale* (Cohen 1992), a Level L fictional book about the changes that happen to a Native American boy when Mother Nature transforms his mud pony into a real one. Both of these books have good character development and connect to social studies, so I knew they would be a great way to integrate instruction. I couldn't find any relevant books for lower levels, so I used the Reading A–Z website (www.readinga-z.com/), which had nonfiction and fiction books relating to animals, plants, and how people live at every level from Level A up. I printed out multiple copies of these books to round out my resources for guided reading groups.

During the unit I also used some fictional guided reading books that had interesting characters but that didn't connect at all to the content areas. My goal was to make as many connections as possible to the content areas, but that didn't mean that absolutely every resource I used would integrate with the content areas.

Writing Workshop

Whenever possible, I connect what we're studying in science and social studies with the writing my ELLs create in the writing workshop. Any month when there's a non-narrative unit, such as expository writing, persuasive writing, or letter writing, I have ELLs use the writing workshop to express what they're learning in the content areas. There are other months when the focus is on narrative writing, such as personal narratives (stories from students' lives) or realistic fiction. It's important for ELLs to have experience writing in a full range of genres, just as the other students at their grade level are doing, so I never eliminate these units to focus solely on nonfiction reading and writing. Instead, during the months when we're working on narrative writing, I help my ELLs see how they can use some of the language we've developed during content-area studies in their narrative writing. For example, after reading aloud the book *Eagle Song* (Bruchac 1997), about a Native American boy who moves to a new school, we brainstormed a list of nouns, verbs, and adjectives related to the topic of moving. I knew this was a topic many of my ELLs could relate to and might want to write about in their narratives. Chapter 5 describes how to use different graphic organizers to develop this kind of language related to a content-area topic.

Minilesson: Modeled Writing

During the minilesson at the beginning of the writing workshop, my modeled writing always matches whatever genre we're focusing on. If it's a narrative focus, then I model narrative writing so that my ELLs are prepared to write their own narratives during independent writing. When I model writing, I make sure that I use a familiar topic and language we've developed previously in vocabulary activities. I want my ELLs to have rich language models that they can draw upon as a support, if necessary, when writing independently.

For our unit on writing personal narratives, I modeled writing a narrative about when I moved to a new city, focusing on my fears about what my new life would be like there. I knew this was an experience many of my ELLs would connect with, and then they could write about a similar experience in their independent writing if they wanted. As I modeled my writing, I showed how I was using many of the nouns, verbs, and adjectives that we had previously brainstormed about the topic of moving.

When we made the transition to expository writing at the end of October, my ELLs had already completed their research about different Native American regions, and they were ready to use their Kidspiration webs to help them add information to their essays. During a series of writing minilessons, I modeled how my ELLs could take the facts from their webs and use them to elaborate each section of their essays about Native Americans. I made my own web on chart paper (Figure 4–7) and next to it I had another piece of chart paper where I had simply copied the basic facts from the web into my writing (Figure 4–8).

I read aloud my writing from Figure 4–8, and the class agreed that by just copying the facts I didn't really explain the information. I then modeled how I could take one of my basic sentences and elaborate it to create more detailed informational writing (Figure 4–9). As always, I made sure my writing also modeled how beginning ELLs could elaborate by adding details to their drawings and adding labels using the vocabulary from the word walls, books, and picture dictionaries.

Minilesson: Shared Writing

After modeling with my own writing, the next part of the minilesson is to have ELLs practice writing with me, often using shared writing. I have my ELLs either help me extend the text I have been modeling or help me compose another text using similar language. This additional practice with the language builds ELLs' ability to write independently in the L2.

For example, after modeling how to transfer basic facts from a web into more detailed informational text, I had the class help me improve the rest of the sentences in Figure 4–8. I read aloud another basic sentence from my modeled writing on the chart and had the students turn and talk with their partners on the rug about how that part could be better. Since the partners were made of mixed L2 proficiencies, they each had someone who could support them linguistically, and beginning ELLs could share their

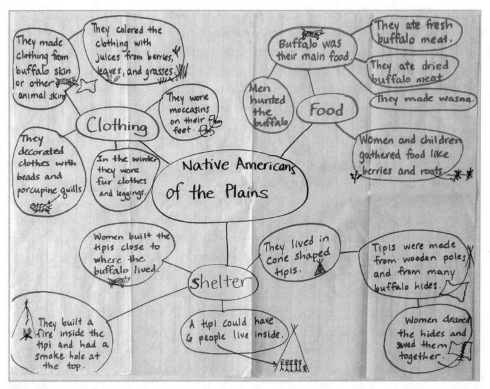

Figure 4–7 *My model of a web*

The web contains the following notes around "Native Americans of the Plains":

Clothing
- They made clothing from buffalo skin or other animal skins.
- They colored the clothing with juices from berries, leaves, and grasses.
- They wore moccasins on their feet.
- They decorated clothes with beads and porcupine quills.
- In the winter they wore fur clothes and leggings.

Food
- Buffalo was their main food.
- Men hunted the buffalo.
- They ate fresh buffalo meat.
- They ate dried buffalo meat.
- They made wasna.
- Women and children gathered food like berries and roots.

Shelter
- Women built the tipis close to where the buffalo lived.
- They lived in cone shaped tipis.
- Tipis were made from wooden poles and from many buffalo hides.
- They built a fire inside the tipi and had a smoke hole at the top.
- A tipi could have 6 people live inside.
- Women cleaned the hides and sewed them together.

They hunted the buffalo. Buffalo was their main food. They ate fresh buffalo meat. They ate dried buffalo meat. They made wasna. Women and children gathered food like berries and roots.

Figure 4–8 *The writing I initially modeled to the class*

The Native Americans of the plains had to use whatever they found on the flat, grassy land for their food. Buffalo were the most important animals on the plains because buffalo gave them lots of meat. Meat from a buffalo could feed a lot of people! They ate fresh buffalo meat, and sometimes they dried it to have meat during the long, cold winters. However, they didn't just eat buffalo meat! Women and children would look all over the plains for things like berries and roots.

Figure 4–9 *Improvements to the basic writing I had modeled*

ideas in their L1. I put my newcomers in triads to give them more linguistic support, and also to give them the option of just listening if they didn't feel comfortable yet participating in this kind of collaborative discussion. Once the partners and triads had a chance to discuss possibilities for adding more detail to the writing, we regrouped and my ELLs gave me ideas for making the text more complete. Approximately the second half of the writing in Figure 4–9 is what my ELLs helped me create through shared writing.

Independent Writing

With the language support from the writing minilessons, ELLs are better prepared to write independently. If your ELLs choose to write about a similar topic as what you modeled, then they'll be able to take advantage of the language they've already developed and use your writing as a guide. Choice is certainly important in the writing workshop, but many ELLs flourish the most as writers when they can choose to write about a topic that has familiar language for them. My experience has been that once ELLs attain approximately an intermediate level of language proficiency, they have a greater base of language structures and vocabulary to draw upon in English, and they feel much more comfortable branching out to different topics when writing on their own.

During the first part of this integrated unit, my ELLs wrote their own narratives, and many of them chose to write about a time when they moved to a new home, using the language we had brainstormed as a class related to moving. Near the end of October we transitioned to writing informational essays. At this point my ELLs had completed their collaborative group research about the way people in a particular Native American region lived, so they were ready to write informational essays based on that research. It was amazing to see how engaged my ELLs were during this independent writing time. As I went around conferring with different students, they were excited to express their knowledge of Native Americans through their writing, and they were able to write extensively on the topic, thanks to the language support they had from their research and Kidspiration webs.

It was through this language support that one of my beginning ELLs from Colombia, Angélica, made a breakthrough in her writing. Angélica arrived to the United States in September, and for the first few months of school she had mainly been writing in Spanish. Her writing in English was limited to using patterned writing with basic sentences and labeling drawings with words in English. As Angélica began this informational essay, she used the research from her Kidspiration web to create a more complete text in English. In Figure 4–10 you can see how Angélica was able to compose more expanded sentences on her own, in addition to using labels and some patterned writing ("They ate _____."). Each page of her writing showed this combination of more original writing with patterned writing. After only two months of learning English, Angélica had enough linguistic support to begin doing this kind of independent writing in English. In addition to her informational essay in English, Angélica wrote a more detailed essay in Spanish about the same topic. This gave her a way to more fully express what she had learned and to continue developing grade-level writing skills.

James, an ELL from Colombia, had arrived to the United States at the end of the previous school year, so he had a slightly higher L2 proficiency level than Angélica. James began the school year writing mainly in Spanish. In October he started using more English when writing his narrative, and by the time he started his informational essay, he was able to write original sentences in English that expressed the many details he had learned about the Tlingit Native Americans of the Northwest. In Figure 4–11

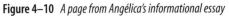

the Native america of the count west, they ate
Fry bread. They ate corn, they ate potatoes, they ate
corn whet, they ate Sherp. When they were
hungry Native america of the Native america
of the south west ate sheep.

Figure 4–10 *A page from Angélica's informational essay*

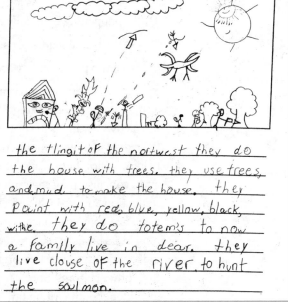

the tlingit of the nortwest they do
the house with trees, they use trees,
and mud to make the house. they
Paint with red, blue, yellow, black,
withe. they do totem's to now
a family live in dear. they
live clouse of the river, to hunt
the soulmon.

Figure 4–11 *A page from James' informational essay*

you can see one page from James' informational essay, where he wrote about the Tlingit's shelter. James' writing shows that developmentally he still wasn't ready to use the past tense, so he would best be classified as a Level 2 ELL. However, his ability to use more expanded sentences in English indicates that he was approaching a Level 3 proficiency. This let me know that using the past tense was something I could begin working on with James.

Interactive Writing

I love using interactive writing with ELLs because there are so many possibilities for reinforcing the learning that takes place in the content areas. And it helps ELLs practice the vocabulary, language structures, and spelling they're learning in English. Interactive writing is very much like shared writing, but the main difference is that with interactive writing ELLs provide some of the spelling and punctuation when writing the text, based on what they're able to contribute at their L2 proficiency level. In shared writing, ELLs provide the ideas for the text, but the teacher does all of the writing work. You can use interactive writing with the whole class, such as at the end of a content-area lesson. Or you can use interactive writing with a small group of ELLs or individual ELLs during independent writing to help them develop their writing skills in English. You can write many different types of short interactive writing texts with ELLs that connect to the content areas:

- Label the content-area vocabulary in photographs, drawings, class murals, or big book illustrations.

- Fill in parts of a graphic organizer related to social studies or science topics, such as a web, T-chart, three-column chart, Venn diagram, or time line (see Appendix G).

- Write a brief summary of the main idea they've learned in math, social studies, or science.

- Write a few details they've learned to support that main idea.
- Keep a daily class journal of scientific observations (for example, what they see happening on a daily basis with seeds they have planted).
- Write a few questions they have about a content-area topic they're studying.
- Write part of an expository text related to a content-area topic.

During independent writing time I often do brief interactive writing sessions to help a small group of beginning ELLs put new language skills into practice. Sometimes the interactive writing is to show ELLs how to use a new sentence structure or how to label their drawings with more vocabulary. In this integrated unit, I knew I would need to help Angélica, James, and other Levels 1 and 2 ELLs in the class write an introduction and a conclusion for their informational essays about Native Americans. Creating an introduction and a conclusion that effectively present and summarize the main ideas of an essay is a complex concept for any student to grasp. It's particularly difficult for beginning ELLs because the language involved is more advanced than what they can produce independently. Also, this organizational concept may be completely new to students from other cultures. So, on two different days I gathered this small group together during independent writing time so we could write an appropriate introduction and a conclusion using interactive writing. I helped guide the organization of the text, and my ELLs came up with the content. Then I wrote the text on the board while they each wrote it in their notebook. I provided the spelling for some of the more difficult words, and I had each of them provide the spelling for some of the high-frequency words and vocabulary words, based on what I felt they would each know at their particular level. Figure 4–12 shows the short conclusion we developed, which Angélica included at the end of her informational essay.

During this unit I also used interactive writing at the end of most of our content-area lessons. For example, after learning about how corn survives in certain environments and how Native Americans used corn for their survival, during science time my ELLs cut out images of the sun, corn, and different animals to create examples of food chains in a particular environment. At the end of science time, we created an interactive

These are all the always that Native Americans of the south west used nature for their food clothin and shelter. thats how they were able to survive for so many years.

Figure 4–12 *Angélica's conclusion, created with interactive writing*

writing piece that summarized what they had learned about the flow of energy in a food chain.

1. First I had some of my Level 1 ELLs show their completed food chains to the class, pointing to how the energy went from one part to the next throughout the chain. I helped these ELLs say each word of the food chain (*sun*, *corn*, etc.).

2. Then I had my Levels 2–5 ELLs formulate complete sentences describing this science concept, and I assisted them in making the sentences grammatically correct. For example, if one of my ELLs said, "Sun give energy to the corn," I would affirm the idea in a grammatically correct way: "Yes, the sun *gives* energy to the corn. Since all food chains start with the sun, let's begin our text with that idea." From our discussion, the complete sentence my ELLs came up with for our interactive writing text was "The sun gives energy to the corn, the corn gives energy to the cow, and finally the cow gives energy to the people."

3. Once we knew what our sentence was going to sound like, I had my ELLs help me with the actual writing. Following is the discussion I had with my class so we could write the text interactively.

   "OK. We're going to write, 'The sun gives energy to the corn,' for the first part of our text." I prepared to write the first word on the whiteboard. "How can I write the first word: *The*?" Since this was a high-frequency word, I knew that my Levels 1 and 2 ELLs would be able to help me, especially since this wasn't the first interactive writing session where they'd provided this word. I called on a Level 1 ELL, and he spelled the word *the* using the letter names in Spanish. "Good. T-h-e, The." I repeated what the student said, using the letter names in English as I wrote the word on the board. I also wrote the word *sun* as I continued saying the phrase aloud. I didn't want students to supply me with the spelling for every single word because that would have been too tedious and time-consuming. "Now we need to write the word *gives*." A number of hands shot up to offer the spelling, but I called on a Level 3 ELL who I knew needed help with subject-verb agreement. The student I called on spelled it as *gibe*, so I repeated the word and asked the student what sound she heard at the end. Her eyes lit up and she told me right away that there was an *s* at the end. I wrote the word on the board, and when I got to the letter *v* I repeated the word again and asked her what letter made that sound. She wasn't sure, but her partner helped by saying it was the letter *v*. I pointed to the letter *v* on our alphabet chart to remind the class what letter represented that sound, and I finished writing the word *gives*. "Great. Now we have 'The sun gives . . . energy to the corn.'" I wrote the rest of the sentence without assistance from any students to keep the activity from dragging on too much. I knew there would be more opportunities for my ELLs to contribute as we wrote the remaining parts of the sentence.

4. As we completed the sentence, I had my beginning ELLs continue to help me with high-frequency words like *the*, *to*, and *and*. Every time we wrote the word *gives*, I emphasized the ending as a reminder to my intermediate ELLs. In the last part of the sentence, I had my advanced ELLs help me with the spelling of *people*, since this is a tricky high-frequency word, and with the spelling of *finally*.

Even though interactive writing comes at the end of content-area time, which coincides with the end of the day, I make an effort to include it consistently. I know it's a highly effective way for ELLs to review content-area knowledge, build academic vocabulary, and practice spelling and language structures all at the same time. That's a great value for about ten minutes of instructional time!

As a final note, when my fourth graders took the state science test later in the spring, there happened to be a multiple-choice question about how energy flows in a food chain. As I circulated around the room during test administration, I saw that nearly every single ELL, including those who had had a lower L2 proficiency in the fall when we studied this topic, answered the question correctly. Having repeated exposure to the science content and language through hands-on activities and literacy activities like interactive writing reinforced the concept for them, and they were able to apply it many months later to the standardized test.

Word Study

Word study can also be integrated with the content areas. You can take a read-aloud, shared reading, shared writing, or interactive writing text that is related to the content areas and use it during word study to examine a particular aspect of spelling or certain language structures. This lets you explicitly examine language using a familiar, content-based text that ELLs already understand.

During this integrated unit, the main language structures I focused on in word study were present-tense versus past-tense verbs because my ELLs needed to use them during reading, writing, social studies, and science. From what I had recorded on the Language Structures checklist, I knew all of my ELLs needed to develop these language structures. I wanted to help my Levels 1 and 2 ELLs expand the verbs they knew in English and understand how they could be used correctly in the present tense. Levels 3 to 5 ELLs needed to develop their ability to correctly use past-tense verbs, including irregular past-tense verbs.

To do this, I used short passages from read-alouds and shared reading texts that my ELLs were already familiar with. I covered up some of the present- and past-tense verbs with strips of sticky notes, and as I reread the passage, I had my ELLs determine what word could go in each blank. Before sharing ideas with me, my ELLs quickly turned and talked with their partners so everyone had a chance to orally share what she thought the covered word was. Even though past-tense verbs are developmentally challenging for Levels 1 and 2 ELLs, it provided good exposure to the language in context, and by using picture clues from the text they were able to share ideas for what the different verbs could be.

After looking at the verbs in a meaningful context, I made charts with my ELLs to compare the structures of present-tense and past tense verbs. This helped my ELLs see that many past-tense verbs use the -ed ending but that there are also a lot of irregular past-tense verbs. Over the next few weeks the students collected examples of regular and irregular past-tense verbs from books they were reading and we added them to the class verb chart. I also created cloze activities for the class to complete based on the verbs they had recorded on the verb chart. For example, with one cloze passage ELLs changed verbs from the present tense to the past tense and put them into a passage about how Native Americans of the Northeast lived. I partnered Levels 1 and 2 ELLs with a Level 3, 4, or 5 ELL so they would have more linguistic support for this learning activity. However, since the verbs were all part of our class verb chart, every ELL was able to use that chart as a reference to complete the activity.

Although we studied verbs explicitly during word study, the goal was for my ELLs to be able to use these language structures correctly during learning activities. For example, during the writing workshop I helped my ELLs use present- and past-tense verbs correctly in their writing. This kept my ELLs accountable for using the language in a meaningful context on a daily basis.

Aside from this focus on language structures, I also used word study to help small groups of ELLs with spelling at their developmental level, using the spelling program my school had adopted. I met with small groups at the beginning of the week, and then throughout the week I had them put the spelling skills into practice with short activities.

The Arts

I was able to incorporate music and art in several ways throughout this period of time. Our music teacher found a song about different Native American tribes for our class to perform as part of an upcoming concert. I put the lyrics on chart paper and we practiced them as a shared reading. This helped my ELLs know how to sing the words accurately and understand the meaning of the lyrics. Practicing the shared reading repeatedly also helped them gain reading fluency.

In science we used art to illustrate different animal adaptations and to draw how humans have changed the environment. The culminating project of creating a shoe box model of a Native American region was another excellent way for my ELLs to tap into their creativity and express what they had learned.

Final Thoughts

I included this particular classroom example to show the different ways you can integrate content areas with balanced literacy components. That doesn't mean it's essential to integrate every single part of the school day for every unit of study. By knowing the possibilities for integrated instruction, you can look at your own units of study and begin imagining little ways you can weave content-area studies in with your literacy components. The more ways you find to integrate your instruction, the more it will benefit your ELLs. Seeing all of my ELLs in the auditorium that November, having the confidence to ask the Native American presenters their questions, showed me just how much they had benefited from the connections I had made between the content areas and literacy. Their content-area knowledge was strong, they had developed more academic language, and they had used this knowledge and language to read and write more complex texts. This made it worth any extra effort to integrate different instructional parts of the school day.

Reflecting on the Keys to Success

Raise the Bar

- Do my content-area and literacy units for each month reflect the learning standards and curricula for my grade level?

- Does my yearlong plan for instruction include *all* of the learning objectives in the curricula for my grade level?

Teach Language and Content Together

- Do I use content-area and literacy instruction to teach my ELLs academic vocabulary?
- Do I plan ways for ELLs to practice that academic vocabulary multiple times during the content-area and literacy components?
- Do I use the Language Structures checklist and other observations of ELLs' language use to plan what language I can teach them during word study, literacy activities, and content-area studies?

Integrate Instruction Thematically

- Do I look across my curricular units each month to plan how I can integrate the content areas with different balanced literacy components?
- Does this integration provide ELLs with multiple ways to hear, speak, read, and write the language?

Differentiate Instruction

- When planning integrated instruction, do I include a range of balanced literacy components that provide time for whole-group, small-group, and individual instruction?
- Do these literacy components use language and concepts developed during content-area studies to make learning more comprehensible and engaging for ELLs?
- Do I incorporate visuals like graphic organizers, pictures, and books with illustrations into my integrated instruction to support ELLs with varying L2 proficiencies?
- Do I incorporate hands-on and collaborative activities in my integrated instruction?
- Do I include ways for ELLs with different L2 proficiency levels to participate during whole-group activities?

Connect Learning to Students

- When integrating instruction, do I relate all new learning to my ELLs' background knowledge about the topic and their life experiences?

Use Students' Native Languages to Support Learning

- Do I encourage ELLs to use their native languages as a way to understand and express their learning of content-area concepts?
- Do I encourage beginning ELLs to participate in their L1 and have other students translate if necessary?

References for Further Reading

Integrating Content-Area and Literacy Instruction for ELLs

Cappellini, Mary. 2005. *Balancing Reading and Language Learning: A Resource for Teaching English Language Learners, K–5.* Portland, ME: Stenhouse.

Freeman, David, and Yvonne Freeman. 2007. *English Language Learners: The Essential Guide.* New York: Scholastic.

Gibbons, Pauline. 2002. *Scaffolding Language, Scaffolding Learning: Teaching Second Language Learners in the Mainstream Classroom.* Portsmouth, NH: Heinemann.

CHAPTER 5

Teaching Academic Language Through the Curriculum

*I*t was May and my ELLs had been learning about different three-dimensional shapes in math, including how these shapes form a part of every community. This connected with our integrated unit in which we were comparing and contrasting life in different world communities. So far my ELLs had learned the vocabulary for three-dimensional shapes such as sphere, cube, rectangular prism, cone, *and* pyramid. *They had also learned the vocabulary for describing these shapes:* edges, faces, vertices, curved surface, *and* flat surface. *Now they needed to learn how to find the volume of a rectangular prism.*

I decided to launch our study of volume with a hands-on collaborative activity. Each group of ELLs got four different rectangular prisms, designed to look like different buildings students could find in a community. I asked my ELLs to think about how much "space" was inside each of these buildings. I didn't want to introduce the word volume *just yet until I saw if any of my students would use that word on their own during the collaborative activity. I told my ELLs they could use the counting cubes in their manipulatives basket or any other strategy to determine the space inside the buildings. I let them know that after about five minutes they would report their findings to the class. My goal was to see if my ELLs would use what they already knew about calculating area (multiplying the length times the width) and just multiply one more dimension, height, to find the volume. I also wanted to see if they would use mathematical language like* length, width, area, volume, cube, *or* rectangular prism *on their own.*

As soon as I gave the groups the OK to start, the room was filled with productive chatter. I listened in to one particular group with three students: Vicente, a Level 4 ELL from Mexico, James, a Level 3 ELL from Colombia, and Fernando, a Level 2 ELL from the Dominican

Republic. In the following conversation, you can see how they used mathematical language as well as a combination of English and Spanish to think through the problem.

Vicente: Oh, I have an idea! I think that to measure all of them we need to put three cubes here [pointing to the length inside the prism] and then multiply the ones that are here [pointing to the width inside the prism] times the ones that are here [pointing to the height inside the prism].

James: Yeah, you should multiply the length by the width, and you should get the area of the inside.

Fernando: So put . . . [indicating that Vicente should fill the base with cubes].

James: So put a lot on the bottom, like to cover the bottom, and then put like up, up, and up [indicating that he should stack enough cubes to reach the top].

Vicente: [Begins to fill the base with cubes.]

James: How many are you putting?

Vicente: Wait . . . [seeing that there are three cubes in the length of the base and three cubes in the width of the base]. So three times three equals nine.

Fernando: Póngalo así para que cubra todo [Put it like this so it covers everything]. . . . Let me see [looking at the base of the rectangular prism].

Vicente: Tiene que caber nueve. Sí, está bien. Yo ahora voy a ponerlo así hasta arriba. [It has to fit nine. Yes, that's good. Now I'm going to put it like this all the way to the top.]

Vicente began stacking enough cubes to reach the top of the shape, cleverly finding the third dimension needed to find volume without having to fill the entire shape with counting cubes. The three students continued working together and correctly found the volume by multiplying the three dimensions, just as Vicente originally proposed at the beginning of the group work. I was thrilled to see how they used words like length, width, area, measure, *and* cubes *as well as their prior knowledge about calculating area to figure out this problem. I was also able to mentally take note of what mathematical language they weren't using, like* height *and* volume. *Everyone participated in this group's collaborative work, regardless of his L2 proficiency level.*

Once each group had a chance to share how it solved the problem with the class, I was able to build upon the students' discoveries to teach them the concept of volume and model how they could use the formula for volume to find how much space was inside a rectangular prism. Through my modeling I reinforced the words length *and* width, *taught them the words* height *and* volume, *and provided the language structures they would need to talk about volume, such as "Volume equals length times width times height" and "The volume is _____ inches cubed."*

Later we continued to use this language as I modeled more examples of finding volume and as my ELLs completed activities related to volume in their math books. We also added these words to our math word wall, and the following day I gave my ELLs time to add the words to their math notebooks, along with their own drawings and explanations.

If we want ELLs to learn all of the content objectives in the grade-level curriculum, we have to be prepared to teach them the *language* they'll need to carry out those objectives. What vocabulary will they need to understand a particular topic? What language structures will they need to express their learning? This math lesson shows just how intricately language is tied to content; I had to incorporate academic language instruction as part of my lesson on volume so my ELLs could understand the math concept and express their learning. This language is something we often take for granted as proficient English speakers, readers, and writers. We set our sights on what we want students to accomplish as learners, overlooking the language they'll need to reach those goals. When we plan for learning, we *must* plan for language; the two cannot be separated when we teach ELLs.

In this chapter I explain how to

- develop language objectives for the content objectives in your curriculum

- teach ELLs the language structures and academic vocabulary they'll need to be successful with the curriculum

Developing Language Objectives

We all know what we're supposed to teach our students in reading, writing, science, social studies, and math because it's outlined for us through state standards and content objectives. We take those content objectives and plan a series of learning activities designed to help students meet the objectives. We also plan assessments to make sure our students are on track for meeting the content objectives (Wiggins and McTighe 2005). But what about the language ELLs need to know for all of this learning? Unfortunately, that's not as clearly laid out for us. It's up to us to think about what we're asking ELLs to do for each learning activity and determine what language structures and academic vocabulary they'll need to know to be successful with the activity. These are referred to as the *language demands* of the curriculum (Freeman and Freeman 2009; Gibbons 1991).

Often, the language demands of the curriculum also match the language needs ELLs have. For example, when I was teaching the integrated unit detailed in Chapter 4, my ELLs had to use a combination of present-tense and past-tense verbs for the content objectives in reading, writing, social studies, and science. Based on my observations, which I had recorded in the Language Structures checklist (Figure 2–7), my ELLs also needed help with these two verb tenses. My beginners needed to work on using the present tense, and my intermediate and advanced ELLs needed support in using regular and irregular past-tense verbs. In this case, the language demands of the curriculum and the language needs of my ELLs overlapped completely. Your ELLs will always have a wide variety of language needs as they develop their L2 proficiency, and you won't be able to address them all during one particular unit of study. Some of them can be addressed through the curriculum each month, and others can be targeted through individual reading and writing conferences, guided reading groups, or interactive writing.

When I prepare to teach each unit of study, I think about what language objectives I'll need to have for the different content objectives. I ask these questions:

- What is the content objective I'm going to teach?

- What learning activities will I have my ELLs do to meet that content objective?

- For those learning activities, what are the *most important* language structures and vocabulary my ELLs will need to understand and use?

Language Structures

Each content objective requires ELLs to use different language structures. These are the grammatical building blocks of language that we use to form sentences and connect sentences together to make a paragraph or longer text. You can use the Language Structures checklist as a reference for examples of language structures your ELLs will need to develop as they learn English. Figure 5–1 shows the language structures I decided to teach my ELLs for the science content objective of understanding how human activity affects other organisms, which was part of the integrated unit I described in Chapter 4. When I thought about the language my students would have to use during the learning activities, I realized they would be talking and writing in the present tense about how people affect the organisms in the environment. They would also need to express the cause and effect of people's actions with different conjunctions such as *when, so, since, as a result*, and *therefore*.

If you've never thought about language in this way, you may feel uncomfortable trying to figure out what language structures your ELLs will need to use. It helps to think about what your ELLs will be doing with the language during a learning activity (the language function). Will your ELLs be *describing* something? *Questioning*? *Explaining*? Each of these language functions leads students to use different types of language structures (Gibbons 1991, 2002). For example, if they'll be describing something, they'll need to use a variety of adjectives. If they'll be *questioning*, they'll need to know how to ask questions in a particular tense (present, past, future) and how to respond to questions using a particular verb tense. If they'll be *explaining* something that happened in the past, they'll need to use regular and irregular past-tense verbs and a variety of conjunctions such as *and, but, so, after, before*, and *because* to transition between ideas.

Content Objective

Identify examples where human activity has had a beneficial or harmful effect on other organisms (e.g., deforestation).

Learning Activities

Read aloud different texts that illustrate human effect on the environment. Using a T-chart, identify the cause and effect of how human activity can have a beneficial or harmful effect on organisms.

Language Objectives

- Language structures: use the present tense; use conjunctions that show cause and effect:
  - *When* humans cut down trees, they destroy a habitat for different organisms.
  - *Since* humans cut down trees, they destroy a habitat for different organisms.
  - *As a result* of deforestation, humans destroy a habitat for different organisms.
- Content-specific vocabulary:
  - deforestation, pollute/pollution, contaminate/contamination, habitat, species, population, organism, food chain/food web, endangered, extinct
- General academic vocabulary:
  - humans, impact, environment, beneficial, harmful, effect, identify, destroy, create, survive, change

---

Figure 5–1 *Example of content and language objectives in science*

After you determine the key language structures your ELLs need to use for a particular learning activity, you'll have to explicitly model them during instruction and plan ways for your ELLs to practice them (Gibbons 1991). The section on modeling and practicing language structures on page 129 gives examples of simple ways to develop language structures in content-area lessons and during different balanced literacy components.

Academic Vocabulary

For each of your content objectives, you'll also need to determine what academic vocabulary your ELLs will need to learn. Academic vocabulary is separated into two types: *content-specific words* and *general academic words*. Content-specific words are used in only one particular subject area, whereas general academic words are used in many different subject areas (Coxhead 2000). Figure 5–1 includes a list of the science-specific words my ELLs needed to know for the content objective. This included words like *deforestation, pollution, endangered,* and *extinct.* These science words are vital to understanding the concept of how human activity affects other organisms in beneficial and harmful ways. General academic words like *environment, beneficial, harmful, destroy,* and *change* are also important for this content objective, but they're not specific science words. ELLs will encounter and use these words in a number of different contexts. I separate vocabulary into these two categories when planning for instruction because there are different approaches to teaching content-specific and general academic words.

Content-Specific Vocabulary

Since content-specific words are used less frequently, you should *explicitly teach* these words to ELLs (Freeman and Freeman 2009). This gives your ELLs a thorough understanding of what the words mean and provides a way for them to practice the words in the content area. Doing this kind of explicit vocabulary instruction increases your ELLs' vocabulary base and also improves their reading comprehension (Goldenberg 2008). Research has found that English-proficient students get the same benefits from explicit vocabulary instruction, so it's worthwhile to dedicate part of each day to teaching content-specific vocabulary. For this reason, I allocate a solid block of time for social studies, science, and math in the daily schedule. I also reinforce content-specific vocabulary during balanced literacy components. See the section "Teaching Content-Specific Vocabulary" on page 141 for teaching strategies.

General Academic Vocabulary

General academic words are used in many different contexts, so your ELLs naturally have greater exposure to them. You can model what these words mean as they come up in discussions or learning activities, but it's not necessary to dedicate as much time to explicitly teaching and practicing the words (Freeman and Freeman 2009). For example, I knew my ELLs would need to understand the difference between the general academic words *beneficial* and *harmful* in order to give examples of ways human actions affect organisms. So when we made a T-chart to compare the two types of human actions, I briefly explained the difference between the two words.

1. First, I wrote a plus sign and a minus sign above the words to illustrate that *beneficial* is something positive and *harmful* is something negative.

2. Then, I wrote down an example for each word based on our read-aloud *A River Ran Wild* (Cherry 2002). Under *harmful* I wrote: "When factories pollute a river, many organisms can die, and they can become endangered or even extinct." Under *beneficial* I wrote: "When people clean up a polluted river, organisms can survive in their habitat again."

3. I pointed to these examples in the book so my ELLs could see the difference with the illustrations. One was clearly something positive and the other something negative.

This quick modeling helped my ELLs understand the two general academic words. The modeling also prepared my students to continue the learning activity of adding more examples to their own T-chart with a partner. When you plan your lessons, there may be certain general academic words you know you'll need to clarify for ELLs, and you can jot these words down in your plans. But you can't anticipate everything. Most likely other general academic words will come up during lessons, which you can explain to your ELLs as needed.

Ultimately, the best way for ELLs to develop high levels of general academic vocabulary is through extensive reading (Freeman and Freeman 2009). As your ELLs read a variety of different texts, they repeatedly encounter these words in context, which helps them construct meaning. This makes it vital for ELLs to have time every day for independent reading so they can gradually expand their vocabulary base (Chen and Mora-Flores 2006).

Incorporating Language into Your Planning

At first glance, planning these language objectives seems time-consuming. Keep in mind that the example in Figure 5–1 is not for just one lesson. We spent several weeks on this content objective, so the language objectives applied to the entire study of the content objective.

There's no right way to record language objectives as you plan for instruction. The easiest approach is often to incorporate them into your personal system for planning lessons. Consider leaving a space in your lesson plans where you can jot down the main language structures and vocabulary you'll want to teach ELLs so they can understand and participate in the learning activity. This makes language instruction a meaningful part of each lesson. You may find that certain language structures will be important for your ELLs to use across multiple subject areas, so they can become a focus for your word study time.

As you get used to thinking about the language structures and academic vocabulary involved in learning, it really becomes second nature. You find yourself automatically considering the language demands of any learning activity. Even for those unplanned teachable moments that arise during the school day, you may notice that you're more aware of what vocabulary you will need to clarify for ELLs or what language structures you will need to help them with. In essence, when you think about the language demands of the curriculum, you put yourself in your ELLs' shoes. You understand how difficult it would be to keep up with the academic work without the appropriate language structures and vocabulary to express your learning.

Modeling and Practicing Language Structures

Once you're aware of the language structures ELLs need to use for a particular learning activity, you can plan how you'll explicitly model them during instruction. Since teaching language structures happens within the context of the lesson, it doesn't take up much additional time, yet those brief moments of modeling language structures make it possible for ELLs to be highly productive during a learning activity. Here I provide several detailed examples of how you can model language structures in different lessons and have your ELLs practice them during collaborative or independent work. You can also reinforce language structures during word study, shared reading, and interactive writing.

Content Areas

Following are the language objectives I had for the math lesson I described at the beginning of the chapter and the ways I taught my ELLs the necessary language structures as part of the lesson.

- Content objective: Use a formula to calculate the volume of rectangular prisms.

- Learning activities: Have students calculate how many counting cubes are necessary to fill a rectangular prism. Then use this concept to develop a formula for finding the volume of a rectangular prism by multiplying the measurements of length, width, and height. Have students use this formula to solve a variety of volume problems in their math book.

- Language structures: Use the present tense (*Volume equals . . .; The volume is . . .*); use the word *times* as a verb

  - Volume equals length × width × height.

  - Volume equals _____ × _____ × _____. (with specific measurements)

  - The volume is _____ inches (or centimeters, meters, feet, etc.) cubed.

- Content-specific vocabulary: *volume, area, length, width, height, inches, feet, centimeters, meters, rectangular prism, cube*

- General academic vocabulary: *building, community, space*

The language structures for this content objective are tricky because they're used in a specific way for mathematics. For example, *Volume equals* is in the present tense, which is a basic language structure, but using the verb *equals* is specific to mathematics. Also, ELLs need to know what word is connected with the symbol for multiplication (×). The symbol in this formula is typically read as *times*. Here the word *times* is used as a verb. This can be confusing for ELLs, since the word *times* is normally used as a noun in other situations, like talking about how many *times* something has happened. Another tricky grammatical point is the word *cubed*. ELLs need to understand that *cubed* refers to the inches; they're counting how many cubes that measure an inch on each side can fit inside a rectangular prism. Understanding the meaning of *cubed* helps ELLs remember to include the word in their calculation, such as "The volume is eighteen inches *cubed*." Aside from these language structures, ELLs also have to use a number of content-specific vocabulary words to express the formula for volume. All of this mathematical language can be quite confusing for ELLs if it's not explicitly modeled and anchored in concrete examples.

1. As I described at the beginning of this chapter, I began by having my ELLs do a hands-on activity to solve a volume problem.

2. After the students shared their solutions for finding the space inside each of the buildings, I was able to build upon their ideas to explicitly model how to find volume, using the buildings and the counting cubes as a concrete visual.

3. I wrote the language structure "Volume equals length × width × height" on the board, and as I read it aloud, I pointed to the manipulatives to connect the abstract language with the concrete concept. We practiced using this structure with each of the buildings (rectangular prisms) I had given the groups to measure. I clarified that the symbol for multiplication is said as *times*, and I wrote the word above the symbol, emphasizing the verb whenever I said the sentence aloud.

4. Then I showed my ELLs how to add specific measurements to the language structure "Volume equals _____ × _____ × _____" as we calculated the volume of other rectangular prisms together. Each time, I pointed to the language structures written on the board and connected the words to the measurements of each side of the rectangular prisms.

5. I modeled how to share the final calculation using the language structure "The volume is _____ inches cubed." I explained *inches cubed* by modeling how it refers to the size of the cubes that fit inside the rectangular prism.

6. When my ELLs worked on volume problems in their math book, I went from group to group helping them verbalize these language structures to express their calculations for volume and their final answers.

7. At the end of the lesson, we reviewed what they had worked on, again using the language structures.

Modeling these language structures didn't take very long. It was simply a matter of having the language structures written out for ELLs to see and making a conscious effort to consistently refer to that language throughout the lesson (Coggins et al. 2007). I also gave my ELLs a chance to practice the language structures as they worked in pairs on more volume problems. These slight modifications gave my ELLs the language support they needed to understand the mathematical concept of volume. Later I put the language structures on chart paper so we could refer to them throughout our unit of study. I also used part of the next math lesson to put the new content-specific vocabulary words on our math word wall and have my ELLs record them in their math notebooks. The section "Explicit Instruction of Vocabulary" on page 144 gives examples of how to do this with key vocabulary words.

Reading Workshop

When you teach your ELLs different reading comprehension strategies, they'll need to use certain language structures to express their thinking. In November one of the reading strategies I focused on with my class was *questioning* to help students understand the nonfiction texts they were reading. When readers ask themselves questions before they read, while they're reading, and after they finish reading, they're actively thinking about the text and making sure they understand it (Keene and Zimmermann 2009; Harvey and Goudvis 2000).

- Content objective: Use the reading comprehension strategy *questioning* to understand a text.

- Learning activities: Using a read-aloud text, model how good readers think of questions as they read. Then have students listen to a new part of the read-aloud and practice asking questions to understand the text. During independent reading, have students practice asking questions with their own books and record those questions in their reading notebooks.

- Language structures: Ask questions in the present and past tense.

  - Understand how to use different question words: *who, what, where, when, why, how.*

  - Understand how to use auxiliary verbs: *do, does, did, can, could, is, are, was, were.*

  - Understand how to form the rest of a question.

I knew that in order to ask questions about a text, my ELLs would need support with the language structures involved in forming questions. My beginning ELLs needed to learn the different question words, and my intermediate and advanced ELLs needed help with the correct formation of questions in the present and past tenses. Although we may take it for granted, forming questions in English is actually quite complex:

- Many questions begin with a word like *who, what, where, when, why,* or *how.*

- These question words are typically followed by an auxiliary verb such as *do, did, can, could, is, was, are, were, will,* or *would.* (*"Why did* explorers travel across the Atlantic Ocean?" or "*What were* the explorers hoping to find?")

- When we ask a yes-or-no question, we don't use a question word, but instead start the question with an auxiliary verb: "*Did* explorers treat indigenous groups fairly?"

- ELLs need to understand that auxiliary verbs are extremely important because they show us if a question is in the present tense, past tense, or future tense. Consider these two questions: "How do people travel from one place to another?" and "How did people travel from one place to another?" The only difference between them is the auxiliary verbs *do* and *did. Do* expresses present tense, and *did* expresses past tense. The main verb, *travel,* never changes tense. If ELLs don't understand the language structures for forming questions, they may think they need to change the verb *travel* to express the tense, or they may not include an auxiliary verb at all. It's very common for ELLs to ask or write questions like these: "How *did* people *traveled*?" or "How people *traveled*?"

The best way to help ELLs with these complicated language structures is to explicitly model them within a meaningful context. This can be effectively done during a reading minilesson focused on asking questions to understand a text.

1. In the reading minilesson I used a book about explorers that I had started reading aloud to the class the previous day. That way, my ELLs were familiar with the book, but they hadn't heard the entire text yet.

2. As I read aloud the next part of the book, I paused several times to model the questions that came into my mind about the explorers. Each time I thought of a question, I wrote it on the board and then continued reading to see if I would learn anything to help me answer my questions.

3. After I had several questions recorded on the board, I pointed out the language structures involved in forming them:

- I explained each question word, and I helped my ELLs distinguish these words by including a little sketch next to some of them, such as a stick person next to the word *who* or a clock face next to the word *when*.

- I pointed out the auxiliary verbs and showed how they tell us if the question is in the present or past tense.

- I also pointed out that the main verb didn't change at all.

4. Then I told the students that as I continued to read aloud the next few pages of the book, I wanted them to ask their own questions to help them understand the text.

5. I showed the class a question tree I had prepared to help us form questions using question words and auxiliary verbs. Figure 5–2 shows the question tree, which had yellow leaves for each question word and orange leaves for different auxiliary verbs. Every time my ELLs shared a question about explorers based on what I was reading, we took the appropriate leaves from the tree and stuck them on the board in the correct order. Then we wrote the complete question underneath the leaves.

This language activity was very fast paced. The focus of the lesson was on the reading strategy of asking questions to understand a text, and I simply included the hands-on activity of combining question words and auxiliary verbs to support my ELLs' language development.

Figure 5–2 *Question tree*

6. During independent reading, my ELLs recorded in their reading notebooks questions they had about the books they were reading. They also recorded what they thought the answers could be based on the text and their prior knowledge.

7. At the end of independent reading, my ELLs shared their questions with their reading partners and talked about possible answers. From listening to these conversations and looking at the questions they wrote in their notebooks, I was able to assess their ability to ask questions in English.

Throughout the month of November we continued working on questioning, and with each lesson I helped my ELLs refine their ability to ask questions in English. Figure 5–3 shows the questions that Julia, a Level 3 ELL from the Dominican Republic, recorded during independent reading one day. I saw that she did an excellent job of asking questions in the present tense, but her second-to-last question showed me that she wasn't sure how to form a negative question. She wrote, "Why *does* the tree *does not* need leaves in the winter?" instead of "Why *doesn't* a tree need leaves in the winter?" This was something I later modeled for the whole class in another reading minilesson, and I also helped Julia with this language use during a reading conference.

Figure 5–4 shows how one of my beginning ELLs, Diana, evolved in her English development throughout the school year. In September, Diana was a newcomer from Colombia and had a Level 1 proficiency in English. When we worked on questioning in November, she mainly wrote questions in Spanish, but from those lessons she was exposed to the language structures for asking questions in English. By March, Diana was independently writing questions in English and explaining possible answers to those questions, as you can see in Figure 5–4. She still needed to work on asking questions in the past tense ("Why the bees *came* to a flower?"), but she was correctly using different

Figure 5–3 *Julia's questions in November*

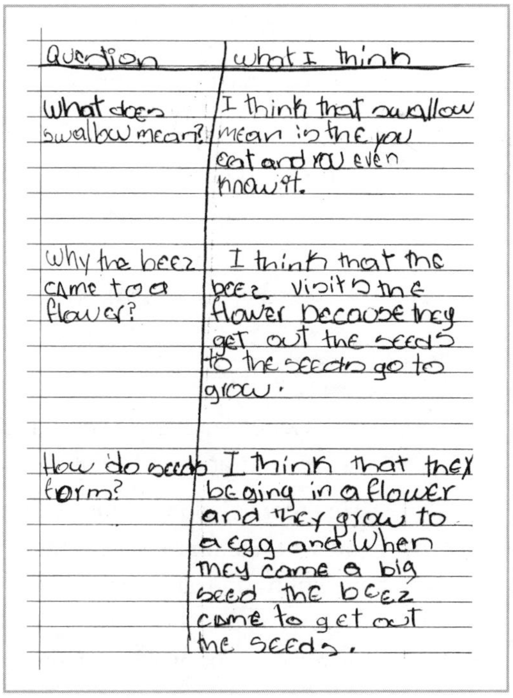

Figure 5–4 *Diana's questions in March*

question words and the auxiliary verbs *does* and *do.* Diana's questions and answers also gave me insight into her misconceptions about seeds, which I addressed with the class as we continued to study that science topic.

Sometimes a reading comprehension strategy doesn't require as much modeling because the language structures are less complex for ELLs. For example, with the reading strategy *making predictions,* modeling the following language structures for the future tenses is more straightforward:

- I think _____ is going to . . .
- I think _____ are going to . . .
- I think _____ will . . .

Whether the explicit modeling of language structures is a brief reference or a more extended look at an aspect of the language, you're preparing ELLs with the language they need to use the reading strategies on their own. Appendix F gives examples of language structures that are commonly used with different reading comprehension strategies. This appendix also shows how you can involve ELLs at different L2 proficiency levels in using the reading strategies.

Writing Workshop

In the writing workshop you can explicitly model certain language structures as part of your minilessons. The example I give here is for a narrative writing unit, and I identify the main language structures my ELLs would need to use for this type of writing.

- Content objective: Using the writing process, produce a personal narrative account that is focused, organized, and elaborated with details that illustrate the action.
- Learning activities: Model how to write a narrative based on a personal experience. Have students practice this type of writing by helping me compose a similar narrative using shared writing. During independent writing, students write their own narratives.
- Language structures:
  - Use the past tense to write a narrative.
  - For beginning ELLs, use basic sentences in the present tense to explain an experience and label a drawing of their narrative with different nouns.
  - Use conjunctions to connect and combine sentences within the narrative (*and, but, so, then, because,* etc.) to make the writing more complex.
  - Use a variety of adjectives, adverbs, and verbs to describe feelings and actions in the narrative.
- General academic vocabulary: ELLs can use vocabulary related to the topics of *moving* and *school* that we previously developed during read-alouds using webs.

In order to help my ELLs with these language structures, I like to have a dual focus to my writing minilessons: I teach my ELLs something that will improve the quality of their writing and also something to improve their language use. In the lesson I describe here, I wanted to help my ELLs elaborate their personal narratives with details that *showed* the action instead of simply telling what happened. Over the past few days I had been modeling different ways to do this elaboration by including descriptions of what people were saying (dialogue), feeling, and thinking. I also wanted to help my

ELLs use the past tense in their personal narratives. So the dual focus for this lesson was elaborating a narrative and using the past tense.

1. In the minilesson I first modeled how to draft a narrative, using details that *showed* the action. To do this, I wrote the first part of my narrative on chart paper, reading it aloud as I wrote each sentence:

   > I walk out of the airport with my husband, pulling my heavy suitcase behind me. I feel butterflies in my stomach when I see how huge New York City is. I think, "I can't believe this is going to be my new home!"

2. I read aloud what I had written so far and asked the class how it sounded. Many of my ELLs identified that I had used elaboration techniques we had previously learned, like adding a description to show how nervous I was feeling and adding my thoughts to show what was happening. Other ELLs commented that I needed to change some words to show that this story happened in the past.

3. I had my ELLs turn and talk with their partners about which words needed to be changed. This was a good way for me to informally assess if they could identify the verbs. Then, with their help, I underlined the verbs and we changed them from the present to the past tense. Since we had already made charts of present- and past-tense verbs in word study, my ELLs were able to use those charts to help them remember the past tense of certain verbs. When I wrote those three sentences, I made an effort to include regular verbs like *walk*, common irregular verbs like *is*, and more difficult irregular verbs like *think*. That way, I could ask ELLs at different L2 proficiency levels to help me change different verbs.

4. Then, using shared writing, we tried out these elaboration techniques by writing a similar narrative based on students' experiences of moving from one place to another. My ELLs shared ideas for how we could add dialogue, thoughts, and feelings to elaborate our shared writing narrative. As we composed the first few sentences together, I also emphasized how we were using past-tense verbs. This supported the lesson's dual focus: practice ways to elaborate a narrative and use the past tense.

5. After the writing minilesson my ELLs worked on their own narratives during independent writing. I circulated around the room, sitting down next to different ELLs to have individual writing conferences with them. It can be tempting to spend an entire writing conference helping ELLs correct all the grammatical or spelling errors you see in their writing. The problem is that this sole focus on language use doesn't help ELLs become better writers. They aren't learning how to focus their writing, organize it, elaborate an idea, add voice to their writing, or expand their word choice. Just like the writing minilessons, writing conferences should have a dual focus on improving the quality of ELLs' writing and improving their language use.

6. I try to find this balance during a writing conference by first focusing on a particular quality of writing an ELL needs to develop. Then at the end of a conference, I point out something about how to use the L2, such as consistently using the past tense. However, I try to limit these comments about language to one particular language structure or one particular type of word an ELL is misusing. If you focus on just one type of error, ELLs can assimilate what you're showing them

and better understand how to use the language. Whatever I teach an ELL about the language needs to be something the student is developmentally ready to tackle (Ferris 2002). For example, I wouldn't push beginning ELLs to use the past tense, because developmentally they're acquiring and using the present tense. Instead, I would help beginners with other aspects of the language, like labeling their drawings with more nouns or using a basic sentence structure in English. On the other hand, ELLs who are at or approaching a Level 3 proficiency are developmentally ready to begin using past-tense verbs instead of present-tense verbs. This makes it very important to continually monitor your ELLs' language use with the Language Structures checklist (Figure 2–7) so you have an idea of what level they're at and what language they are developmentally ready to use in the L2.

7. At the end of independent writing I always give my ELLs a few minutes to do a quick edit. No matter what stage they're at in the writing process, it's helpful to provide this time for ELLs to reread what they wrote and make corrections based on what they know about the language. In the case of this lesson, where I was modeling how to write a narrative in the past tense, I told my ELLs to be on the lookout for how they used the past tense. Quick edits aren't limited to editing for the language structure we happen to be studying at the moment. My ELLs know that I expect them to check for everything they've learned about the language throughout the school year, including the spelling of high-frequency words, the spelling of other words they've studied, and punctuation. They can use our high-frequency word wall and our language charts to help them. At the beginning of the year I break this up for ELLs. First they reread their writing to look for punctuation mistakes, then for spelling, and finally for specific language structures. The less experience ELLs have with this kind of editing, and the younger they are, the more structured the quick edit needs to be.

8. You can occasionally use the share time at the end of the writing workshop to regroup the class and teach the students something specific about the way they're using language in their writing. This is like having a language minilesson with the class. It can remind your ELLs about an aspect of the language that you taught at the beginning of the writing workshop, or it can address something else you observed your ELLs misusing during independent writing. I often use this time to teach my ELLs certain high-frequency words that I see many of them misspelling. If you choose to wrap up the writing workshop with a language minilesson, it should be something that the majority of the class needs help with. You can target more individual needs through writing conferences.

Word Study

Based on what you're studying in different subject areas, there may be some key language structures that you want to focus on for a longer period of time, such as how I focused on present- and past-tense verbs during one of my integrated units. You can work in depth with ELLs on these language structures in a number of ways. ELLs benefit from whole-to-part-to-whole instruction, where you begin with a familiar text, then study a particular aspect of the language in it, and afterward put that language into context again (Bear et al. 2007). Here I describe some of the learning activities that follow this model. These activities take a familiar text (the whole) and help ELLs examine one aspect of the language (the part). The ultimate goal is to bring this language back to a meaningful whole by having ELLs use these language structures during reading, writing, social studies, science, and math. Since the language structures you examine in word study are necessary for your content objectives, ELLs will have opportunities to use them during different learning activities. Make explicit connections between the work they've done in word study and the language you want them to use for a learning activity.

Cloze Activity

I like taking a text ELLs are familiar with, such as a read-aloud or shared reading, and covering up the words that relate to whatever language structures we're studying. This is known as a *syntactic cloze* (Gibbons 1991). You can cover up certain verbs, nouns, adjectives, pronouns, conjunctions, prepositions, prefixes, or suffixes. Then, as I read aloud the text and we come to one of the covered words or word parts, I have ELLs discuss with their partners what it could be, and we see if their predictions are correct. This helps ELLs use context clues from the text, as well as what they know about how language works, to determine the missing words or word parts.

For example, in March I used the book *The Tiny Seed* (Carle 2001) as a read-aloud so we could review the ways seeds are dispersed. Later I used the book to cover up words for comparatives (*taller than*) and superlatives (*the tallest*). I wanted my ELLs to understand these language structures because they were used very frequently in the nonfiction science books my students were reading. Following is one of the pages where I covered up the comparatives and superlatives with strips of sticky notes:

> It is Summer. Now the tiny plant from the tiny seed is all alone. It grows on and on. It doesn't stop. The sun shines on it and the rain waters it. It has many leaves. It grows _____ and _____. It is _____ than the people. It is _____ _____ the trees. It is taller than the houses. And now a flower grows on it. People come from far and near to look at this flower. It is the _____ flower they have ever seen. It is a giant flower. (13)

When we came to each covered word, I asked my ELLs to turn and talk with their partners about what was missing, and then I uncovered the word to see if they were right. We then made a chart of the language structures used for comparatives and superlatives. Whenever my ELLs found other examples in their nonfiction books, they shared them at the end of independent reading and we added them to the chart.

You can also give your ELLs copies of a cloze text to complete with a partner or collaborative group. The cloze text can have blanks for the language structures you've been studying as a class. I like to cover up several different types of language structures so that ELLs at different English proficiency levels are developmentally able to figure out at least some of the missing words. For example, I might cover up comparatives and superlatives for my intermediate and advanced ELLs but also cover some basic nouns or plural noun endings for my beginning ELLs.

Lift a Sentence from a Text

Using a familiar text, you can take one of the sentences with a particular language structure and write it on chart paper. Then your ELLs can help you create sentences about a familiar topic using the same language structure. For example, after doing the cloze activity described previously, I wrote the sentence "It is taller than the people" on chart paper. Underneath this sentence I wrote the language structure with blanks so we could make our own sentences: "_____ is taller than _____." We replaced the word *taller* with other adjectives to make different sentences related to the science topics we were studying.

Sentence Scramble

Using a familiar read-aloud or shared reading, write one of the sentences on a sentence strip. Then cut it into individual words and mix them up. Have your ELLs help you place the words in the original order. Manipulating the words in this way helps ELLs develop a sense for word order in English (for example, the subject comes before the verb, and adjectives typically come before the noun).

Shared Writing Focused on Language Structures

After focusing on a particular language structure from a familiar text, you can use shared writing to create a text with your ELLs that uses the same language structure. For example, I wanted to help a group of first- and second-grade ELLs use different prepositional phrases, so I read aloud the book *Rosie's Walk* (Hutchins 1971). This wonderful picture book has a series of prepositional phrases that describe where Rosie the hen goes on her walk through the farm, such as around the pond, over the haystack, past the mill, through the fence, and under the beehive. We made a list of these prepositional phrases on the board. Using shared writing, we created our own story about where we walked in the school to get to the playground using some of those same prepositions: "We walk *through* the hall, *past* the office, *around* the corner, *through* the main door, and *under* the big tree to get to the playground." The next day my ELLs took this shared writing text and illustrated each part of the story to show what the prepositional phrases meant. This helped them develop their understanding of prepositions and also gave them a familiar text to read in English.

Language Search

Once ELLs have examined a language structure with you through different activities, you can have them search for other examples. They can look in their books, their writing, and the print in the classroom. For homework they can look for examples in their neighborhoods and homes. Then you can chart these examples as a class so ELLs can refer to the language for future use. For example, when we were studying contractions, I had my ELLs search for examples of contractions in the books they were reading and in the classroom. We made a list of those contractions, and then we examined which two words had been combined to make each contraction. I took this list and made a magnetic chart that my ELLs could manipulate to match individual words with their contraction. This became a reference for when my ELLs were doing their own writing and gave them a visual understanding of how contractions are formed, which can be a difficult concept for ELLs.

Shared Reading

You can use shared reading as a time to point out language structures that often make a text confusing for ELLs. These may be the same language structures you're teaching ELLs in other lessons, or they could be other language structures that come up in the shared reading that ELLs will need help understanding. Here I describe some of the language structures that can make a text confusing for ELLs. Once you know these potential difficulties, you're prepared to point them out to ELLs while reading the text together.

Referents

When reading a text, ELLs may not recognize words that refer to something already mentioned (Gibbons 1991). These referents could be:

- Personal pronouns (subject): *I, you, he, she, it, we, they*

- Personal pronouns (object): *me, you, him, her, it, us, them*

- Possessive pronouns: *mine, yours, his, hers, ours, theirs*

- Possessive adjectives: *my, your, his, her, its, our, their*

- Demonstrative pronouns: *this, that, these, those*

- Indefinite pronouns: *some, most, all, few, several, both, each*

The following excerpt from the book *Animal Senses* shows how referents are commonly used in a text: "Even if an animal is hidden and quiet, *its* enemies may still find *it. That's* because *its* smell can be carried through the air" (Hickman 1998, 24).

You may need to help your ELLs understand that *its* and *it* are referring to *an animal* from the beginning of the first sentence. The word *that's* is referring to *its enemies may still find it*. Clarifying what these ambiguous words refer to greatly increases ELLs' reading comprehension. You can also help ELLs with referents during guided reading groups and reading conferences.

Conjunctions and Transition Words

Conjunctions are words that connect one part of a sentence with another, or show a relationship between different parts of a sentences, such as *and, but, or, so, either . . . or, both . . . and, not only . . . but also, because, since, if, unless, although,* and *whereas.* Transition words are used to show a relationship between sentences and between paragraphs, such as *first, next, then, and then, finally, before, after, in addition, however, on the other hand, for the same reason, meanwhile,* and *therefore.* If ELLs don't understand the meaning of different conjunctions and transition words, they won't be able to understand the relationship between ideas throughout a text (Gibbons 1991). Conjunctions and transition words are widely used in academic texts, and even lower-level texts use a number of them, such as this excerpt from the picture book *Snakes!*: "Snakes are hunters. Some hiss loudly *before* they strike their prey. *But* most hide silently in water, trees, or burrows—*and then* attack" (Rudy 2005, 16).

By pointing out the words *before* and *and then*, you can help ELLs understand the sequence of what snakes do to catch their prey. The word *but* is important for ELLs to understand the contrast between the snakes that hiss loudly and the majority that don't make any noise at all. By understanding the meaning of different conjunctions and transition words, ELLs can begin using them in their own writing, making it more fluent and complex.

It's important to note that this excerpt also has a number of referents that could be unclear for ELLs. They need to understand that the words *some, most, they,* and *their* all refer to *snakes.*

Passive Voice

The passive voice is a very common language structure in academic texts (Scarcella 2003). It can be confusing for ELLs because the passive voice doesn't clearly state who or what is doing the action (Freeman and Freeman 2009). Shared reading is a good time to help ELLs figure out the missing subject of the passive voice. Consider the following excerpt from the textbook *Social Studies: New York*:

> Once at Ellis Island, immigrants *were asked* questions about what they planned to do in the United States. They *were also checked* by a doctor. The government did not want people with certain diseases coming into the United States. If you passed the inspections, you were free to enter the United States. If not, you could *be sent back* to the country you had left. (Scott Foresman 2004, 308)

Here, ELLs need to question, "Immigrants were asked questions *by whom?*" It doesn't say in the text, so they have to infer that it was an immigration officer controlling the people who came through Ellis Island. The second sentence is also in the passive voice, but here the writer tells who is doing the action: "They were also checked *by a doctor.*" However, the sentence would be easier for ELLs to understand in the active voice: "A doctor also checked them." In the last sentence, ELLs need to think, "You could be sent back *by whom?*" They need to infer that the same people who asked immigrants questions upon their arrival could decide to send the immigrants back to their countries. Briefly modeling how to understand the passive voice during a shared reading shows ELLs how they can do the same thinking when they read a text on their own. You can also help ELLs with this during guided reading groups and reading conferences.

Interactive Writing

Finally, you can support your ELLs with how they use different language structures during interactive writing. In Chapter 4 I shared an example of how I used interactive writing to help my class write a sentence that summarized the concept of food chains. As we determined how to write each part of the sentence, I pointed out the subject-verb agreement, such as "the sun *gives,*" not *give.* This was something a number of my ELLs struggled with. During interactive writing you can explicitly point out any language structures that you've observed your ELLs need to develop, including the use of prepositional phrases, different verb tenses, possessive nouns ("the *student's* book"), how to form contractions, or relative clauses ("The sun, *which provides energy for plants,* is the beginning of every food chain."). If you know that many of your ELLs need to work on certain language structures, you can help ELLs create an interactive writing text that includes those particular structures.

By incorporating these different ways of teaching language structures in your literacy and content-area instruction, you give your ELLs the tools they need to be more successful with the curriculum.

Teaching Content-Specific Vocabulary

When you think of teaching vocabulary, you may remember your own experiences from elementary school. I clearly remember my teacher assigning a weekly list of vocabulary words and having the class write dictionary definitions for them as homework, even though we hadn't learned those words yet in class. I was able to memorize all the definitions and sample sentences to get excellent grades on vocabulary quizzes, but I was rarely able to explain what the words meant or use them in my speaking and writing. Learning a word means understanding its meaning, understanding how it relates to other words or concepts, and knowing how to use it in the context of a sentence (Wong-Fillmore and Snow 2000). The decontextualized vocabulary instruction I experienced isn't beneficial for *any* student, and certainly not for ELLs, because it doesn't provide a complete understanding of words and how to use them.

In the rest of this chapter I describe how you can teach ELLs vocabulary within the meaningful context of content-area and literacy activities. I provide specific examples of ways you can introduce key vocabulary words, explicitly teach ELLs these words, and different ways for ELLs to practice the words. The research-based practices I describe are supportive of ELLs and take advantage of what they know in their L1 (Marzano and Pickering 2005). The same vocabulary practices that help ELLs learn new words also help English-proficient students (Goldenberg 2008), so you can use these ideas in any classroom setting.

Introducing Vocabulary

Once I've determined which content-specific words I want to teach for a particular content objective, I like to find out what background knowledge my ELLs have for these words before I formally teach the vocabulary to the class. Do they already know the words in English or in their native language? Do they have a full understanding of what those words mean? When they talk about the topic, do they use more general words instead of the content-specific words? Following are a few learning activities you can use to determine what your ELLs already know about the new vocabulary. Then you can build off their background knowledge to explicitly teach them the words.

Prereading Book Talk

I often start the study of a new topic through a read-aloud or shared reading. Before beginning to read, I have my class look at the cover of the book and think about what it's going to be about. I have my ELLs turn and talk with their partners to discuss their predictions about what will be in the book and what they already know about that topic. I listen in to the different partnerships and then regroup the class. I have my ELLs share their ideas, and from that discussion I get a very good idea of what they know about the topic as well as the content-specific vocabulary they're able to use.

For example, to launch our study of how humans affect the environment, I read aloud the book *A River Ran Wild* (Cherry 2002).

1. I first read aloud the title, and we talked about what *ran wild* meant, translating it into Spanish for the beginning ELLs.

2. I pointed to the main picture on the cover, which shows a group of Native Americans in a mountainous area with a beautiful river below them.

3. I asked students to turn and tell their partners what they thought the book would be about. Since we had already been studying Native Americans, I heard my ELLs use a number of content-specific words related to this topic to make their predictions.

4. When I had the students turn back toward me, I told them to look at the smaller pictures on the cover that made a border around the main picture. I pointed out that the pictures weren't showing Native Americans; they showed other people, other objects, and even a factory blowing black smoke into the air. There was a murmur among the class as they saw these images.

5. I had them turn back to their partners to see if they had any new ideas about what would happen in the book. This time they thought something was going to happen to the river and that maybe other people would come and take the river from the Native Americans.

I listened to the partners talking, and I didn't hear any of my ELLs use the specific words *explorer, colonist, colonies,* or *pollution,* but since many of the partnerships had talked about the idea of other people coming to this river and taking it from the Native Americans, I knew they had some prior knowledge about this part of history. I also knew that just because my ELLs didn't use those specific words in their discussion, it didn't mean they weren't familiar with the words. When learning English, ELLs are able to recognize and understand many words (their receptive language) that they don't currently use when they speak (their productive language). This let me know that as we read aloud the book, I would need to emphasize those content-specific words so that with time they would become a part of my ELLs' receptive *and* productive language. From this brief prereading discussion I had an idea of my ELLs' ability to use vocabulary related to this topic, and I had a good idea of what words I would need to explicitly teach them.

Prereading Vocabulary Predictions

Another possibility for a prereading activity is to post a short list of content-specific and general academic words on the board, some of which are in the reading and some of which are not. After you show ELLs the cover of the read-aloud or shared reading book, they can turn and talk with their partners to make predictions about which of the posted words will be in the text.

1. For example, when I read aloud the book *Snakes!* (Rudy 2005), I put this list of words on the board: *predator, prey, disappear, fly, eggs, monkeys,* and *endangered.*

2. My ELLs discussed with their partners which words they thought would be in the text, and they had many different opinions. From the discussion, most ELLs thought the book would have the science words *predator, prey, eggs,* and *endangered.* There was more debate about whether the words *disappear, fly,* and *monkeys* would be in the book.

3. Listening to my ELLs' discussion let me know how well they understood the meaning of the science words. When we regrouped, I took a moment to briefly explain any unfamiliar words.

4. As I read aloud the text, the students listened to see which words were actually there. Whenever my ELLs heard one of the words, they gave the thumbs-up sign. If they heard one of the words they weren't expecting, I had them turn and talk with their partners about the surprise in the text. During the read-aloud they were able to confirm some predictions, like *predator, prey,* and *endangered.* There were also some surprises, like with the word *disappear.* The book explains how some snakes camouflage so well with their environment that they seem to disappear. Another surprise was when I read that some snakes can eat animals as large as monkeys. Most of my ELLs thought this word wouldn't be in the book. The word *fly* wasn't in the book, and afterward we talked about words that describe how snakes move.

This activity was an effective way to see what my ELLs knew about these science vocabulary words, and at the same time it supported their reading comprehension. Later during science time we explicitly studied these science words more in depth, based on the background knowledge my ELLs had shown during this read-aloud.

Collaborative Content-Area Activity

Planning a collaborative activity to launch the study of a new social studies, science, or math topic is another effective way to see what vocabulary your ELLs are currently able to use. An example of this is the activity I described at the beginning of this chapter. By listening to each group, I had a good idea of what math vocabulary the students were already using and what I would need to explicitly teach them. In social studies or science you can launch a new unit of study by distributing to each group some photographs, images, hands-on materials, or realia related to the new topic. Have your ELLs discuss what they already know about those things. Listening to their conversations will tell you what vocabulary your ELLs are able to use and what background knowledge they have.

Content-Area Word or Picture Sort

Another possibility for content-area collaborative work is to give partners or groups of ELLs a word or picture sort before you begin teaching about the topic in class (Bear et al. 2007). The idea is to have students sort the words or pictures based on what they already know about the word meanings and the topic. This is a great way to preview vocabulary they'll be learning throughout the unit of study. I type up a list of the key words we'll be studying for a particular topic, such as those in Figure 5–5 (page 144), and I have the collaborative groups cut them apart into miniature word cards. Sometimes I include a little sketch with the words. Other times I just use the words.

- Open sort: One way to have your ELLs sort the words is through an open sort where they group the words together however they want and then explain to the class why they arranged the words that way. This is an excellent communicative activity because ELLs have an opportunity to orally discuss with their partner or group how they think they should organize the words and justify their idea based on what they know about the vocabulary. Beginning ELLs should always have the option to express these justifications in their native language so they can fully participate in using higher-order thinking skills. When I created the word sort in Figure 5–5, I intended the categories to be *producers, consumers,* and *decomposers* to help my ELLs learn the meaning of these three

bacteria	rabbit	cactus
snake	earthworm	wildflower
fish	grass	hawk
mold	deer	bear
corn	human	maggot
plankton	fungi	wolf
insect	lizard	berries

Figure 5–5 *Word sort for* producers, consumers, *and* decomposers

important science words. However, when I first gave the sort to my ELLs, I let them do an open sort to see how they would separate the words into categories on their own. Interestingly, many of my ELLs sorted words based on what belongs in different ecosystems, and others made examples of food chains. Most ELLs were unsure of what to do with the words related to decomposers. When you see how students group words and discuss their meanings, it gives you insight into their understanding of the words.

- Closed sort: Alternatively, you can have your ELLs do a closed sort where you give students the specific categories for grouping words. This type of sort also encourages oral communication as ELLs work together to discuss the appropriate category for each word. With the sort in Figure 5–5, I gave the class the three category names without explaining their meanings, and as partners discussed how to sort the words I was able to see if they had any background knowledge about the words *producers*, *consumers*, and *decomposers*. I also saw if they were able to make predictions about what the words might mean. Afterward, I regrouped the class and had students share their ideas. ELLs at any proficiency level can share ideas with the class, but you may need to specifically call on beginners who are reluctant to raise their hands. For example, you can ask a beginning ELL an either-or question such as "Is a cactus a *producer* or a *consumer*?" The beginning ELL can either verbalize or point to the correct category name. Then another student can expand on why the word goes in that particular category.

Explicit Instruction of Vocabulary

Once ELLs have had a chance to share what they already know about certain words and hear the words in context, you can help them develop a stronger understanding of the content-specific words. Marzano and Pickering (2005) have an effective step-by-step system for developing ELLs' understanding of a new word. I like to do this explicit vocabulary instruction during social studies, science, and math time, which is why I allot a solid block of time to these content areas in my daily schedule. Remember that you want to spend time explicitly helping ELLs develop an understanding of the most important content-specific words. There will be many academic words related to a particular topic you're studying, so choose the most critical ones for them to understand in depth through the following sequence of steps.

1. Describe or Explain a New Content-Specific Vocabulary Word

When you explain the meaning of a new word, connect it to what you've learned about your ELLs' background knowledge. Your explanation can include an example of how to use the word in a sentence. I also like to draw a picture to help my ELLs visualize what the word means. I write the new word on an index card and place it in a pocket chart, along with the picture card and the explanation. I use a pocket chart for the word cards and picture cards so that later on my ELLs and I can interactively manipulate them during different vocabulary activities. To help beginning ELLs understand the new vocabulary word, partner each ELL with someone who can explain the meaning of the word in his native language.

Whenever possible, I make the word cards bilingual so my ELLs can make connections between English and their native languages. For our study of producers, consumers, and decomposers, many of the key vocabulary words we studied were similar in English and Spanish: *producer—productor, consumer—consumidor, herbivore—herbívoro, carnivore—carnívoro, omnivore—omnívoro, decomposer—descomponedor.* These are referred to as *cognates*. After I displayed the bilingual word cards in the pocket chart, one of my ELLs raised his hand and commented on how similar the words were in the two languages. He couldn't believe how many parallels there were, and seeing those connections helped him learn the words in English. To us, the cognates may seem obvious, and it's easy to assume that ELLs will automatically make these kinds of connections between their L1 and the L2. However, research shows that many ELLs don't recognize how their native language can help them in learning English (Freeman and Freeman 2009). They often see the two languages as separate worlds that have nothing to do with each other. By displaying vocabulary in both languages, you can make those connections more explicit for ELLs. That way they can take advantage of what they know in the L1 to help them learn the L2, whether they're in a bilingual, ESL, or mainstream classroom.

When explaining a new vocabulary word, it's also important to point out to ELLs any tricky pronunciations or spellings (Scarcella 2003). For example, with a word like *amphibian*, ELLs may not have learned yet that *ph* in English is pronounced as /f/. Or if you're introducing a word like *export*, explain that the pronunciation is different if it's a verb or a noun. Say these sentences to yourself to hear where the emphasis is:

Oil is an important éxport.

The United States will expórt many goods this year.

Native English speakers automatically make this distinction in pronunciation without even thinking about it. By drawing ELLs' attention to these details of pronunciation and spelling, in the meaningful context of learning relevant vocabulary words, we can help them develop the phonological aspect of the L2 (Scarcella 2003).

2. Have ELLs Come Up with Their Own Explanation or Example of the Word

In pairs, your ELLs can think of another way to explain the word or another sentence that uses the word. You don't want your ELLs to copy the example you gave because then you won't know if they really understand the word. For the word *producer*, my explanation was "Producers are plants that use the sun's energy to produce (make) their own food." When my ELLs turned and talked about this word with their partners, they created their own sentences, such as "Grass is a producer," and "Every plant in the world is a producer because they can make their own food." It's very helpful for beginning ELLs to have a native language partner so they can give the example or explanation in their L1. If your ELLs have difficulty with this activity, explain the word in another way or give them more examples to clarify.

If age appropriate, each ELL can record the word and her own example or explanation in a notebook. Beginning ELLs can write the explanation in their native language. Marzano and Pickering (2005) recommend that students have a vocabulary notebook with sections for each subject area. You could also have ELLs create a vocabulary section within each of their notebooks so that everything related to one subject is together. Primary-grade ELLs can keep an ongoing vocabulary journal. You can give younger ELLs printouts of the new vocabulary words as you teach them, and they can cut and paste the words into their vocabulary journal in the section for that topic. Underneath each vocabulary word I like to include a short sentence based on an example the class brainstormed together. That way, when students are ready to cut and paste, they have the word as well as how it's used in context.

3. Have Primary- *and* Upper-Grade ELLs Draw a Picture to Represent the Word

A picture is essential in helping ELLs remember what the word means. Since some words can be difficult to represent pictorially, ELLs can draw a symbol or a situation related to the word or dramatize the word using cartoon bubbles (Marzano and Pickering 2005). Even though you've already given ELLs a pictoral example in the first step, it's important that students create their own visual representations in their notebooks or vocabulary journals to make sure they really understand the word.

Practicing and Extending Vocabulary

Once ELLs have been introduced to the content-specific vocabulary, they need opportunities to practice the words multiple times in meaningful contexts (Freeman and Freeman 2009; Marzano and Pickering 2005; Goldenberg 2008). ELLs rely on this practice to solidify their understanding of the words and incorporate the words as part of their speaking and writing. It's also important to help ELLs make connections between these words and other academic vocabulary.

There are many opportunities to help ELLs practice and extend their understanding of the words. If you integrate content-area instruction with literacy components, then you're already planning learning activities where your ELLs can use this vocabulary. Following are some specific ways you can practice and extend your ELLs' use of the vocabulary during content-area instruction and some of the literacy components.

Cloze Activity

Before doing a content-area read-aloud or shared reading with the class, you can cover up a few vocabulary words with sticky notes. When you come to those words during the reading, have your ELLs predict what vocabulary word should be there based on the context. This is referred to as a *semantic cloze* (Gibbons 1991; Cappellini 2005). ELLs can briefly turn and talk with their partners to make their predictions before you reveal the word. If the word is different than what they predicted, you can take a moment to discuss it with them and then continue reading.

Tallying Words

Whenever ELLs hear, read, or say one of the vocabulary words you've displayed on your word walls or in pocket charts, they can add a tally mark next to the word. Some teachers like to put a sticky note next to each vocabulary word where they can record the tallies, and other teachers prefer to have students do this tallying next to the vocabulary words in their notebooks. The important thing is to encourage ELLs to recognize when they hear the word or read the word. If ELLs encounter the word outside of school, they can share this with the class at the beginning of content-area time and explain how the word was used.

Matching Words and Pictures

Using the content-specific words that are displayed in the pocket chart, I often have ELLs do a quick matching activity with the word cards and picture cards to help them review these words. Sometimes I remove the picture cards and have different ELLs match the pictures to the word cards, each time explaining what the word means. Other times I reverse the process and remove the word cards so my ELLs can match them to the pictures. Surprisingly, one type of matching may be easier for some ELLs than the other, so it's helpful to do both.

Word and Picture Sorts

You may have already given your ELLs a word or picture sort *before* launching the study of a particular topic to see what prior knowledge they had about the words and the concepts. Once you begin explicitly teaching the content-specific vocabulary, you can give your ELLs the same words and pictures to sort again. This is an excellent activity to help ELLs review what they've learned about the words and clarify any confusion they may have. I like to do this collaborative activity during science, social studies, and math time.

Connecting Words

Using the content-specific words displayed on your word wall, have your ELLs physically take several of the word cards off and formulate a sentence that connects those words. Or you can take off two words of your choice and have ELLs turn and talk about possible sentences that include both words. For example, I took the word cards for *consumer* and *producer* out of the pocket chart and had partners think of how they could connect the words. Some ideas they had were "I'm a consumer and I eat producers like fruits and vegetables" and "Producers are different from consumers because they can make their own food." This works very well at the end of social studies, science, or math time as a way to review the vocabulary words. Sometimes I like to give the class a connecting-words challenge, where I take three or more words from the word wall and see if they can find a way to combine all of them in a sentence. When I took the words *herbivore, carnivore,* and *consumer* out of the pocket chart, one sentence my ELLs created was "Herbivores and carnivores are both consumers, but herbivores only eat plants and carnivores only eat meat." Students love a challenge, and I've found that the more words I challenge them with, the more intent they become on finding some way for them to all fit together!

You can record some of their sentences on chart paper with shared writing. You can also have ELLs do a connecting-words activity for homework, using the vocabulary they've recorded in their notebooks for a particular topic. Specify how many words you want them to connect or how many sentences you want them to write that combine different words. Beginning ELLs can do the same activity by explaining in their native language how the words are connected or by drawing a picture that shows the relationship between the words.

Webs

Creating webs is an effective way to help ELLs extend their vocabulary base related to a particular word. You can take any word you've been working on and help them brainstorm other words that connect with it. These words could be nouns, verbs, adjectives, adverbs, or prepositional phrases. For example, after learning about the concept of family in the social studies curriculum, you could first make a web of nouns related to family, such as *mom, dad, brother, sister, grandma, grandpa, aunt, uncle,* and *cousin.* After creating the web, I like to write a language structure below it to show my ELLs how the words go together, such as "Some families have a _____" or "In my family I have a _____." You can create a quick sketch on the web next to each word to clarify its meaning. In this case it's important for ELLs to know which words refer to males and females, so you could show this by writing the words for male family members in blue and the words for female family members in pink.

On another day, you could make a web of verbs or verb phrases related to what a family does, such as *helps with homework, works, plays sports, reads a book, goes to the park, laughs, eats dinner together, eats breakfast together,* and *cleans the house.* A language structure ELLs could use to combine this vocabulary is "In my family, my [family member] [verb]" or "My family [verb]." Again, a quick sketch helps ELLs remember what these words mean. You could also make a web of adjectives that describe a family, such as *happy, helpful, caring, loving, nice, funny, silly,* and *serious.* A sentence structure to practice with ELLs could be "My [family member] is [adjective]." Figure 5–6 shows an example of these webs and language structures.

This vocabulary can be a reference for ELLs as they do their independent writing because it gives them a wealth of familiar words to choose from, as well as sample sentences to remember how the words can be combined together. Using the language structures and vocabulary in the webs, you can also model for ELLs how to form more complex sentences, such as "In my family my brother helps with homework and plays games. He is helpful and funny." Beginning ELLs can take home a copy of these webs and create different sentences using the vocabulary for homework. They can also illustrate the different words on the webs. Intermediate and advanced ELLs can add more words to the webs and write expanded sentences about the topic.

Hierarchical Graphic Organizers

Hierarchical graphic organizers also help ELLs extend their knowledge of a content-specific word by recording other academic vocabulary words that are related to it (Rea and Mercuri 2006). Typically I do this kind of activity after reading aloud a content-area text or after doing a content-area shared reading text with the class. For example, after I read aloud the nonfiction book *Birds* (Stewart 2001), my first-grade ELLs helped create a hierarchical graphic organizer about the physical structures birds have and the function of each structure. Figure 5–7 (page 150) shows how the graphic organizer looked after ELLs brainstormed ideas.

In Figure 5–7 you can see that I added connecting words between the main concepts and the vocabulary words. That way, my ELLs had a model for how to create a

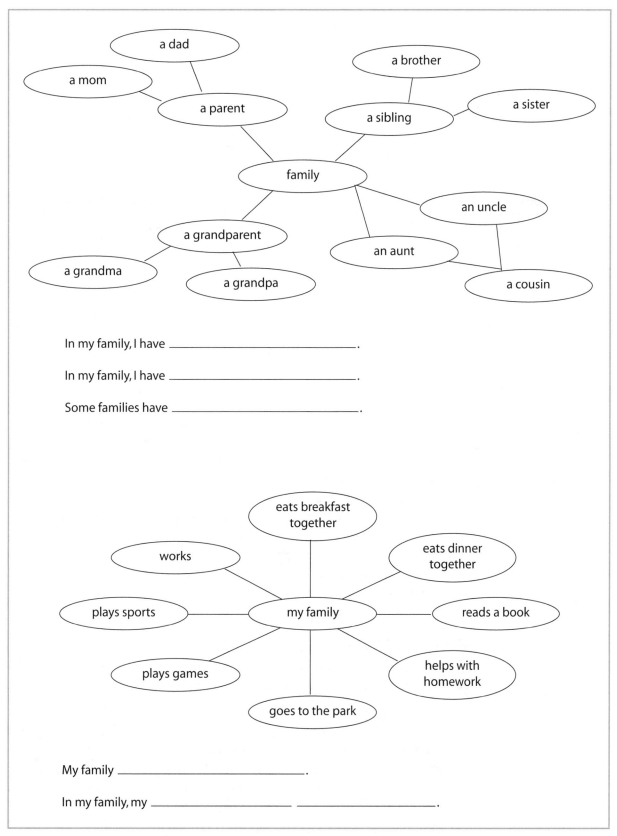

In my family, I have _____.

In my family, I have _____.

Some families have _____.

My family _____.

In my family, my _____ _____.

Figure 5–6 *Webs with language structures*

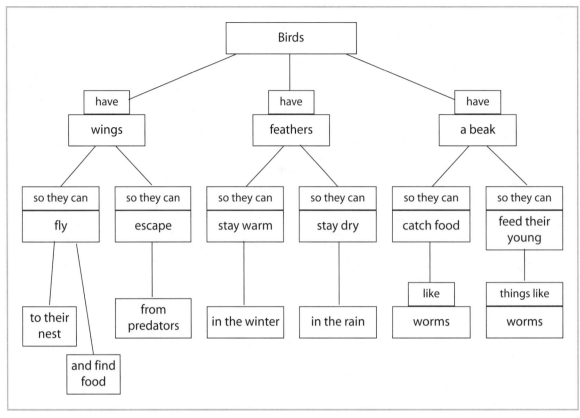

Figure 5–7 *Hierarchical graphic organizer created with ELLs*

complete sentence using the words in the graphic organizer. You can help ELLs read the different sentences that can be made from the graphic organizer, such as "Birds have wings so they can escape from predators." This helps review the concepts and the vocabulary and also helps ELLs verbalize complete sentences using the academic vocabulary. For homework, ELLs can take home a copy of the graphic organizer and illustrate the different words. If age appropriate, they can also write as many sentences as possible using the language in the graphic organizer and illustrate the meaning of each sentence. Intermediate and advanced ELLs can add more examples or write more expanded sentences about the topic.

Other Graphic Organizers

Following are some other ways you can use graphic organizers with ELLs to explore the meaning of vocabulary words or to examine the parts of a word:

- Use a web to record synonyms and antonyms for a particular word.
- Use a web to brainstorm words that have the same prefix or suffix. For example, if you put the word *consumer* in the center of a web, you can explain to ELLs how the *-er* suffix changes a verb, *consume*, into a noun, *consumer*. ELLs can think of other similar nouns that end in this suffix, such as *teacher, learner, writer,* and *painter.*
- Use a chart to record multiple meanings of a word.
- Use a Venn diagram to compare and contrast the meanings of two different content-specific vocabulary words.

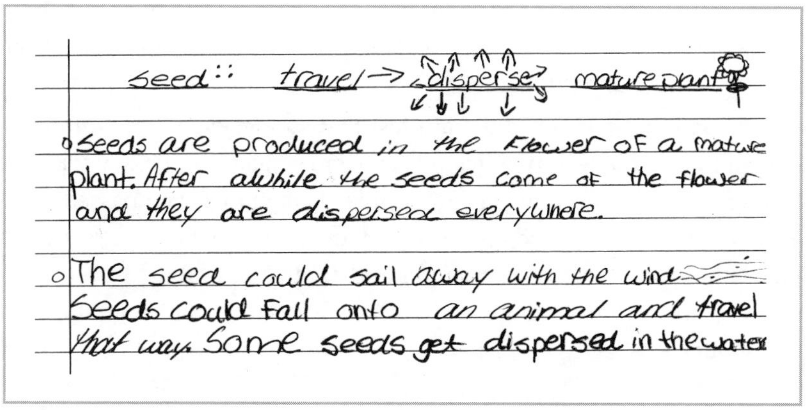

Figure 5–8 *Interactive writing that Miguel recorded in his science notebook*

Appendix G lists other possibilities for building language with ELLs using graphic organizers and provides reproducible versions to use with your ELLs.

Use the Words in Interactive Writing

At the end of social studies or science time, you can do an interactive writing session with ELLs to help them summarize what they're learning and to use the content-specific vocabulary. Doing this on a regular basis helps ELLs strengthen their understanding of key concepts and retain the key vocabulary. Figure 5–8 above shows two related interactive writing sessions that one of my Level 4 ELLs, Miguel, recorded in his science notebook. We had been learning about seed dispersal, and over a period of several days we did several read-alouds and shared readings related to the topic. For the first interactive writing session we recorded the key vocabulary of *seed, travel, disperse,* and *mature plant,* and the class came up with two sentences that explained the main idea of how seeds leave a mature plant. In the second interactive writing session the class listed three examples of ways seeds are dispersed.

Art Projects

You can have your ELLs use art to illustrate something they're learning about in science, social studies, or math. Then help them label the art with content-specific vocabulary words or with sentences using the vocabulary words that explain the concept. For young ELLs, you can use interactive writing to collaboratively write these words or sentences on index cards or sentence strips. Then display the interactive writing along with the students' artwork.

Final Thoughts

When you develop language objectives, you make language instruction a meaningful part of your ELLs' learning. This doesn't mean your teaching needs to change radically. The suggestions in this chapter illustrate simple ways you can weave language structures and vocabulary into the literacy and the content-area instruction you're already doing. When you focus on language on a daily basis, you'll see the positive effect it has on your ELLs' language development and on their academic success.

When I listened to my ELLs collaboratively discussing that math problem in May, I couldn't help but reflect on how far they had come linguistically and academically since the beginning of the year. With the exception of two beginning ELLs, every single ELL in my class passed the standardized math test that spring, even though most of them were required to take the test in English. They were similarly successful with the standardized science test in the spring, and a number of my ELLs even passed the English language arts test, a standardized test designed for students who are already proficient in English. Emphasizing language structures and academic vocabulary every day during instruction was critical for my ELLs to experience success in the content areas and to improve their literacy skills in English.

Reflecting on the Keys to Success

Raise the Bar

- Do I create language objectives to go along with the content objectives in my *grade-level* curriculum?

Teach Language and Content Together

- Do I identify what language structures my ELLs will need to understand and use for a particular content objective?
- Do I identify what content-specific and general academic vocabulary my ELLs will need to understand and use for a particular content objective?

Integrate Instruction Thematically

- Do I have my ELLs use the language they developed during social studies, science, and math in different literacy activities throughout the school day?

Differentiate Instruction

- Do I include ELLs with different L2 proficiency levels in class discussions?
- Do I know what language each ELL is developmentally ready to use on her own in a learning activity, based on my assessment of her L2 proficiency level?
- Do I plan ways to teach my ELLs that language as part of my whole-group lessons, read-alouds, shared reading, interactive writing, and word study?
- Do I teach language structures and vocabulary in a visual way by writing down examples and connecting the language to images or hands-on materials?
- Do I use collaborative learning structures so my ELLs can discuss vocabulary words and practice the new language?

Connect Learning to Students

- Do I use students' background knowledge to help them learn new vocabulary and language structures?

Use Students' Native Languages to Support Learning

- Do I make bilingual vocabulary cards so ELLs can make connections between the two languages?

- Do I have ELLs use their native languages to explain the meaning of new vocabulary words?

- Do I allow ELLs to take advantage of their native languages to express their ideas during collaborative activities?

Be Consistent

- Do I consistently teach language as a meaningful part of my instruction?

References for Further Reading

Developing Academic Language with ELLs

Freeman, Yvonne S., and David E. Freeman. 2009. *Academic Language for English Language Learners and Struggling Readers: How to Help Students Succeed Across Content Areas.* Portsmouth, NH: Heinemann.

Gibbons, Pauline. 1991. *Learning to Learn in a Second Language.* Portsmouth, NH: Heinemann.

————. 2002. *Scaffolding Language, Scaffolding Learning: Teaching Second Language Learners in the Mainstream Classroom.* Portsmouth, NH: Heinemann.

Marzano, Robert J., and Debra J. Pickering. 2005. *Building Academic Vocabulary: Teacher's Manual.* Alexandria, VA: Association for Supervision and Curriculum Development.

Snapshots of Differentiated Instruction with English Language Learners

Keys to Success with ELLs

Throughout this book I've described how you can incorporate certain keys to success in your teaching to make your classroom a place where your English language learners develop academically and linguistically. I've shown how you can

- *raise the bar* by teaching your ELLs grade-level content and holding them accountable for their learning, which ensures that your ELLs can be academically competitive with their English-proficient peers

- *teach language and content together* by weaving academic language instruction into each of your lessons, which helps your ELLs develop both conversational and academic English language proficiency in a meaningful way

- *integrate instruction* by combining content-area studies with literacy activities, which gives your ELLs multiple opportunities throughout the school day to learn and use the academic language, develop content-area knowledge, and increase their literacy skills

- *differentiate instruction* by using visual supports, modeling, hands-on experiences, and collaborative learning structures with your whole-group, small-group, and individual instruction

- *connect learning to students* by building off their background knowledge and incorporating their experiences in your instruction, which gives your ELLs a familiar context for new learning and shows them that their experiences are an important part of the classroom

- *use students' native languages to support learning* through collaborative work and instructional materials; the research is clear that using your ELLs' native language supports their development in English because knowledge and skills transfer from one language to another

- *be consistent* by setting up a predictable daily schedule, routines, and rules in your classroom

- *involve families* from day one, keeping close communication with them regarding their children's progress and how they can be a part of their children's education, which shows your ELLs that there is a strong partnership between home and school and can increase your ELLs' academic development

The Classroom Setting for the Snapshots of Instruction

In this final chapter I give snapshots of instruction in action, showing how these Keys to Success can come together to make your teaching supportive of ELLs. The examples I share all took place in my classroom, showing how I taught my ELLs during a read-aloud, a shared reading, a reading workshop minilesson, a reading conference, guided reading groups, a writing workshop minilesson, and writing conferences. The examples are all from a particular week during the month of March in my fourth-grade classroom. I've used the same techniques and approaches with ELLs in primary as well as upper grades, so the ideas from these examples can be adapted to working with ELLs across grade levels. The students involved in the instruction were the ELLs I described in my whole-class profile in Chapter 2, although by March some of my ELLs had moved away and other newcomers had joined our class. At this point in the year I had twenty-six ELLs who spanned Levels 1–5 in their English proficiency: three students were at Level 1, five students were at Level 2, four students were at Level 3, nine students were at Level 4, and five students were at Level 5.

During the month of March we were preparing for the state science test, so in these examples you can see how I integrated science instruction with different balanced literacy components. Every week I focused my science instruction on key topics I needed to review with the class. The week I highlight in these snapshots was a time when I reviewed concepts related to plants.

Before each example I give a brief description of what the literacy component entails and whether it's whole-group, small-group, or individual instruction. You can also refer to Chapters 3 and 4 for more detailed descriptions of each of these literacy components. After each example I provide a commentary that highlights what made the instruction supportive for ELLs. I also point out how I included ELLs from every L2 proficiency level through the types of questions I asked them and through the paired work and group work I used (Gibbons 2002). Although it's beyond the scope of this book to go into great detail about how to implement each instructional component, these snapshots will give you an idea of what differentiated instruction can look and sound like in a classroom with ELLs.

Read-Aloud

Read-alouds are a time when you read a text to the whole class, pausing occasionally to model different reading comprehension strategies that you're using to understand the text. In this example you can see how I use these think-alouds to model for my ELLs what's going through my mind as I read. In italics I indicate which reading comprehension strategies I was modeling to the class. During the read-aloud I also provided several opportunities for my ELLs to turn and talk with their partners about certain parts of the book. It was critical for my ELLs to try using some of the reading comprehension strategies within the supportive structure of talking with a partner. I used a consistent cue, "Eyes on me," to bring my ELLs' attention back to me after talking with their partners. Read-alouds are also a good time for vocabulary development with ELLs, so you can see in the example how I included a prereading vocabulary activity and discussed vocabulary during and after the read-aloud as well.

During the month of March I chose read-alouds that connected with science topics. Many of the read-alouds were nonfiction, but I also included some fictional texts. In this example I read aloud the fictional book *Carlos and the Squash Plant / Carlos y la planta de calabaza* (Stevens 1993), which is a beautifully illustrated bilingual book about a boy who discovers one day, to his complete horror, that a squash plant is growing out of his ear. The content objective of a read-aloud is always to help ELLs use a variety of reading comprehension strategies to understand a text. For this particular read-aloud my language objective was to help my ELLs with vocabulary related to plants.

Teacher: I have a new book to read aloud to you today [holding up the book for the class to see]. The title is *Carlos and the Squash Plant / Carlos y la planta de calabaza*. One of the interesting things about this book is that it's written in two languages, English and Spanish, just like many of you have chosen to write in two languages this year. Let's look at the cover. What do you see here? [I call on James, one of my Level 3 ELLs, who's from Colombia.]

James: There's a boy outside working with his dad.

Teacher: Yes, maybe that boy is Carlos, and that could be his dad [pointing to the illustration]. We'll have to see when we start reading. What else do you see? [I call on Angélica, a Level 2 ELL from Colombia, even though she hasn't raised her hand. I know she has the vocabulary base to be able to name different things in the cover illustration.]

Angélica: I see a boy and some different food.

Teacher: Yes, that's true. There's a boy holding a basket [pointing to the illustration] with different types of food. What do you see in his basket?

Angélica: I see some corn. Oh, and tomato.

Teacher: [Paraphrasing and pointing to the illustrations] Yes, there are ears of corn and also tomatoes. Do any of you know what these vegetables are called [pointing to the yellow squash and the zucchini squash]? [No one knows their names.] These are both types of squash, like the word in the title. I wonder why the title is called *Carlos and the Squash Plant / Carlos y la planta de calabaza*. Turn and tell your partners what you think the book is going to be about. *(reading strategy: making predictions)* [I point to the sentence strip we have posted in the classroom that shows the language structure for making predictions: "I think _____ is going to . . ." and "I think _____ are going to . . ."]

My ELLs turn to face their partners sitting next to them on the rug. My Level 1 ELLs are in triads for extra linguistic support. I listen in to the predictions my ELLs are sharing with their partners.

Teacher: Eyes on me [cue to stop their conversations and turn back to face me]. I heard many of you say that you think Carlos is going to help his family plant squash seeds on their farm. Miguel had a different prediction. Would you like to share it with the class? [Miguel is a Level 4 ELL from the Dominican Republic.]

Miguel: I think there's going to be some big problem with Carlos because characters always have some kind of problem.

Teacher: That's true. Many fictional books have a problem that the characters need to solve. While I read you this book, let's see if your predictions are correct.

Now, I have a list of words here [pointing to the whiteboard on the easel]. I want you to decide with your partner which words you think might be in this book [reading aloud the list]: *roots*, *hide*, *stem*, *leaves*, *bathtub*, and *photosynthesis*. Turn and talk with your partner. [I wait to explain the meaning of the words until I hear the partners' conversations.]

I listen in to the different partnerships discussing the words. Many ELLs are talking about the words *roots*, *stem*, and *leaves*, saying that they think these words will definitely be in the book since it looks like it's about plants. There's more debate about the words *hide*, *bathtub*, and *photosynthesis*. Many ELLs have a difficult time trying to explain the word *photosynthesis* to their partners, so I know I need to go over that word with the class.

Teacher: Eyes on me. So, it sounds like most of you think we'll find the words *roots*, *stem*, and *leaves* in this book since they're all parts of a plant. [I quickly make a sketch of a plant, labeling each part with the three words.] How many of you think we'll hear the word *hide*? [I act out the word. My ELLs follow our routine of giving a thumbs-up or a thumbs-down based on their prediction of whether or not the word will be in the book.] What about the word *bathtub*? [I make a little sketch of a bathtub next to the word. Again, my ELLs signal their predictions, and most think this word won't be in the text.] Now, I heard many of you trying to remember exactly what *photosynthesis* means. We learned about photosynthesis way back at the beginning of the year. Vicente had a good way of explaining it to his partner. Vicente, would you like to share your explanation?

Vicente: Photosynthesis, it's when the plants make food for themself.

Teacher: Exactly. Photosynthesis is what plants do to make their own food using energy from the sun. [I write this short definition next to the word and add a little sketch of a plant and the sun.] Plants don't need to go to the store to buy food like we do! They just have to take the energy that comes from the sun, and then inside their leaves they change that energy into food. So, do you think this book is going to have the word *photosynthesis*? [Some ELLs give the thumbs-up, but others aren't so sure. They know I try to trick them with the words I put on my list!] All right, let's start reading the book and see if our predictions are correct. If you hear any of these words while I'm reading, give me the thumbs-up sign.

I start reading aloud the book. I gesture the action in some parts of the story as a way to explain words on the fly without having to constantly stop the reading. It's important to not break up the reading too much; otherwise you lose fluency and it's hard to hold onto the meaning of the text. Here I describe the places where I paused to think aloud or to have my ELLs turn and talk.

On the first page of text I read about how Carlos helps his brother and father in the garden, but that Carlos hates taking baths after working outside. The text says that Carlos' mother always tells him to take a bath and wash his ears, warning him that if he doesn't, a squash plant will grow from them, but he never listens to her advice.

Teacher: So, one of your predictions is correct. This must be Carlos working with his father, and we learned that he also has a brother. So far there isn't any problem, but I think there could be a problem with Carlos not taking a bath like his mother tells him to. Let's see what happens. *(reading strategy: making and confirming predictions)* [I continue reading the next pages of text until I get to the part where Carlos discovers that a squash plant has started to grow out of his ear.]

> A tiny light green stem with two pear shaped leaves was growing in his right ear. (7)

Teacher: Oh my goodness! I can't believe Carlos has a plant growing out of his ear! This is definitely a big problem for Carlos. *(reading strategy: monitoring for comprehension)* And I saw many of you give me the thumbs-up sign; you found two of the words from our list! This sentence had the words *stem* and *leaves*, just like you predicted. [I point to the stem and the leaves in the illustration.]

So, what do you think Carlos is going to do about this problem? Turn and talk with your partner. *(reading strategy: making predictions)* [My ELLs turn and talk with their partners to make predictions based on what's happened so far in the story.]

Teacher: Eyes on me. [I decide to ask Juan, a Level 1 ELL from Puerto Rico, to share his prediction, so I ask him a yes-or-no question.] Juan, do you think Carlos is going to tell his mom about the plant? [I point to the picture of Carlos, his mom, and the plant.]

Juan: No [smiling and shaking his head].

Teacher: Who agrees with Juan that Carlos isn't going to tell his mom about the plant? [Most students raise their hands.] OK, let's see what Carlos does about his problem. [I read further into the story.]

Hmm, many of your predictions are correct. Carlos was too afraid to tell his mother. *(reading strategy: confirming predictions)* [I continue reading aloud.]

> The next morning when the sun felt warm on his face, his right ear was itching more than ever. He jumped out of bed and looked in the mirror. The green plant that had been merely a tiny shoot the day before had grown to about four inches in length. Three more leaves had joined the first two. (13)

Teacher: This page gave me a really great picture in my mind. *(reading strategy: visualizing)* I can imagine Carlos itching his ear and feeling how much the plant has grown. It's not a tiny shoot, which is a new plant just starting to grow. Now it's four inches long! That's about as long as this crayon here. [I hold up a crayon to my ear to show what that would look like.] And it has three more leaves. How can Carlos hide this from his parents? *(reading strategy: questioning)* [I continue reading aloud.]

I'm not going to show you the picture on this next page just yet. Listen and see what picture you get in your mind. *(reading strategy: visualizing)*

Carlos woke up late. His head felt heavier on one side. A long green vine with yellow blossoms trailed down to the floor. He tried pulling it out, he tried breaking it off, he tried stomping on it with his foot, but nothing would rid him of the squash plant, which was now several feet long. (20)

Teacher: Turn and tell your partner what you were visualizing in your mind as I read this part. [My ELLs turn and talk to describe the pictures they have in their minds, and each partner adds different details until together they have a more complete image of what was happening on this page.]

Teacher: So, what were you visualizing? [I have a few ELLs at different proficiency levels share their descriptions. We make a connection to math by measuring two feet with a yardstick and holding it up to our ears. I also ask the class to infer why Carlos couldn't pull the plant out of his ear. This requires background knowledge about the function roots have to anchor a plant into the ground (or in this case, an ear!). Then I reveal the picture on page 20 so my ELLs can compare it with the pictures in their minds. I continue reading aloud the next page.

Coiling the squash plant on top of his head, he pulled the hat down over both ears and walked into the kitchen. (21)

Teacher: Hmm. Coiling. That's a tricky word. What do you think it could mean, based on this sentence and what you see in the picture? Turn and talk with your partner. *(reading strategy: determining word meaning)* [My ELLs turn and talk to determine the word meaning, and when we regroup they share how they figured out the word meaning from the context and the picture. We act out the word *coiling*.]

I finish reading aloud the remaining pages of the book, where Carlos finally decides to take a bath and wash his ears, and he's able to get rid of the plant in his ear.

Teacher: So Carlos has solved his problem. But when it says that his mother winked at Papá, what does that make you think? *(reading strategy: inferring)* Turn and talk with your partner. [I point to the sentence strip that has a language structure for making inferences: "This makes me think that . . ."]

[While talking with their partners, my ELLs make inferences to read between the lines of what really happened: that Carlos' parents knew all along that he had the plant growing in his ear, but that they wanted him to learn the lesson on his own. I have several ELLs share their inferences with the class to make sure everyone understands what the author was trying to express at the end of the book.]

Teacher: So, let's look back at our list of words. Which words weren't in the book?

We discuss how the author never used the word *roots*, even though they were the biggest part of Carlos' problem. The roots made it impossible for him to get the plant out of his ear. We also discuss how the word *photosynthesis* wasn't in the book, but that it must have been happening because it was the process that gave the plant the food it needed to grow bigger and bigger. The word *hide* wasn't there at all, but of course it's what Carlos was trying to do the whole time so his family wouldn't find out about the plant.

Commentary

- For this read-aloud I used a bilingual book that connected to many of my students' cultural experiences. It also affirmed the importance of knowing how to write in two languages, and I was able to encourage my ELLs to use their language skills to continue writing bilingual pieces, as many of them had done throughout the year.

- The book had beautiful illustrations on each page, but it also had a significant amount of text, which most of my students couldn't have read independently. This made it ideal to use as a read-aloud. The detailed pictures supported my ELLs in the beginning stages of L2 proficiency.

- The vocabulary activity I included before reading aloud the book helped my ELLs think about words that were important in the text. It also helped them review some key science words that we would be using throughout the week. Putting sketches next to each word helped beginning ELLs understand them.

- Providing multiple opportunities for my ELLs to turn and talk about the book promoted oral language development. Only a few students could orally share with the whole class, but with this communicative structure every ELL had a chance to speak six different times during the read-aloud time.

- Since less advanced ELLs were each sitting next to a partner with a higher L2 proficiency level, they had linguistic support for discussing the book. In most cases beginning ELLs had a native language partner who had a higher proficiency in English. That way beginning ELLs could share complex ideas in their L1 and also have support for understanding the L2. I also put my beginning ELLs in triads so they had two partners for additional linguistic support. This took some of the pressure off the beginning ELLs who were culturally unfamiliar with participating in this kind of collaborative work structure. If necessary, they could simply listen to the other two partners discuss the text until they felt more comfortable joining in.

- When my ELLs shared ideas with the whole group, I made an effort to include beginning ELLs. Even if they didn't raise their hands, I still wanted them to contribute to the discussion. For example, I asked Juan a yes-or-no question so he could share his prediction with the class. This made every ELL an active part of the class discussion and validated every ELL's ability to contribute.

- Whenever necessary I used gestures to explain particular words while I was reading. This helped ELLs understand the text and kept the read-aloud fast paced since I wasn't stopping constantly to explain each new word.

- I also used physical objects like the crayon and the yardstick to help my ELLs visualize what was happening in the text.

- The think-alouds modeled for my ELLs the type of reading strategies I wanted them to use. The turn-and-talk moments gave ELLs a chance to try those same reading strategies in a supportive environment. I showed my ELLs some of the language structures they could use to start their discussions for making predictions and inferring based on language we had posted from previous reading lessons.

- My ELLs knew exactly what to expect during read-aloud time. I had consistent routines in place such as how to identify vocabulary words during the read-aloud by giving the thumbs-up or thumbs-down signal, how to turn and talk with a partner, and what cue to listen for to stop talking with their partners.

Shared Reading

Just like with a read-aloud, shared reading is also done with the whole class. The difference is that the students read the text with you instead of you reading it aloud to them. So the text has to be large enough for the whole class to see. In this example of shared reading you'll see how I read a nonfiction text with my ELLs, pausing in key places so we could use different reading comprehension strategies to help us understand the meaning of the text. The focus of a shared reading in the upper grades is mainly on reading comprehension, whereas in the primary grades there's a greater focus on helping students learn concepts about print like directionality, one-to-one correspondence, and text features. There's also more emphasis in the primary grades on helping students learn decoding skills and develop reading fluency. Even so, shared reading at all grade levels is meant to help students understand the text, so many of the techniques I describe here can be adapted to primary-grade students. Shared reading is also a great time to work on vocabulary development with ELLs at any grade level, and in this example you can see how I helped my ELLs determine the meaning of new words during our reading of the text. You'll also see how I helped my ELLs understand some ambiguous grammatical aspects of the text.

Throughout the month of March I used different texts for shared reading, including several science-related big books, excerpts from our science textbook, and several articles about science topics from children's magazines. In this example I used an online quiz called "Plant Power" from the *National Geographic Explorer!* website: magma .nationalgeographic.com/ngexplorer/0604/games/game_intro.html.

The quiz provided ten questions about plants, all connected to the concepts we were reviewing. After we answered each question there was a paragraph explaining the science concept. One of the difficult things about reading a nonfiction text is that there's a lot of information and vocabulary packed into just a few sentences. Students need to learn how to read a nonfiction text in a way that lets them assimilate all the information, pausing more often to make sure they understand what they're reading. By using the text on this website as a shared reading, I was able to help my ELLs do this kind of careful reading to unpack the meaning of each science question and then to summarize the important information from each paragraph of nonfiction text.

For this shared reading session I hooked up a laptop computer to an LCD projector so I could show the website on the screen in the classroom. This made the text large enough for all of my students to read. I planned to focus on the first four questions and explanations from the website, which all had to do with different plant parts and their functions.

- Content objective (shared reading): Use multiple reading strategies to understand a nonfiction text: making predictions, making connections to background knowledge, determining word meaning, synthesizing information.
- Content objective (science): Understand the parts of a plant and their functions.

- Learning activities: During science time, do a shared reading of the text "Plant Power," focusing on the first half of the text, which is about plant parts and their functions. Then, have ELLs collaboratively summarize what they learned about the function of the roots, stem, leaves, and flower. Use shared writing to record the class' summaries for each plant part. (Shared writing is when students provide the ideas for a text, and the teacher writes the text on the board or on chart paper.) Finally, have each ELL create a vocabulary flipbook that illustrates each plant part and explains its function.

- Language structures: Use the present tense to explain what the plant parts do. Verb agreement could be difficult for some ELLs: "The stem *carries* water and nutrients to the plant," (not *carry*).

- Content-specific vocabulary: *plant, roots, stem, leaves, flower, seeds, soil, nutrients, photosynthesis, reproduce*

Teacher: Today we're going to read something I found on the *National Geographic Explorer!* website. [There's a murmur of excitement as I project the website on the screen. Next to the title "Plant Power" there's an introductory paragraph and a vivid photograph of a plant.]

Let's read this introduction together to find out what "Plant Power" is going to be about. [Together we read the introduction. As soon my ELLs read in the introduction that it's a game about plants, they can't wait to start reading.]

So here it asks us how much we know about our silent green neighbors. [I emphasize the final three words.] What does this mean? [I call on Diana, a Level 2 ELL from Colombia, because I think that from the clue "green" she should be able to guess that it's referring to plants.]

Diana: The plants?

Teacher: Yes. Since the whole paragraph is talking about plants [I point to all the places in the text where the word *plant* appears], the author wanted to use a different way to talk about plants: silent green neighbors.

What do you think this game is going to ask us about plants? Turn and talk with your partner. *(reading strategy: making predictions)* [My ELLs talk with their partners and come up with ideas such as food chains, seeds, parts of a plant, and ecosystems.]

Let's see if your predictions are correct. [I click on the link to the next page, which brings up the first question.]

Most plants have parts that absorb water and minerals from the soil.
What are these parts called? (1)

We read the two sentences slowly enough to think about what they are saying. When we come to the question, I ask my ELLs what "these parts" refers to. Together we point to the end of the first sentence where it says, "parts that absorb water and minerals from the soil" (1).

Teacher: And one of your predictions is correct! This question is about parts of a plant. *(reading strategy: confirming predictions)* OK, so now we understand that the question is asking what plant part absorbs water and minerals from the soil. What does *absorbs* mean? *(reading strategy: determining word meaning)* [I call on Samuel, a Level 3 ELL from Colombia who has his hand raised, and then Jason, a Level 5 ELL from Mexico, elaborates on that idea.]

Samuel: That it takes in the water and minerals.

Jason: Yeah, it can suck up all the water and minerals like a sponge.

Teacher: Exactly. And the word is very similar in Spanish: *absorber*. [I act out the word *absorb* with my fingers as if they're taking in the water and minerals from the soil.]

Well, our choices for the answer are *branches, feet,* and *roots*. Turn and tell your partner what you think the answer is. [The class unanimously agrees that it's roots and some students say how easy the first question was. I remind them that something is easy only when you've learned the information and the vocabulary! I click on the link to the next page, which tells us we got the right answer and displays a short paragraph about roots.]

Let's read this text together. [My ELLs quietly read aloud the text with me.]

Class: Way to dig in! [I pause and laugh at the play on words with "dig in" and explain it to the class.] Roots soak up water and important nutrients from the soil. [I pause briefly to point out that *soak up* is a synonym for *absorb*.] They also anchor the plant in the ground.

Teacher: Hmm, that was a tricky word in that last sentence. It looks like it should be pronounced "an-chor," but it's really "an-kor" with a /k/ sound. What do you think *anchor* could mean from what's written in the rest of the sentence? *(reading strategy: determining word meaning)* [Students turn and talk with their partners. Then I call on Edwin, a Level 5 ELL from Mexico, so he can share his idea.]

Edwin: I think it means that it holds the plant in the ground. Like how the roots were holding the plant in Carlos' ear.

Teacher: Great connection to our read-aloud book! The roots anchor, or hold, the plant in the ground. [I act this out.]

So, from what we read in the text, how many different jobs do the roots have? Turn and talk with your partner. *(reading strategy: synthesizing information)* [My ELLs turn and talk about what they think based on this text. I call on a Level 1 ELL to share the number of jobs based on what he and his partner discussed, and he says the number *two* in English. Using a pointer, I underline the text to count each job and point out that the word *also* indicates that there is a second job.]

OK, should we try another question? [I click on the link to take us to the next part of the quiz and a photo appears of bright green leaves.]

[Asking one of my Level 1 ELLs] Is this a photo of a *stem* or *leaves*?

Student: Leaves.

Teacher: Good; let's see what it asks us about leaves.

Many plants use their green leaves to soak up sunlight. Then they turn it into food and oxygen. What is this process called? (3)

Teacher: Let's make sure we understand the second sentence. When it says *they*, what is it talking about? [I call on one of my Level 3 ELLs to see if she knows the referent, and she indicates that it's talking about the plants.]

Exactly. So the text is saying, "Then *the plants* turn it into food and oxygen." What does *it* refer to? [I hear my ELLs rereading the first sentence to themselves. I call on a Level 4 ELL, who says the word *it* is talking about the sunlight.]

You're right, *it* means the sunlight. The whole sentence is saying, "Then *the plants* turn *the sunlight* into food and oxygen." So, we need to decide what the process is called where plants turn sunlight into food and oxygen. [I make a quick sketch of this on the board.]

Let's look at the choices: *chlorophyll, photosynthesis,* or *sun bathing.* Turn and talk with your partner.

Most of my ELLs remember that this process is called photosynthesis, especially since we talked about this word during our read-aloud of *Carlos and the Squash Plant / Carlos y la planta de calabaza* (Stevens 1993). However, a few ELLs are convinced that the answer is chlorophyll, a related science vocabulary word. The class votes and we decide to enter *photosynthesis* as our answer on the website. The next page confirms our answer and has the following paragraph explaining this science concept.

> You sure are bright! Most plants make their own food, using a process called photosynthesis. Their leaves contain a substance called chlorophyll. It traps energy from sunlight. The plant then turns this energy into food and oxygen. Chlorophyll also gives plants their green color. (3)

As we read the first sentence, I see if the class can figure out the play on words with *bright.* Then we carefully read each sentence, pausing as needed to discuss the vocabulary. When we get to the part that mentions chlorophyll, we pause our reading and I use the sketch I made about photosynthesis to illustrate that chlorophyll is something inside the leaves that traps energy from the sunlight. After reading these sentences that are packed with important information, I have my ELLs turn and talk with their partners to synthesize this information in their own words. *(reading strategy: synthesizing information)* I hear some of my beginning and intermediate ELLs use their native languages to explain this complex concept.

We do the same type of reading and discussing with the next two questions. The following day during shared reading time, we look at the remaining six questions, which touch upon the topics of seed dispersal, pollination, and plant survival.

Commentary

- This shared reading helped my ELLs use a number of reading strategies to understand all the information that's packed in a nonfiction text. My ELLs were able to use their prior knowledge about plants and their familiarity with the science vocabulary to help them understand the questions and explanatory paragraphs. This also enabled us to review the concept of plant parts and their functions.

- During the shared reading I read aloud the text and my ELLs quietly read along with me as they looked at the text on the screen. This gave them a chance to practice reading the nonfiction text in a supportive environment where they were hearing me read it at the same time. However, ELLs who didn't feel comfortable reading aloud in English just listened to me read and followed along. This helped my beginning ELLs connect the oral language they were hearing with the written language they were seeing.

- During the shared reading I occasionally stopped to make sure my ELLs understood key words. This expanded my ELLs' academic vocabulary and reminded them of strategies they could use to figure out the meaning of new words. When applicable, I made connections between cognates in the L1 and L2, such as *absorb* and *absorber.*

- I also pointed out the use of synonyms, such as *absorb* and *soak up*. Academic texts often use a variety of synonyms and ELLs need to recognize that the different words are all referring to the same thing.

- In several paragraphs I explained expressions and play on words, since this kind of language use is very advanced.

- In some of the paragraphs I helped my ELLs determine what pronouns like *these, they,* and *it* were referring to. Texts that use a number of these referents can be very confusing for ELLs. I helped my students see how they could refer to the previous sentences to figure out what the words meant.

- I again used the turn-and-talk structure so every ELL had a chance to share ideas orally at multiple points during the shared reading. This developed my ELLs' speaking skills and gave them a chance to use the academic vocabulary about plants.

- I made an effort to include ELLs at all different L2 proficiency levels in the whole-class discussion. For example, I asked one of my Level 1 ELLs an either-or question about whether the photograph showed a stem or leaves. I asked another one of my Level 1 ELLs a question that required a one-word answer about the number of jobs roots have. Although the language was simplistic, these questions related to key academic vocabulary and concepts.

- By focusing on how to carefully read questions and consider possible answers, this shared reading was a meaningful way to help my ELLs understand how to read similar kinds of questions on the state science test.

- Using this website was motivating for my ELLs, and it also provided them with clear photographs that were a visual support for each paragraph of text.

Connection to Science Activity

This shared reading activity took place during the first part of our science time, and the information in the "Plant Power" text helped my ELLs remember the function of roots, the stem, leaves, and flowers. For the rest of our science time I had my ELLs work collaboratively in groups to record what they remembered about the function of each plant part. I circulated to see how much vocabulary they were able to recall from the text and how accurately they were summarizing the science concepts. Then I regrouped the class and had different ELLs share their summaries. We used these ideas to create a shared writing text that accurately described the function of each plant part. With shared writing my ELLs provided the ideas and I wrote them on chart paper along with a sketch of each plant part. Finally, I had my ELLs create vocabulary flipbooks with this information. I modeled how they could fold a blank piece of paper in half and then cut the top flap into four strips. That way they could write the four plant part names on the strips, along with a drawing. Then I modeled how they could lift each strip and underneath write an explanation of the plant part's function, based on our shared writing. Beginning ELLs copied the shared writing in their flipbooks, but I encouraged my Levels 3–5 ELLs to explain each function in their own words.

Reading Workshop Minilesson

The reading workshop is a time for students to take reading strategies they've seen and used with you during read-alouds and shared reading and put them into practice with their independent reading. The reading workshop begins with a brief minilesson to teach the whole class a particular strategy you want the students to use and to give them a chance to practice it with you before starting their independent reading. During this nonfiction unit of study in March, I wanted to use my minilessons to center on four reading comprehension strategies: visualizing, determining word meaning, determining importance, and synthesizing information. Each week I focused in depth on one of these reading strategies to help my ELLs understand their nonfiction books during independent reading. We had studied all these strategies in earlier units of study, but I cycled back to them periodically throughout the year to improve my ELLs' ability to use them with increasingly more difficult texts.

The minilesson I describe here shows how I worked with my class on determining the meaning of "tricky words." I spent a solid week working on this until I assessed that my ELLs were doing it independently.

- Content objective: Students will recognize when they don't understand part of a nonfiction text and determine the meaning of the difficult words by rereading the text, using picture clues, using context clues, and using the glossary.

- Language structures: Ask and answer questions about word meaning: "What does _____ mean?" "I think it means _____. "Use the structure of the sentence to think about what an unknown word could mean (is it a verb, noun, adjective, etc.?).

My minilesson followed the format developed by the Teachers College Reading and Writing Project (Calkins et al. 2003, 2006). The lesson began with a *connection* to build off my students' prior experiences. In the *teach* part of the lesson I explicitly modeled the reading strategy for them. In the *active engagement* part of the lesson I provided an opportunity for my ELLs to practice the reading strategy with me. The lesson ended with a *link*, where I reminded the students how they could use the reading strategy in their independent reading. In the transcript of this lesson, I indicate where each of these components began as I worked with my ELLs on determining word meaning.

Teacher: When you come to the meeting area today, you'll need to bring your reading notebook and a pencil. [I model these materials for the class and I call each group of students over to the rug.]

(Connection) Yesterday we talked about how we should have a picture in our mind as we read, and that picture helps us understand all the details we're learning in our nonfiction books. Last night before I went to sleep I started reading this book *From Seed to Plant* (Gibbons 1991). [I show the class the book.] As I was reading, I had a really good picture in my mind of what the information was all about. But then I got to a part where all of a sudden my picture stopped. I didn't understand what the words meant, so I had no picture in my mind! Has that ever happened to you? Do you get to parts you where you can't imagine what's happening anymore? [Students nod their heads.] Since you've started

reading your science nonfiction books, I've noticed that a lot of you get to parts that are confusing.

(Teach) So today I'm going to remind you of the strategies we learned earlier in the year to figure out tricky words. We're going to use those strategies with our science books so that we understand everything we read. Do you remember this chart that we made earlier in the year? [I point to the chart I have posted on the easel. Students nod their heads.] Let's reread the chart to remember all the strategies we can use to understand a confusing part.

Oh no! I lost the picture in my mind! How can I get it back?

1. STOP and reread the part carefully.
2. Look at the pictures.
3. Think: "What would make sense here?"
4. Try to explain it in your own words.
5. Keep reading.

Teacher: [Explaining each step of the chart] First, you can stop and reread the confusing part. Then, you can look at the pictures to see if that helps you understand the words. You can think, "What would make sense in this part of the book?" It also helps to try to explain what you read in your own words. Finally, you can keep reading to see if you learn anything else that helps you understand.

I'm going to read aloud part of this book *From Seed to Plant*, and I'll show you the part where I lost the picture in my mind last night. Then I'll show you what I did to understand it better, using some of these strategies.

I read aloud the first four pages, and after each page I pause to describe the good picture I have in my mind of what the text means. When I read aloud pages 5 and 6, I stop to show the class that this part has words that made it difficult for me to understand at first.

A flower is made up of many parts. Before a seed can begin to grow, a grain of pollen from the stamen must land on the stigma at the top of the pistil of a flower like itself. This is called pollination.

Teacher: This is the part where I lost the picture in my mind; there were so many words I didn't understand. First let me go back and reread it more carefully. [I point to the strategy chart to indicate that I'm doing the first step. I reread the two sentences more slowly.]

Hmm, I understand the first sentence. A flower has many different parts. So this next sentence must be talking about those different parts. But there are so many words I don't understand. Let me try looking at the pictures. [I point to the second strategy on the chart.]

Well, the picture here has a lot of labels to help me understand these words. So let's see, "Before a seed can begin to grow, a grain of pollen from the stamen [pausing to look at the picture to see where the stamen is labeled] must land on the stigma [pausing again to see where the stigma is labeled] at the top of the pistil [pausing to see where the pistil is labeled] of a flower like itself."

So, before a seed can grow, this is what happens: the pollen from the stamen [pointing] has to get on the stigma [pointing]. And the stigma is right here, at the top of the pistil [pointing].

Now I just need to understand that last part of the sentence: "of a flower like itself." Let me think; what would make sense here? [I point to the chart.] Maybe "like itself" means that this pollination has to happen with the same kind of flower? I think I need to keep reading to see if the next part of the book helps me understand this. [I point to the last step on the chart.]

Do you see what I did?

- On the first few pages of the book, the picture in my mind was great. I understood everything I was reading.

- But as soon as I came to a part where I lost my picture, I stopped and I reread the sentences carefully. [I point to number one in the chart.]

- I was still confused, so then I looked at the pictures, and that helped me understand some of those difficult words. [I point to number two in the chart.]

- Once I saw the pictures, I tried to explain it in my own words to make sure I understood. [I point to number four in the chart.]

- The last part of the sentence didn't have a picture to help me, so I thought about what would make sense there. [I point to number three in the chart.]

- Now I have an idea of what it could mean, so I just need to keep reading to see if I learn anything more about pollination. [I point to number five in the chart.]

(Active engagement) Now I want you to try it. Let's keep reading this book. As you listen, make sure you have a good picture in your mind of the information. If we come to a part we don't understand, then we'll try to figure it out using these strategies.

I read aloud the next few pages, and there aren't any parts that are confusing for the class. The pages talk about how the wind can blow pollen and how bees, insects, and hummingbirds can also carry pollen. Page 10 has some new vocabulary on it, so I plan to use that page for my ELLs to figure out the meaning of the text:

If pollen grain from a flower lands on the pistil of the same kind of flower
it grows a long tube through the pistil into an ovule. This is the beginning
of a seed.

Teacher: Hmm, this part is a little confusing, and I lost the picture in my mind again. What about you? [Many students nod their heads.]

I wrote this page on chart paper so you can all see the sentences. Let's reread this part together. [The class reads the two sentences with me.]

OK, now I want you to turn and talk with your partner and use some of these strategies to see if you can understand what it means.

My ELLs turn and talk with their partners. I hold up the book so they can all see the illustration on this page. I hear partners saying the words *pistil* and *ovule* and I see them pointing to the labels in the illustration. Then I hear partners trying to explain what this all means. I see them acting out the order of how everything happens, starting with the pollen landing on the pistil, and then motioning how the tube goes down into the ovule.

Teacher: OK, eyes on me. What did you do to understand this part of the book? [I call on Marcos, a Level 4 ELL from the Dominican Republic.]

Marcos: We looked the pictures with the words, and that helped us understand those science words.

Teacher: Yes, this picture has labels for *pistil* and *ovule*, which helps us understand the science words. Where is the pistil? [I call on a Level 1 ELL, who points to the pistil labeled in the picture.] And where is the ovule? [I call on a Level 2 ELL, who points to the ovule labeled in the picture.]

What else did you do to understand this part? [I call on Miguel, another Level 4 ELL from the Dominican Republic, who has his hand raised.]

Miguel: We tried to explain the whole thing. Like we said, "What does this mean?"

Teacher: I saw many of you explaining this information in your own words to make sure you understood it. Some of you were even acting it out with your partner. [I have Miguel and another ELL share what they now understand about this page.]

(Link) When you're reading independently today, you need to watch out for parts that you don't understand. If you don't have a picture in your mind, then you need to stop, reread, and try these strategies to figure it out [pointing to chart]. In your reading notebooks you can record important information you're learning from your nonfiction books. You can also include pictures that show the information. [I hold up an example from my own reading notebook. This type of reading response is something my ELLs are already familiar with from previous lessons.]

After the reading minilesson my ELLs sit with the groups I have created, which I formed on the basis of common science interests. Within a minute or so they are settled into their seats, reading nonfiction books from their baskets. They have their reading notebooks open so they can record the important information they are learning.

Figure 6–1 shows how Vicente, a Level 4 ELL from Mexico, used his reading notebook during independent reading that day to record what he was learning from his nonfiction science book and how he visualized the information.

Commentary

- This lesson was part of a multiday focus on determining the meaning of tricky words in a nonfiction text. This reading strategy is essential for ELLs because they will always encounter unfamiliar words as they develop their academic language proficiency in the L2. Science texts in particular have many vocabulary words that are new for ELLs. They need to have ways to figure out those words and understand the key information in the nonfiction texts. During other minilessons that week we reviewed other ways to figure out a tricky word, such as using print strategies like breaking a word into chunks, looking for familiar words within a word, and getting clues from prefixes and suffixes.

- I kept the minilesson focused on determining word meaning. This helped my ELLs understand what was going on in the lesson. I first modeled this reading strategy and then had my ELLs practice it with me. Then I told them to try it with their independent reading.

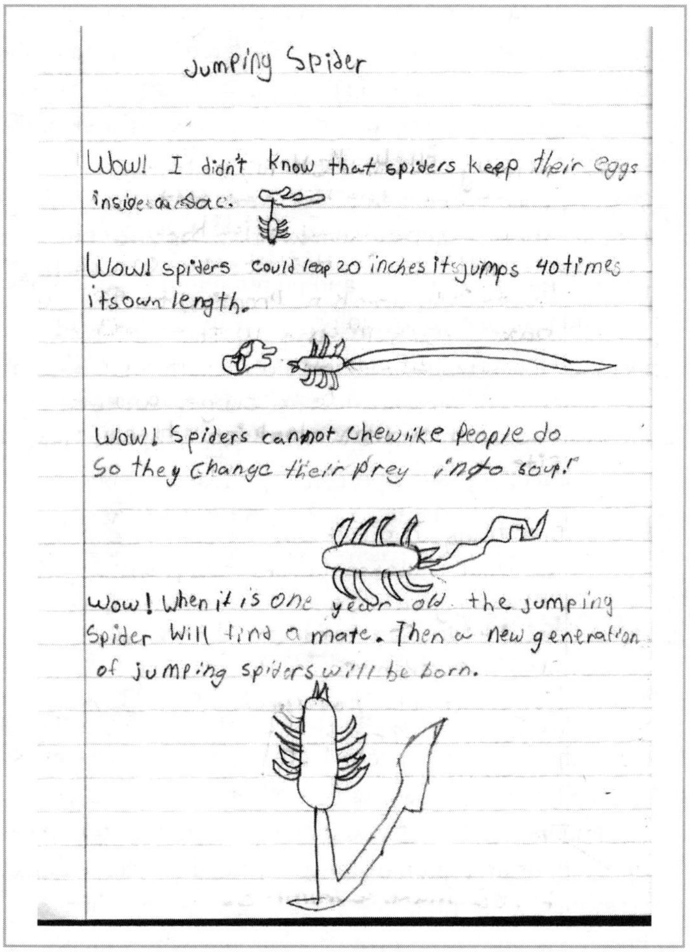

Figure 6–1 *Vicente's reading notebook*

- I chose a book for this minilesson that was related to our review of seeds and plants. Normally I use a read-aloud or shared reading text that I've already read with the class, but in this case it needed to be a new text so we could practice what to do when we came to a confusing part. If I had used a familiar text, we would have already talked about the meaning of those difficult parts. However, since the book *From Seed to Plant* (Gibbons 1991) related to what we were reviewing that week in science, it had many familiar words and concepts that made it more comprehensible for my ELLs.

- Since I was reviewing several ways to determine word meaning, I had them written on a chart and I referred to the chart throughout the lesson. This was an important visual support so my ELLs could see which strategies we were using.

- When it was time for my ELLs to practice figuring out the meaning of one of the confusing pages, I had the sentences written on chart paper so everyone could see them.

- As with the read-aloud and shared reading, having time for ELLs to turn and talk with their partners gave every ELL a chance to orally communicate. Partners combined their language skills to figure out the meanings of the science words and then explained the information in their own words.

- I expected ELLs at every proficiency level to participate in practicing this reading strategy. Every ELL needed to know how to determine word meaning, regardless of his reading level. By adjusting the types of questions I asked, I was able to include ELLs at every proficiency level in the class discussion. For example, I included beginning ELLs by having them point to labeled words in the picture to indicate word meaning. Then intermediate and advanced ELLs explained the meaning of the whole text in their own words, using more extended language.

- Acting out the meaning of the text and pointing to the illustrations gave everyone a better understanding of the information about pollination.

- This minilesson helped ELLs remember how to determine word meaning, but the teaching didn't stop here. My ELLs needed individualized support to really put this into practice with their own reading, especially with more difficult nonfiction texts. I provided this support through reading conferences and guided reading groups while the class was reading independently.

Reading Conference

After the reading minilesson, my ELLs began independently reading the nonfiction science books they had chosen from the book baskets available in the classroom library, shown in Figure 6–2. All of these baskets related to concepts my ELLs needed to review for the science test, and they contained books at a wide range of reading levels.

At the beginning of our nonfiction reading unit I had asked my ELLs to give me a list of the topics they were most interested in reading, based on the book baskets I had created. From those preferences, I formed small groups who would read books from each basket during independent reading time. Each week I formed new groups so my ELLs would read from four different baskets by the end of the month. As they read these books during independent reading, my ELLs recorded important information they were learning about the topics, and at the end of each reading workshop they shared their books and thoughts with the other students in their groups. Later my ELLs used the information from these books to write feature articles about the different science topics during writing workshop.

During independent reading on this particular day I circulated around the room to make sure everyone was working productively, and then I decided to start some reading conferences. Reading conferences are a way to sit down with individual students, check up on how they're reading, and help them with a particular need they have in reading. In my assessment binder I have a reading conference form for each of my ELLs (see Appendix D) and my Language Structures checklist for the whole class in the front cover (Figure 2–7). On the reading conference form I take note of what I teach my ELLs about reading and language, as well as any observations I have. On the Language Structures checklist I record any grammatical aspects that I notice my ELLs are using or developing. This helps me plan for future instruction.

From the notations in my assessment binder, I knew which ELLs I hadn't met with yet that week in a reading conference, and James, a Level 3 ELL from Colombia, was one of them. I sat down next to James to have a reading conference with him. He was reading a nonfiction book from the "Ecosystems Around the World" basket called *Life in a Coral Reef* (Brinkworth 2003).

Figure 6–2 *Nonfiction book baskets for independent reading*

Teacher: Hi, James. What book are you reading today?

James: See—it's called *Life in a Coral Reef*. [He shows me the cover of the book.]

Teacher: What an interesting topic. What have you learned so far? [I want to get an idea of what information James has understood from this book. It's a Level K book, which is at his independent reading level. However, the vocabulary in the book could make it difficult for him to fully understand the text.]

James: I'm reading this part here, and I learned that the colors of the fish attract them.

Teacher: [Paraphrasing] Oh, so the colors of the fish attract each other?

James: Yeah.

Teacher: Is that what you put here? [I point to the writing and drawing in James' reading notebook, which is on his desk.]

James: Yeah. The fish send message to other fish.

Teacher: Can you show me the part of the book where you learned that?

James: It's right here. It says [reading aloud], "Thousands of different kinds of fish live around coral reefs. Most of these fish are very colorful. Their different colors help them recognize each other. Their colors also help them send messages to each other. Colors tell the fish which other fish are safe, and which other fish are unsafe" [10].

Teacher: So from what you just read here, what kind of messages do they send to each other?

James: [James isn't sure. The sentence about messages has stood out to him, but James hasn't connected it to the next sentence, which indicates that the colors of fish send messages about which ones are safe or unsafe.]

Teacher: In a nonfiction book, all of the sentences in a section connect to each other because they're all about the same topic. So the next sentence might tell you more about those messages.

James: [Rereads the two sentences.] Oh, so the message is about what fish are safe and what are the enemies!

Teacher: Exactly. The colors of the fish let them know who is safe and who is unsafe. That's very important for the fish to know so they can survive in the coral reef! When you're reading nonfiction, you need to think about how all of the information in a section goes together.

James: OK.

Teacher: Before I leave, were there any words you had difficulty reading in this book?

James: Yeah, there's this one word here. [He shows me the word *surface* on the previous page in the sentence "Fish, worms, snails, shrimp, clams, crabs, and birds all make their homes near the ocean's surface" (9).]

Teacher: Hmm, that word's tricky, right? [James nods his head in agreement.] Well, let's try what we talked about today in the reading lesson. First try rereading the sentence. [James rereads it.] So all these things that you drew [pointing to his reading notebook where he had sketched the different animals that live in a coral reef], like the birds, worms, and fish, "make their home near the ocean's surface." Hmm, what would make sense here?

James: Like the, like the top part of the ocean?

Teacher: Exactly! It's the top part of the ocean; animals like birds and worms aren't going to live all the way down at the bottom of the ocean. [I gesture to explain the word meaning.] So, all you had to do was reread it and take a moment to think about what made sense.

James: Yeah!

Teacher: Why don't you keep reading and try to do this with other difficult words you find. Stop, reread the sentence, and think about what it could mean from the pictures and the other words. Your book also has a glossary, so you can use that to find the meaning of some of the important words. [I show James the glossary.]

Commentary

- When I sat down with James to talk with him about what he was learning, I noticed that he wasn't combining all the information on the page to have a complete understanding of the topic. He was simply keying in to certain sentences that seemed interesting to him. So, I decided to focus the reading conference on *synthesizing information* to help James see that in nonfiction texts the information in each section is all connected.

- Since our reading lesson that day had been about determining word meaning, I wanted to briefly check with James to see if he had had trouble with any words. It turned out that there was a word James wasn't sure of, and with just a little prompting he figured it out on his own. This helped James see that it's worth pausing for a moment to better understand the words in a text. The conference helped James learn a new vocabulary word in English. Other times reading conferences have a different linguistic focus, such as helping ELLs read unfamiliar language structures, decode in the L2, learn how to read certain high-frequency words, or understand certain expressions. Having a dual focus on content (in this case a reading strategy) and language helps maximize learning in the L2.

- When I took notes in my reading conference form (Appendix D), I recorded what I taught James about reading: how to synthesize information and how to determine word meaning using context clues. In the language section of the reading conference form I jotted down the vocabulary word we had discussed: *surface*.

- On my Language Structures checklist I noted that James wasn't consistently making nouns plural, which is a beginning structure that he should have been using at this point ("The fish send *message* to other fish"). This was actually the case with several other ELLs in the class, including a few students who had a more advanced L2 proficiency than James. I knew I would need to point this out in whole-class activities like shared reading and interactive writing, as well as in more individual activities like independent writing.

Guided Reading

During independent reading I also meet with one or two guided reading groups. This is when I bring together a small group of students who are all reading at a similar level. In this transcript I worked with three Level 2 ELLs who were starting to show some of the characteristics of a Level 3 proficiency. Angélica and Diana were both from Colombia, and Brando was from Ecuador. These three ELLs were independently reading nonfiction books at approximately Level G. In our guided reading group session I gave them multiple copies of the book *Earth's Water* (Scraper n.d.), which I had printed out from www.readinga-z.com/. This is a Level H nonfiction text, slightly higher than what this group of ELLs could currently read on their own. My goal was to give these students just enough support so they would be able to read this text independently. In this example you can see how I provided that support by building their background knowledge about the properties of water and the water cycle and by previewing key vocabulary in the text through a picture walk. Since my class was going to be studying concepts related to water the following week in science, this was an excellent way for me to preview the concepts and language with this small group of ELLs.

After doing this book introduction, I had my ELLs read the book on their own and listened to each one read aloud quietly to me. If they struggled with reading or understanding part of the text, then I guided them to use different reading strategies. After my ELLs read the book, I regrouped them so we could discuss the text, and I taught them something about reading and language based on the needs I had observed when they read aloud to me.

I began by calling over this small group of ELLs and giving each of them a copy of the book *Earth's Water*. They sat in a circle on the rug.

Teacher: I have a new nonfiction book for you to read today. [I hand out a copy of the book to each ELL.] What's the title of the book?

Angélica: *Earth Water*.

Teacher: Yes, *Earth's Water*. [I emphasize the correct pronunciation of the first word.] Do you know why there's an apostrophe and an *s* at the end of the word *Earth*? [I point to this part of the title.]

Diana: I think is because the water is from the earth.

Teacher: That's a great way to explain it. The apostrophe and the *s* tell us that the water belongs to the earth. Let's read the title together.

All: *Earth's Water.*

Teacher: What do you think you're going to learn in this book?

Angélica: Maybe we learn about where is water.

Diana: Or what happens to water, like how it go up in the clouds.

Teacher: Like the water cycle we learned about earlier in the year! Do you remember the names for each part of the water cycle?

Brando: [Shares one of the words in Spanish, *evaporación*, but says he can't remember the name of the part where it goes into the cloud or when it rains.]

Teacher: Yes, *evaporation* is when water heats up and turns from a liquid into a gas. [I sketch this part of the water cycle on a small whiteboard that I have next to me.] Does anyone remember the names of the other parts of the water cycle?

No one can recall the words *condensation, precipitation,* or *runoff.* I remind them of these words as I add to my sketch of the water cycle. There's a chorus of "Oh yeah!" from the group as the language and concept come back to them. I have these ELLs explain the water cycle to me in their own words to make sure they understand what happens in each part.

Teacher: OK, let's take a quick picture walk through the book and see if any of your predictions are correct. Then you'll read the book on your own. [We open to the first page with text. Each page has a photograph and text beneath it.] What do you see here?

Angélica: Oh! Is like my prediction! I see the ocean, lake . . .

Teacher: Yes, it looks like this part is all about where you can find water on Earth. I also see a river. What do you see on the next page?

Diana: There's water in all the cups.

Teacher: Yes. Is water a liquid or a solid? [The group responds that it's a liquid. I point out this boldfaced word in the text on that page.] Ooh—and what do you see here? [I point to the adjacent page.]

Diana: Now is an angel! Like the water is *congelado* [frozen]. [The photo on this page shows an ice sculpture carved into the shape of an angel.]

Teacher: Yes, the water is *frozen.* When water freezes [pointing to the boldfaced word in the text], it turns into ice, which is a solid [pointing to the boldfaced word in the text].

We continue this quick picture walk so I can see what vocabulary my ELLs already know in English and Spanish and build language from their responses. I make sure I preview the main vocabulary words related to water that appear in the text. Then I tell them to read the book on their own.

My ELLs turn their backs to the inside of the circle so they're a bit separated from each other. During this time I sit next to each student and listen to him or her softly read aloud part of the text to me. This lets me see what each ELL is doing while reading. If the student gets stuck on a particular word or doesn't understand a part, I'm there to guide him or her, reminding the student of what reading strategies he or she can use. For example, when Diana reads aloud to me, she isn't sure how to read the word *container* in the sentence "Liquid takes the shape of the container it's in" (7). Diana has difficulty decoding this longer word, so I prompt her to break the word into parts. After I help her sound out each part ("con-tain-er"), she recognizes the familiar word. She points to the photograph and explains what the word means. I remind Diana that she can also use the photographs to help her understand difficult words, and then I have her continue to read.

As I listen to each ELL read aloud, I record my observations of his or her reading ability and language use in my reading conference form (Appendix D). In Diana's case, I take note of how I have helped her use the print strategy of breaking a word into parts, and I indicate that she needs to continue practicing this. Additionally I note that her reading fluency is improving in English. When Diana reads aloud to me, I also notice that she isn't pronouncing the final *s* in a number of words, including third-person verbs such as *melts*. Using this language structure correctly is something typical of a Level 3 ELL, and at this point in the year she is showing signs of transitioning from a Level 2 to a Level 3. Helping her with this aspect of the language is appropriate for her developmental level.

Brando finishes reading the book before I have a chance to listen to each ELL read, but he knows the routine: he can either reread the book or return to some of his favorite parts to read them again. Once I meet with each student, they turn back into the circle so we can talk about the book together. I have them summarize the important information they learned about water, and when necessary I help them use science vocabulary words from the text. Based on the difficulties I have observed while listening to my ELLs read, I decide to help the group use a combination of print strategies to understand some of the more difficult words in the book. On the language side, I have noticed that Diana, Angélica, and Brando all need to focus on reading the final *s* or *es* in words such as *takes*, *melts*, and *freezes*. We briefly work on reading these words, making an effort to pronounce the final sound. I compare the meaning of *I take* with *It takes* within the context of this book. This is a first step in helping my ELLs learn this aspect of English language use.

Commentary

- With this guided reading session I had high expectations for my ELLs. I helped them use the same reading strategies as the rest of the class, just with a text appropriate for their reading level in English.

- I used a book that integrated with our upcoming science study of water. This provided a way for these Level 2 ELLs to build the academic language necessary for understanding the science concepts. I spent about fifteen minutes meeting with this group, since I took a few extra minutes at the beginning to go over the concepts and language of the water cycle.

- By previewing the science concepts and language with me in guided reading, my ELLs were better prepared to understand the science concepts in whole-class learning activities the next week. It also increased their participation in class discussions.

- When Angélica read aloud the title, I was able to emphasize an important language structure: using the possessive *s*. I reread the title correctly and then asked why the apostrophe and the *s* were at the end of the word *Earth's*. This helped my ELLs think more critically about the language, and they learned how to read a word that has the possessive *s*, which can be very confusing for ELLs.

- Through the picture walk my ELLs had a chance to use their background knowledge to talk about the language and concepts they would encounter in the text. The picture walk also helped me point out key vocabulary words and connect them to the text. This enabled my ELLs to successfully read a nonfiction text at a level that was slightly higher than their independent reading level.

- I encouraged my ELLs to express their ideas in Spanish as well as English. Brando was able to share the word *evaporación* in Spanish to talk about the water cycle, and then I helped him recall the word in English. These words happen to be cognates, so I could point out the connection between the two languages.

- As I listened to each ELL read aloud, I took note of the student's reading ability *and* language use. Based on these observations I decided to help the group with a reading strategy (determining word meaning) and an aspect of the language (reading the final *s* or *es* in words, particularly verbs in the third person). This developed language in a meaningful context.

- The guided reading session relied on familiar routines to eliminate the need for explaining procedures. My ELLs knew the routines for previewing the book, reading it independently, reading it aloud to me, and what to do if they finished early. This maximized what we were able to accomplish in a short period of time.

Guided Reading with Level 1 ELLs

When I meet with a group of Level 1 ELLs, the guided reading session has a different format because these students are just beginning to develop a vocabulary base in English and learn the sounds of the language. I choose a book at a beginning reading level that has clear pictures, patterned writing, and important vocabulary for my newcomers to learn. I first do a picture walk to help them learn the key vocabulary and connect that vocabulary with the written language in the text. Then we do an echo reading where I read each sentence, and they repeat it after me, following along with the text in their copies of the book. This is a supportive way for Level 1 ELLs to read a new text and try out the sounds of the language. Since these books are short, we usually have time to read through the book again, this time using shared reading. This releases a little more of the reading responsibility to my ELLs, because they're reading it at the same time as me instead of hearing it first and then echoing it.

I typically meet with the group of Level 1 ELLs the next day for a very short guided reading session where we do another shared reading together and I have them try to read the text with a partner. I listen in to each partnership to see how well they're able to read the new high-frequency words and vocabulary words in English. I take note of their reading and language development in my conference notes.

Writing Workshop Minilesson

The writing workshop begins with a minilesson where you teach your whole class something about writing and have the students practice it with you. The minilesson is followed by a block of time where children have the opportunity to write independently, putting into practice what you taught them during the minilesson. During the month of March my ELLs wrote feature articles during the writing workshop, patterned after the type of articles found in magazines like *Scholastic News* and *National Geographic Explorer!* To get a feel for this type of writing, we analyzed a number of articles from the magazines we had in the classroom to see what nonfiction features the authors used, such as headings, subheadings, photographs, charts, and captions. We also looked carefully at the way authors shared the information in a more conversational tone, instead of just presenting the information. Each ELL chose a particular science topic based on the nonfiction books they had been reading in independent reading. For the first few days of writing workshop they used those books to record more information about their topics using a graphic organizer with boxes and bullets (see Appendix G). In the boxes they recorded their section headings and in the bullets they recorded the specific information they wanted to include for each section.

In the minilesson detailed here, I wanted to show my class how they could take the information they had gathered from their nonfiction books and turn it into a text for a feature article by adding their reaction to the information. That conversational voice differentiates a feature article from other types of informational writing. Again, my minilesson followed the format developed by the Teachers College Reading and Writing Project: connection, teach, active engagement, and link (Calkins et al. 2003, 2006).

- Content objective: Use the writing process, which consists of prewriting, drafting, revising, editing, and publishing, to produce informational texts that are focused, organized, and elaborated with relevant details and that have voice.

- Learning activities: Use daily minilessons to model each step of the writing process and have ELLs practice each step with me. Have each ELL independently write her own feature article about a particular science topic using information from nonfiction books.

- Language structures: Use the present tense to explain the science information; use verb agreement; ask questions in present and past tense; use contractions.

- Content-specific vocabulary: Use relevant science vocabulary from the nonfiction books.

Teacher: When you come to the meeting area, please bring your writing notebook where you have the information for your feature article. [I hold up my notebook as a model and have each group of ELLs come to their rug spots.]

(Connection) Over the past few days you've been gathering information for each section of your feature article. Now all that information is in your writing notebook. [I show my writing notebook as an example.]

(Teach) Today I'm going to show you how you can take the information from your notebook and use it to write a feature article. When we looked at the different feature articles from *National Geographic Explorer!* one thing we noticed was that the authors didn't just tell us the information. They wrote it like they were talking to us about the information. It was more like a conversation. So today we're going to take the information in our notebooks and try to write it in a way that is more like a conversation. Let me show you how I did that with my own writing. Remember, my feature article is about plants. One of the sections in my article is about how seeds are dispersed. Here you can see what I wrote in my notebook for this section. [I point to the chart in Figure 6–3 (page 180), where, on the left side, I've written information in a notebook. I read aloud the information, pointing to the writing in the chart as I read it aloud.]

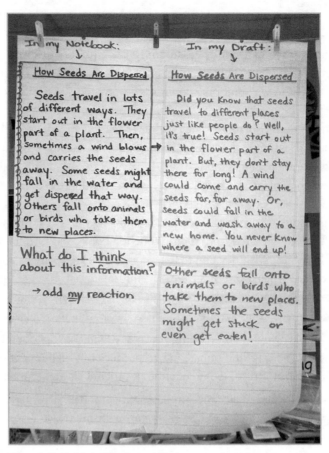

Figure 6–3 *Modeled writing for a minilesson*

So, this is the information I learned from the different books I've read about seeds and plants. It's good information, but it doesn't sound as interesting as the articles we read in *National Geographic Explorer!* To make it sound more like a conversation, I have to imagine that I'm talking to someone about this information. Listen to what I wrote in my draft. [I read aloud the text on the right side of the chart, where I've used the information to write a feature article in a more conversational style.] Do you see how I make it sound more like a conversation? I started off with a question, and I tried to explain the information as if I were talking to my friend about it.

(*Active Engagement*) Let's make a list of ways we can make our writing sound more like a conversation. [On the whiteboard I make two categories: "Ask the Reader a Question" and "Add Your Reaction." Under each category my ELLs help me make a list of possible language structures they could use in their feature articles.]

Ask the Reader a Question

- Did you know that . . . ?
- Do you know that . . . ?
- Have you ever wondered . . . ?

Add Your Reaction

- Wow!

- I can't believe . . .

- It's amazing (unbelievable, surprising, etc.) that . . .

- It's interesting how . . .

- That's incredible (disgusting, scary, unusual, etc.)!

Teacher: Now I want you to try this with your own information. Open your writing notebook to one of the pages where you have information for a section of your feature article. [I model this with my own writing notebook, which I have on my lap.] Take a minute to read that information to yourself so you remember what you wrote there. [ELLs quietly read their writing.]

OK, now I want you to do two things with your partner. First, read the information to your partner exactly as it's written in your notebook. Then, try to explain the information to your partner so that it sounds more like a conversation. You could start it with a question and also add your own thoughts about the information.

Who would like to try this with me? [I want to model this new kind of partner work so my ELLs know exactly what to do. A number of ELLs volunteer, and I call on Julia, a Level 4 ELL from the Dominican Republic.]

OK, Julia. What's your feature article going to be about?

Julia: It's about ants, and this section is all about ant tunnels.

Teacher: Great! Why don't you read aloud the information you gathered in your notebook.

Julia: OK! [Reads aloud the information.]

Teacher: I just learned some new information about ants from you. Now, the second step. Try to tell me about this information like you're having a conversation. You could start with a question, and you could also include your reaction to the information.

Julia: I think I'm going to start with a question. Did you know that ant tunnels are about one meter long? They have so much room in there because they need room for the queen and the babies and the worker ants.

Teacher: I love how you start with a question and then explain it with this information. Is there anything else you want to say about this part?

Julia: I could say, "That is so amazing!" because I never know that about ant tunnels.

Teacher: Absolutely. Those are all ways for you to make your feature article interesting for people to read. [I thank Julia for sharing with me and then address the whole class.] Do you see how Julia first read me her information, and then she told me about it in a conversation with me? She started with a question, and she also added her reaction to the information. [Students nod their heads.] You can do the same with your partner. Give your partner ideas for how to make his or her information sound more like a conversation. Turn and talk with your partner. [Students turn to their partners and start following these two steps.]

[I circulate to each of the partnerships, listening to them talk about their information. When I hear partners that are having difficulty, I help them use ideas

Figure 6–4 *Vicente, Angélica, and Jason draft their feature articles*

on the board to add more voice to their information. This communicative practice lasts for about four minutes.]

OK, eyes on me. It was very interesting to listen to you talk with your partner, because I heard you share the information in a conversational way. [I point to the board where we have our list of language structures, and I give specific examples of what I heard different ELLs say.]

(Link) Today during independent writing you can start drafting each section of your feature article. As you write, try to take the information from your notebook and make it sound more like a conversation, using these techniques we talked about here.

I send my ELLs back to their desks group by group so they can start the independent writing time as shown in Figure 6–4 above. For this writing unit I have them sitting with the other students who are writing about a similar topic. That way, my ELLs have access to their nonfiction book basket in case they need to look for more information. And if they need help they can consult the other group members who have been reading the same books.

Commentary

- This lesson provided support for ELLs by first modeling the teaching point and then having them practice it. I often use shared writing to have students practice a writing skill with me. In this lesson, however, I wanted each ELL to orally try out this style of writing using the information he had gathered for his particular feature article. I've found this kind of oral rehearsing activity to be very effective with ELLs. It helps them think through how they could use the language to express an idea. Since oral language skills are often more developed for ELLs than their writing skills, they can use the oral language as a stepping-stone to writing the language. Sharing orally with a partner gives them someone who can offer other ideas for how to express their ideas through language.

- I explicitly modeled the new routine for the turn-and-talk time with Julia. I wanted my ELLs to see exactly what they were expected to do and how I wanted them to use the language. That way everyone was highly productive.

- Through the turn and talk, every single ELL had a chance to orally communicate in a meaningful way for an extended period of time, helping them all build speaking skills and use the academic vocabulary related to their science topics.

- The lesson included a number of visual supports, including the chart with my modeled writing and the list of language structures we wrote on the board.

- Listing these possible language structures provided my ELLs examples of the type of language they could use in their own writing. More advanced ELLs could, of course, branch out to use other language structures, but it gave ELLs at earlier proficiency levels the support they needed to add more voice to their writing.

Writing Conferences

Once my students had settled in to do their independent writing, I started having writing conferences with different ELLs. Writing conferences are a way to sit down next to individual students to help them with any specific writing needs they may have. You can use writing conferences to help ELLs develop the quality of their writing *and* the way they use the L2 in their writing. When I have writing conferences I take an assessment binder with me, which has a writing conference form for each ELL (Appendix D) and my Language Structures checklist for the whole class tucked in the front cover (Figure 2–7). On the writing conference form I take note of what I teach my ELLs about writing and language use as well as any observations I have. On the Language Structures checklist I record any grammatical aspects that I notice my ELLs are using or developing. This helps me plan for future instruction.

Sometimes I use my writing conferences just to quickly touch base with different ELLs to make sure they're on the right track. Other times I sit down with them for about five minutes to help them with a particular aspect of their writing. Here I give an example of each type of conference.

Quick-Check Writing Conference

As I circulated around the classroom, I noticed that Samuel, a Level 3 ELL from Colombia, was reluctant to start writing. Samuel had come to my classroom with lower literacy skills in Spanish, as seen in his letter in Chapter 2. Even though he had progressed greatly in writing since the beginning of the year, he still was hesitant about his ability to express himself in writing.

Teacher: Hi, Samuel. What are you doing with your writing?

Samuel: I don't know what to write.

Teacher: Let's look at your notebook. What sections are you going to have in your feature article?

Samuel: It's about reptiles, and I have a section about snakes and a section about alligators.

Teacher: Well, let's start with the section about snakes, because I heard you talking about that with your partner during the lesson. What do you want to tell people about snakes?

Samuel: When we were on the rug, I was thinking I could say [switches to a narrating voice], "The snakes like to eat eggs and their favorites are birds' eggs. But you know what's really scary about snakes? They can't chew eggs. They swallow them!" But I don't know if I should write that.

Teacher: Wow! I love the way that sounds. It's like you're talking to me, explaining the interesting things you've learned about snakes.

Samuel: Could I write it like that?

Teacher: Of course. It sounds like a great start to your section about snakes. But remember, don't worry right now about the spelling. If you're not sure how to spell a word, then just circle it. The important thing is to get your ideas written down on paper so you can share all of this amazing information with other people.

Samuel: [Nods his head] I'm going to write it here in English. [Begins writing intently.]

Commentary

- When I prompted Samuel to orally tell me what he was thinking about writing, I discovered that he already had a strong, detailed idea in mind, and I was impressed that he was able to use a conversational voice when expressing the information he knew about snakes. He was really applying what we had practiced in the lesson.

- Samuel's oral language skills were stronger than his writing skills, so he felt more comfortable getting started when he could share his ideas orally. Orally rehearsing this idea with me simply helped him think about how he could express his ideas in English, and it gave him the confidence to write it down in the L2.

- At the end of this brief conference I reminded Samuel not to worry about spelling at this stage of writing. By circling words he was unsure of as he drafted his writing, Samuel could focus on getting his ideas onto paper. Then during editing time he could focus on including the correct spelling.

- On my writing conference form I recorded that Samuel was still hesitant about writing, but that having him use oral rehearsing seemed to help with his elaboration. On the Language Structures checklist I quickly marked that I heard Samuel correctly using contractions (*don't, it's, can't*), which is typical of a Level 3 proficiency.

Writing Conference with an ELL with Limited Formal Education

For the next conference I was working with Fernando, a Level 2 ELL from the Dominican Republic. Throughout the year I had worked with Fernando on developing literacy skills in Spanish and transferring those skills to his reading and writing in English. Whenever I had writing conferences with Fernando, I helped him apply his developing knowledge of spelling, high-frequency words, vocabulary, and writing conventions to his independent writing in English. I also wanted him to develop qualities of writing such as focus, organization, and elaboration.

I began by sitting down next to Fernando and asking him what he had written in his notebook. He had copied some simple sentences about bees from the nonfiction books he had read into his notebook. These sentences came from books I had found about bees at early reading levels. As soon as I had discovered how interested Fernando was in bees, I wanted to make sure he had texts he could more or less read independently about this topic.

In his notebook Fernando had copied some sentences about the food bees eat and what they look like. He had also drawn pictures to go with this information. His writing was clearly organized into these two sections, and he had a solid focus for his feature article. I decided that with this writing conference I could help Fernando develop more language to elaborate each of these sections.

Teacher: Fernando, it looks like you have two sections here. This section is about what bees eat and this section is about what bees look like. [I point to his notebook.]

Fernando: Yeah.

Teacher: Which section do you want to start drafting today?

Fernando: Umm . . . what bees look like.

Teacher: OK, great! So let's think of everything you know about what bees look like.

Fernando: [Opens one of his books about bees and points to different parts of the photographs.] Bees are yellow and black. And they have wings.

Teacher: [I decide to use interactive writing to help Fernando get some basic sentence structures down in writing. Then he can use those structures to add more details to his writing in English.] Those are all good details. Let's try writing the first detail you said: "Bees are yellow." [I have a piece of paper with me so I can write the sentence at the same time that Fernando writes it on his draft paper.]

OK, *Bees*. Do you need to look at your word list to remember how to spell *bees*? [Note: When Fernando started reading about bees, I helped him create a word list of important words he was learning how to read. One of those words was *bees*.]

Fernando: No! I remember! [He starts his sentence by writing each letter in the word *bees*.]

Teacher: Great! You've learned that word already. OK, "Bees *are* yellow." Hmm. Any idea how to write *are*?

Fernando: [Writes the letter *r* in his notebook.]

Teacher: Yes, you heard the /r/ sound in there. Very good. This is a tricky word to spell because there are some other letters around the letter *r*. Look at how I write this word. [I write the word *are* in my notebook after the word *Bees*, and Fernando writes it the same way in his notebook.]

Now the last word: *yellow*. [Fernando's eyes light up as he remembers that the word *yellow* is in his book about bees. He looks for the word in his book, finds it, and completes the sentence.]

All right. Read the sentence to me.

Fernando: "Bees are yellow."

Teacher: Now, let's think of other words you could use in this kind of sentence.

I help Fernando brainstorm other adjectives about bees, like *black, small, fast, scary,* and *cool*. I model how he can use that same sentence structure to explain the other adjectives about bees. Fernando and I do the same kind of interactive writing for one more sentence structure, "Bees have _____," and we make a list of some of the things bees have, like *wings, a stinger,* and *stripes*. I end the conference by reminding Fernando that he can always look at the nonfiction books about bees to add other vocabulary words into his writing. He can also add drawings to each sentence to illustrate what they mean and label things in the drawings. When I leave Fernando to meet with another student, he is intently working on writing more sentences for this section of his feature article.

Commentary

- Even though his literacy skills were significantly lower than those of most of his peers, Fernando was still working on the same type of writing as the rest of the class: feature articles.

- This writing conference gave Fernando the linguistic support he needed to write about bees. The interactive writing helped Fernando purposefully use what he already knew about English sounds, letters, and words. Since the writing was interactive, I was able to provide the parts that he hadn't learned yet. Between the two of us, we wrote the basic language structures he needed to get started with his feature article.

- The words we brainstormed for the language structures also helped Fernando add some voice to his writing ("Bees are cool.").

- I was happy to see how Fernando was able to write some of the vocabulary words he had learned from his reading. One of the words he had seen over and over again was *bees*, and he was able to spell that word correctly without looking back at his word list. This reinforces how beneficial integrated instruction can be, particularly for ELLs with low native language literacy levels.

- My conference with Fermando didn't just focus on building his language skills in English. I also thought about his writing skills. I made sure his writing had a focus and was organized in sections. Then, I used this conference to help him elaborate one of those sections. ELLs with limited formal education need help developing more basic skills, but they should also be supported with the academic expectations of their grade level.

Published Writing

Over the next two weeks my ELLs drafted their feature articles, revised them so they were organized and detailed, and edited for spelling, grammar, and punctuation. Figure 6–5 shows the two-page feature article that Samuel published about reptiles at the end of this writing process. Samuel's feature article shows just how much he had progressed with his writing skills and with his English proficiency since September. In Chapter 2 I included the letter Samuel wrote on the first day of school, when he was a Level 1 ELL. He had written his letter in Spanish, and his native language literacy skills were below grade level. Throughout the year I supported Samuel in learning English and in developing his literacy skills. Samuel's feature article shows his growth in both of these areas. He clearly communicated detailed information about reptiles through his writing in English. His writing is focused and organized, and his voice comes through in several parts. Samuel also improved his understanding of writing conventions such as letter formation and punctuation.

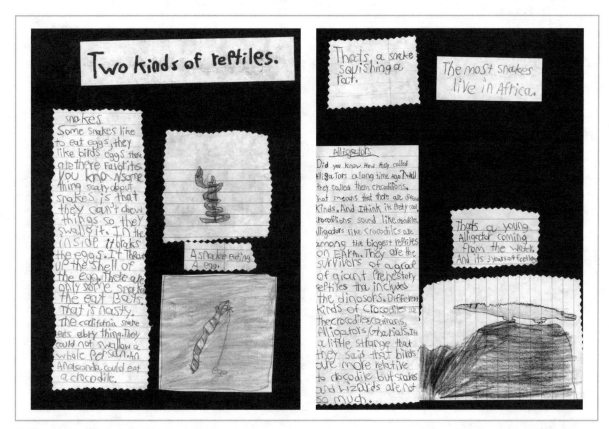

Figure 6–5 *Samuel's feature article*

Based on the characteristics TESOL identifies for each English proficiency level (Figure 2–6 on page 40), Samuel could now be described as having a solid Level 3 proficiency in English. He was able to write in expanded sentences. While his writing had grammatical errors, the text maintained much of its meaning. Samuel was also using language structures typical of Level 3, such as subject-verb agreement ("the snake *eats*") and basic contractions (*it's, that's*).

In Chapter 2 I also analyzed an initial writing sample by Edwin. I assessed Edwin as having approximately a Level 3 proficiency in English at the beginning of the school year. At that time, Edwin needed support to focus, organize, and elaborate his writing in English. He also needed to develop some language structures from earlier proficiency levels and develop his spelling skills. Figure 6–6 shows Edwin's published feature article about ants. You can see how Edwin had also progressed significantly from September to March. His writing is much more focused, it's organized into sections, and it's elaborated with excellent detail and voice.

Based on the characteristics TESOL identifies for each English proficiency level, Edwin could now be described as having a Level 5 proficiency in English. He was writing extensively in English, used a variety of sentence lengths with a wide range of complexity, and his writing was approaching what would be comparable to the writing of an English-proficient peer. There were very few grammatical errors that would indicate that a student learning English wrote this feature article. Edwin also used a number of expressions that showed a sophisticated grasp of English.

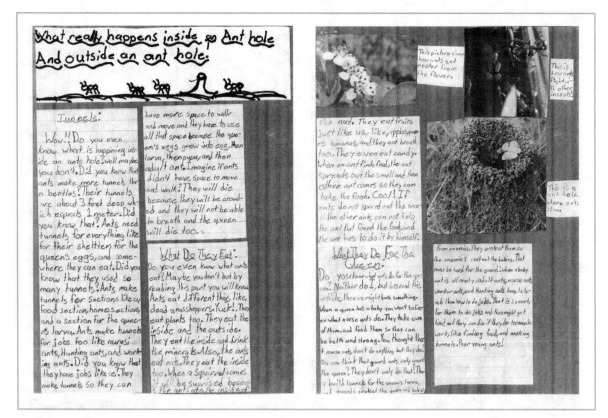

Figure 6–6 *Edwin's feature article*

Final Thoughts

From these snapshots of my classroom in action, you can see how the Keys to Success that I've discussed throughout the book have grounded my approach to teaching ELLs.

- Raise the bar: I made sure I taught my ELLs the grade-level curriculum, and I assessed how they were progressing with each content objective. I fully expected them to achieve the same standards as their English-proficient peers, and I hoped they would even exceed those standards.

- Teach language and content together: I included language objectives as a natural part of every lesson. My ELLs were learning the academic vocabulary and language structures they needed to be successful with the content objectives.

- Integrate instruction: I combined my content-area instruction with the balanced literacy components whenever possible. My ELLs were hearing, speaking, reading, and writing language connected to the content areas at multiple times throughout the day and over an extended period of time. This helped them understand the content more deeply, internalize the academic language, and also develop their literacy skills.

- Differentiate instruction: I used a balance of whole-group, small-group, and individual instruction to meet each of my ELLs' needs. I also used a number of supports in my teaching, including visual aids, explicit modeling, hands-on activities, collaborative partner work, and collaborative group work.

- Connect learning to students: When I taught a new concept, I tied it to what my ELLs already knew about the topic. If I saw they lacked certain background knowledge, then I helped them build it through our learning activities.

- Use students' native languages to support learning: I set up native language partnerships and encouraged my ELLs to use both of their languages to express their ideas and their learning. I also encouraged my ELLs to read and write in both languages because I knew that any literacy skills they developed in their L1 would transfer to English. I made bilingual word walls to help my ELLs learn new content-area vocabulary, and whenever possible I clarified concepts in my students' L1 or had another student summarize the concept in the L1.

- Be consistent: The routines and rules I incorporated in my daily schedule were very predictable, so my ELLs always knew how the classroom worked and what they needed to do. I used familiar language for my cues to get the class' attention and to transition from one activity to the next. I also had predictable homework procedures in place so my ELLs knew what assignments they would have each day and how they were supposed to complete them, based on their proficiency levels in English. This helped my ELLs be academically productive at school and at home.

- Involve families: From the first day of school I began an ongoing communication with my ELLs' families. I let them know right away how their children were progressing in school and what they could do to support learning at home. I provided different ways for families to be involved with their children's education, regardless of their proficiency in English, many of which I detailed on the Family Survey (Appendix C).

This is the framework I've relied upon over the years to guide the way I teach ELLs, but I don't think there will be a time when I feel like I've done everything possible to meet each student's needs. By the end of the school year I've inevitably started a mental list of all the things I plan to do differently the next time around. I'm always learning about new techniques that I want to add to my toolbox of instructional strategies or meeting new students whose needs challenge me to rethink some of my approaches. But whatever I change about my teaching each year is always grounded in what I know is good practice for ELLs. I may decide to try a new approach to introducing academic vocabulary or experiment with a new structure for collaborative learning, but these changes just refine the way I implement the Keys to Success. My hope, always, is that the changes I make will help more of my ELLs experience even greater success in the classroom.

On the last day of school with the class you've accompanied throughout this book, I had my ELLs write about special moments from the year. Samuel decided to write his thoughts in a letter that he addressed to me, which you can see in Figure 6–7 on page 190. When I read his letter I could sense how proud Samuel was of his accomplishments—and rightly so. He was now bilingual, literate in English and Spanish, and at grade level in all the content areas. What really touched me, when I got to the end of his letter, was Samuel's understanding that I had always tried to help the class and had tried to push them forward. For me, that's ultimately what the Keys to Success are about—transforming our teaching day by day so that every ELL knows we are committed to him achieving academic and linguistic success.

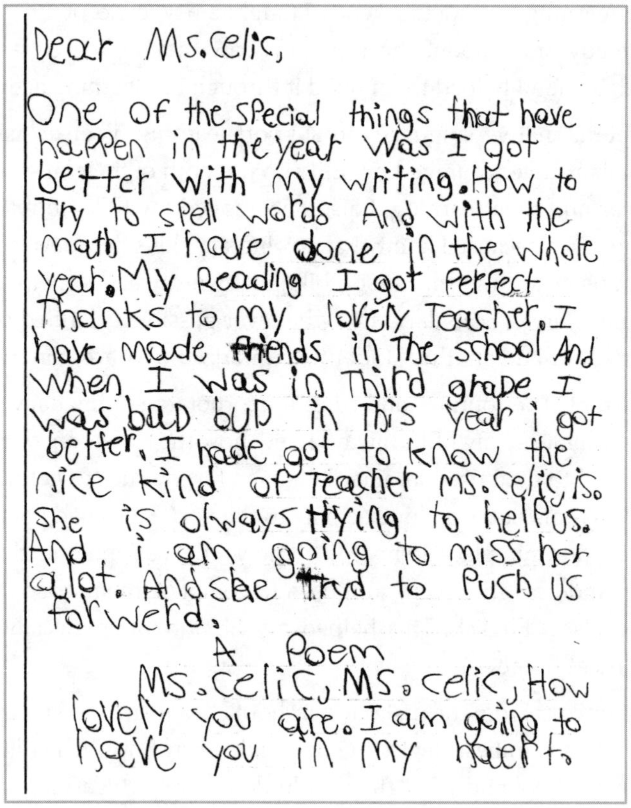

Dear Ms. Celic,

One of the special things that have happen in the year was I got better with my writing. How to Try to spell words And with the math I have done in the whole year. My Reading I got perfect Thanks to my lovely Teacher. I have made friends in the school And when I was in Third grape I was bad but in this year i got better. I hade got to know the nice kind of teacher ms. celic is. She is olways trying to helpus. And i am going to miss her alot. Andshe tryd to Push us forwerd.

       A Poem
Ms. celic, Ms. celic, How lovely you are. I am going to have you in my haert.

Figure 6–7 *Samuel's letter*

Appendices

Student Names	Native Language(s)	Country of Origin	L2 Proficiency Level	# of Years Learning L2							
1											
2											
3											
4											
5											
6											
7											
8											
9											
10											
11											
12											
13											
14											
15											
16											
17											
18											
19											
20											
21											
22											
23											
24											
25											
26											
27											
28											
29											

Appendix A–1 *Whole-Class Profile*

Student Names	Native Language(s)	Country of Origin	L2 Proficiency Level	# of Years Learning L2	Concepts About Print	Reading Level L1	Reading Level L2	Letter Name Identification L1	Letter Name Identification L2	Sound Identification L1	Sound Identification L2	High-Frequency Word Assessment L1	High-Frequency Word Assessment L2	Spelling Assessment L1	Spelling Assessment L2	Writing Level L1	Writing Level L2	Math Class Work	Special Services	Other
1																				
2																				
3																				
4																				
5																				
6																				
7																				
8																				
9																				
10																				
11																				
12																				
13																				
14																				
15																				
16																				
17																				
18																				
19																				
20																				
21																				
22																				
23																				
24																				
25																				
26																				
27																				

Appendix A–2 *Primary-Grade Whole-Class Profile*

Student Names	Native Language(s)	Country of Origin	L2 Proficiency Level	# of Years Learning L2	Reading Level L1	Reading Level L2	Language Arts Standardized Test Results L1	Language Arts Standardized Test Results L2	Writing Level L1	Writing Level L2	Spelling Assessment L1	Spelling Assessment L2	Math Grade	Math Standardized Test Results	Science	Social Studies	Special Services	Other
1																		
2																		
3																		
4																		
5																		
6																		
7																		
8																		
9																		
10																		
11																		
12																		
13																		
14																		
15																		
16																		
17																		
18																		
19																		
20																		
21																		
22																		
23																		
24																		
25																		
26																		
27																		

Appendix A–3 *Upper-Grade Whole-Class Profile*

Student Name: _____   Date: _____   Overall Proficiency Level: _____

	Characteristic Features of Speaking and Writing	Conversational Vocabulary	Academic Vocabulary	Language Structures Used When Speaking and Writing
Level 1 Starting	Often silent; responds nonverbally through gestures, pointing, nodding, yes-or-no answers, and drawing. May speak in single words, simple two-word phrases, or memorized chunks of text. May answer yes-or-no and either-or questions. Writing in the L2 may involve labelling with letters or sounds, labeling basic vocabulary, or filling in simple form sentences.	Learning common high-frequency words and everyday vocabulary in the school setting to express basic concrete needs.	Learning basic content-specific vocabulary, but may not be speaking or writing this vocabulary just yet.	Uses common nouns: *dog, boy, book* Uses regular plurals: *dogs, boys, books* Uses basic prepositions: *in, on, at* Uses verb *to be: I am happy.* Uses basic sentence structure (SVO): *I am a girl. I play soccer.* Uses basic commands: *Look! Help!*
Level 2 Emerging	Speaks and writes in phrases or short sentences. Makes basic errors that often interfere with communication.	Developing conversational language to communicate simple and routine experiences.	Beginning to use some content-specific and general academic vocabulary and expressions, but lacking a range of vocabulary beyond the basic.	Uses subject pronouns: *I, you, he, she, it, we, they* Uses statements: *there is/are, here is/are* Uses present tense Makes negative statements: *That is not my paper.* Uses present progressive tense: *We <u>are going</u> to the party.* Uses prepositional phrases: *in the book, on the bed* Uses basic adjectives: *big* instead of *huge, enormous* Uses coordinating conjunctions: *and, or, but*
Level 3 Developing	Speaks and writes in expanded sentences. Makes grammatical errors that may interfere with communication, but maintains much of the meaning.	Has a foundation for conversational language to communicate familiar matters that are regularly encountered.	Increasingly using content-specific and general academic vocabulary and expressions.	Uses possessive pronouns: *mine, yours, his, hers, ours, theirs* Uses habitual present tense: *He <u>goes</u> to Mexico every summer.* Uses past tense: *I <u>played</u> with my friend.* Uses subject-verb agreement: *She <u>likes</u> science.* Uses adjectives correctly: *the <u>beautiful red</u> flowers* Uses more coordinating conjunctions: *so, yet* Uses subordinating conjunctions: *because, when, before, after* Uses basic contractions: *I'm, it's, can't, didn't* Uses comparatives: *This magnet is <u>stronger than</u> the other one.* Asks questions in future tenses: *Will you go to the museum?* or *Are you going to go to the museum?*
Level 4 Expanding	Speaks and writes using a variety of sentence lengths of varying complexity. Makes minimal grammatical errors that do not interfere with the overall meaning.	Has a strong command of conversational language to communicate both concrete and abstract situations. Can apply language to new situations.	Using a wider range of content-specific and general academic vocabulary and expressions.	Uses reflexive pronouns: *myself, yourself, himself, herself, itself, ourselves, themselves* Uses abstract nouns: *democracy, freedom, trust* Uses irregular past tense: *I <u>found</u> the book and I <u>bought</u> it.* Uses gerunds: *<u>Voting</u> is a responsibility citizens have.* Uses superlatives: *Which planet is <u>the largest</u> in our galaxy?* Uses adverbs: *quickly, carefully, well* (instead of *good*) Uses synonyms and antonyms Use more coordinating and correlative conjunctions: *however, therefore, either...or* Asks question in past tense: *Where did the colonists settle?*
Level 5 Bridging	Speaks and writes extensively using a variety of sentence lengths of varying complexity. Speaking and writing approach comparability to English-proficient peers.	Near English-proficient command of conversational language, communicating in a wide range of situations and understanding implicit meaning.	Nearing English-proficient command of content-specific and general academic vocabulary and expressions.	Uses perfect tenses: *has been, had been, will have been* Uses conditional perfect tense: *If I <u>had checked</u> my answer, I <u>would have gotten</u> it correct.* Uses auxiliary verbs and contractions: *could/couldn't, would/wouldn't, should/shouldn't* Uses a wider range of adverbs: *already, still, often* Uses relative pronouns: *who, whom, whose, which, that* Uses more subordinating conjunctions: *although, whenever, until, whereas, even though* Uses the passive voice: *The seed <u>was planted</u> in the garden.* Uses metaphors and similes

Appendix B–1 *What to Expect from ELLs at Each Proficiency Level (Source: Gottlieb et al., 2006; Cappellini, 2005)*

Language Structures																			
Level 1	Common nouns (*boy, dog, school, bathroom*)																		
	Regular plurals (*boys, dogs, pencils, books*)																		
	Basic prepositions (*in, on, at, to*)																		
	Verb *to be* (*I am happy.*)																		
	Basic sentence structure (SVO) (*I play soccer.*)																		
Level 2	Subject pronouns (*I, you, he, she, it, we, they*)																		
	Statements (*There is/are, Here is/are*)																		
	Present tense																		
	Negative statements (*That is not my paper.*)																		
	Present progressive tense (*I am going to school*)																		
	Prepositional phrases (*in the book, on the bed*)																		
	Basic adjectives (*big* instead of *huge*)																		
	Coordinating conjunctions (*and, or, but*)																		
Level 3	Possessive pronouns (*mine, yours, his, hers, ours, theirs*)																		
	Habitual present tense (*He goes every summer.*)																		
	Regular past tense (*I played with my friend.*)																		
	Subject-verb agreement (*She likes science.*)																		
	Uses adjectives correctly (*the beautiful red flowers*)																		
	More conjunctions (*so, yet, because, when, before, after*)																		
	Basic contractions (*I'm, it's, can't, didn't*)																		
	Comparatives (*better than, faster than*)																		
	Asks questions in future tense (*Will you help me?*)																		
Level 4	Reflexive pronouns (*myself, yourself, himself, herself*)																		
	Abstract nouns (*trust, freedom, happiness*)																		
	Irregular past tense (*found, brought, went, saw, were*)																		
	Gerunds (*Going to the park is fun.*)																		
	Superlatives (*the best, the fastest, the most difficult*)																		
	Adverbs (*quickly, carefully, well*)																		
	Synonyms and antonyms																		
	Advanced conjunctions (*however, therefore, either … or*)																		
	Asks questions in past tense (*Where did you go?*)																		
Level 5	Present perfect (*I have learned a lot.*)																		
	Past perfect (*I had lived in Mexico.*)																		
	Future perfect (*I will have been here for four years.*)																		
	Conditional perfect (*If I had tried, I would have won.*)																		
	Auxiliary verb contractions (*couldn't, wouldn't, shouldn't*)																		
	Wider range of adverbs (*already, still, often*)																		
	Relative pronouns (*who, whom, whose, which, that*)																		
	Advanced conjunctions (*although, whenever, whereas*)																		
	Passive voice (*The houses were built quickly*)																		
	Uses metaphors and similes																		
Overall Proficiency Level:																			
Key: blank square = structure not evident; D = developing structure; S = secure structure																			

Appendix B–2 *Language Structures Checklist (Source: Adapted from Cappellini, 2005)*

Child's Name: _____   Parents' Names: _____
Nombre de su Hijo/a   *Nombres de los Padres*

Language(s) Spoken at Home: _____
Idioma(s) Utilizado en Casa

1. What do you feel would be helpful for me to know about your child?
   ¿Qué creen Uds. que sería importante que yo supiera sobre su hijo/a?

2. What are your child's interests?
   ¿Cuáles son los intereses de su hijo/a?

3. What concerns do you have about this school year?
   ¿Qué les preocupa sobre este año escolar?

4. How would you like to be involved in your child's education this year?
   ¿Cómo querrían participar en la educación de su hijo/a este año?

At School *En la Escuela*:

☐ Volunteer for class trips *Hacerse voluntario/a para viajes de clase*

☐ Help with class celebrations *Ayudar con las celebraciones de clase*

☐ Attend after-school workshops to learn how to help your child in school
   Asistir a talleres al final del día escolar para saber cómo Ud. puede ayudar a su hijo en la escuela

☐ Come to class to talk about your country *Venir a clase para hablar sobre su país*

☐ Come to class to talk about your profession *Venir a clase para hablar sobre su profesión*

☐ Come to class for our writing celebrations *Venir a clase para nuestras celebraciones de escritura*

☐ Come to class to listen to children read *Venir a clase para escuchar a los niños leer*

At Home *En Casa*:

☐ Cut and staple copies of books for our class to read
   Cortar y grapar copias de libros para que nuestra clase pueda leerlos

☐ Prepare book order forms *Preparar los pedidos de libros*

☐ Read with your child at home *Leer con su hijo/a en casa*

☐ Help your child with homework *Ayudar a su hijo/a con su tarea*

Other *Otra*:

Reading and Language Conference Notes for _____

Date: _____ Text: _____
Observations:

Reading Teaching Point:

Language Teaching Point:

Date: _____ Text: _____
Observations:

Reading Teaching Point:

Language Teaching Point:

Date: _____ Text: _____
Observations:

Reading Teaching Point:

Language Teaching Point:

Date: _____ Text: _____
Observations:

Reading Teaching Point:

Language Teaching Point:

Date: _____ Text: _____
Observations:

Reading Teaching Point:

Language Teaching Point:

Date: _____ Text: _____
Observations:

Reading Teaching Point:

Language Teaching Point:

Date: _____ Text: _____
Observations:

Reading Teaching Point:

Language Teaching Point:

Date: _____ Text: _____
Observations:

Reading Teaching Point:

Language Teaching Point:

Writing and Language Conference Notes for _____

Date: _____ Type of Writing: _____ Observations: Writing Teaching Point: Language Teaching Point:	Date: _____ Type of Writing: _____ Observations: Writing Teaching Point: Language Teaching Point:
Date: _____ Type of Writing: _____ Observations: Writing Teaching Point: Language Teaching Point:	Date: _____ Type of Writing: _____ Observations: Writing Teaching Point: Language Teaching Point:
Date: _____ Type of Writing: _____ Observations: Writing Teaching Point: Language Teaching Point:	Date: _____ Type of Writing: _____ Observations: Writing Teaching Point: Language Teaching Point:
Date: _____ Type of Writing: _____ Observations: Writing Teaching Point: Language Teaching Point:	Date: _____ Type of Writing: _____ Observations: Writing Teaching Point: Language Teaching Point:

Connections between the content arreas:

Language focus:

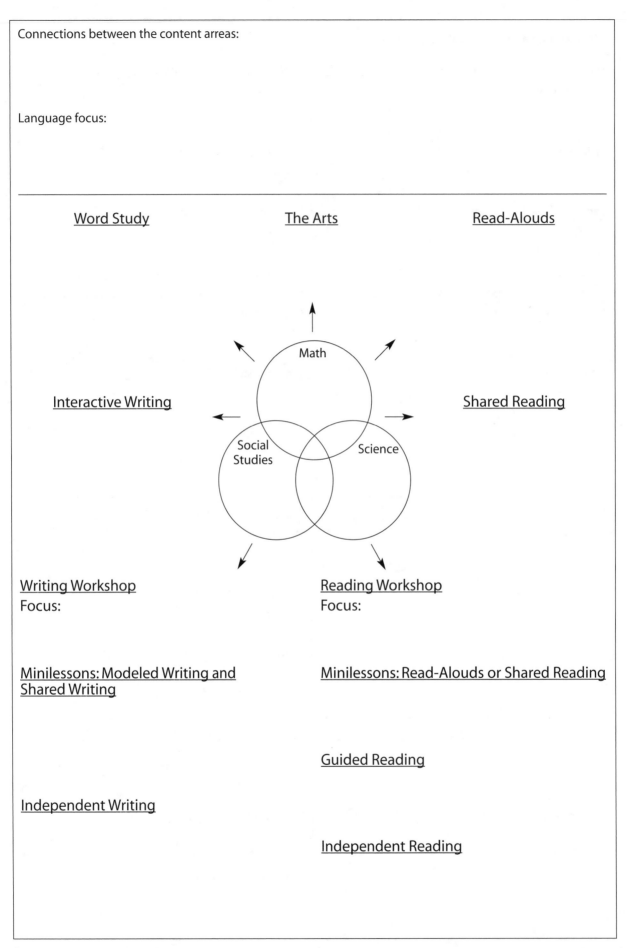

Word Study   The Arts   Read-Alouds

Interactive Writing   Shared Reading

Writing Workshop   Reading Workshop
Focus: Focus:

Minilessons: Modeled Writing and   Minilessons: Read-Alouds or Shared Reading
Shared Writing

                                        Guided Reading

Independent Writing

                                        Independent Reading

Developing Language Through Reading Comprehension Strategies

Making Predictions

Questions

- To make a prediction
  - What do you think will happen next?
  - What do you think is going to happen?
  - What do you think the book is going to be about?
  - Where/when do you think _____ is going to _____?
  - How do you think the story will end?
- To support a prediction with text evidence
  - Why do you think _____ is going to _____?
  - What makes you think that will happen?
- To revise a prediction
  - *Now* what do you think is going to happen?

Prompts for Responses

- To make a prediction and support it
  - I think _____ is/are going to _____ because _____.
  - I think _____ will _____ because _____.
- To revise a prediction
  - At first I thought _____, but now I think _____ because _____.
  - Before I thought _____ was/were going to _____, but now I think _____.
  - Before I thought _____ would _____, but now I think _____.

Language Structures

- Future tenses
  - subject + *to be* + *going to* + infinitive verb: I think *they are going to clean* the river.
  - subject + *will* + infinitive verb: I think *they will clean* the river.
- Develop a list of action verbs so ELLs have language to express what they think will happen.
- Point out the use of these irregular verbs in the present and past tenses:
  - *is/was*
  - *are/were*
  - *will/would*
  - *think/thought*
- Point out how to use transition words to show a change in ideas: *before, at first, but then, now, in the end*

Involving ELLs at Every English Proficiency Level in Making Predictions

Examples are with the nonfiction book *A River Ran Wild* (Cherry 2002).

Level 1

Ask a predicting question to get a yes-or-no response.

- Question: "Do you think the people [pointing to the townspeople in the picture] will clean the river [acting out cleaning garbage from the river]? Yes [thumbs-up] or no [thumbs-down]?" Point to the next pages, which are still hidden from view, to clarify that you are asking about something that will happen later in the book.

- Response: Student either gives the thumbs-up or thumbs-down sign or says the word *yes* or *no*. Then have other students expand on the prediction, or have the Level 1 ELL expand on her idea in the L1 and have another student translate if possible.

Ask a predicting question by giving an either-or choice.

- Question: [Pointing to the next pages, which are still hidden from view] "Do you think the river is going to be *clean* or *dirty*?" You can write the two words on the board and act them out or point to pictures in the book that illustrate each word.

- Response: Student either points to the word or says the word. Then have other students expand on the prediction, or have the Level 1 ELL expand on his idea in the L1 and have another student translate if possible.

Level 2

Ask a predicting question and expect a short phrase or sentence as a response. Students will rely heavily on the language prompts to structure their responses.

- Question: "What do you think is going to happen to the river [pointing to the river]?"

- Response: [With teacher guidance to use the prompt] "I think the people are going to . . ." The student may need to finish the sentence in the L1 or get help from the teacher or classmates to finish the sentence in the L2.

Level 3

Ask a predicting question and expect a complete sentence as a response. Students will rely less on the language prompts but may need help using academic vocabulary. They may also make common grammatical errors.

- Question: "What do you think will happen next?"

- Response: "I think the people is going to clean up the river because now is so dirty."

Levels 4–5

Ask a predicting question and expect a complete sentence as a response. These ELLs have a broader academic vocabulary base and more complex grammatical structures to draw upon, so they can express more complete justifications for their predictions (at an age-appropriate level). Questions for these ELLs can either be the same as for earlier levels or include more academic vocabulary.

- Question: "What do you think will happen now that the colonists have arrived on the Native Americans' land?" (Or more simply "What do you think will happen next?")

- Response: "I think the colonists are going to try to take the land from the Native Americans, because in another book I saw that the colonists didn't respect the Native Americans. They usually took their land after a while."

Making Connections to Self, Text, and World

Questions

- What does this page/paragraph/chapter/section/book make you think of? Why?
- What does this remind you of? Why?
- Connection to self
  - Does this remind you of something in your life?
  - Have you ever _____? (comparing own experience to something in the book)
- Connection to world
  - Does this remind you of something else you know?
- Connection to text
  - Does this remind you of another text?

Prompts for Responses

- This makes/made me think of _____ because _____.
- This reminds/reminded me of _____ because _____.
- When I read _____, it reminded me of _____.
- I've also _____. (comparing own experience to something in the book)
- _____ is like what we read in _____ because _____.
- _____ is different from _____ because _____.

Language Structures

- Point out the use of these verbs in the present and past tenses. The present-tense verbs are in the third person (ending in *s*), which can be difficult for ELLs to include in their language use.
  - *makes/made*
  - *reminds/reminded*
- Develop ELLs' ability to tell about something they've done, seen, or learned in the past, using verbs in the past tense: "This reminds me of one time when I looked out my window and I saw that it was snowing, just like Peter. I was so excited to go to the park with my dad."
- Make an ongoing chart of verbs comparing the present- and past-tense forms to help ELLs understand how to correctly use verbs in each tense. You can have one chart for regular verbs and another for irregular verbs.
- Present perfect:
  - Subject + *has/have* + participle: "*I have seen* a big snowstorm too, just like Peter" or "*I've seen* a big snowstorm too, just like Peter."

Involving ELLs at Every English Proficiency Level in Making Connections

Examples are with the fictional book *The Snowy Day* (Keats 1976).

Level 1

Ask a making-connections question to get a yes-or-no response.

- Question: "Here Peter is playing in the snow [point to picture and act out]. Do you like the snow? [Point from the picture to the student, giving the thumbs-up and thumbs-down signals.]
- Response: Student either gives the thumbs-up or thumbs-down sign or says the word *yes* or *no*. You can follow this up by asking other students if they have any personal connections to what's happening in the text. Or have the Level 1 ELL expand on his idea in the L1 and have another student translate if possible.

Ask a making-connections question by giving an either-or choice.

- Question: "On this page Peter sees the snow! Does this remind you of *winter* or *summer*?" You can write the two words on the board and act them out.
- Response: Student either points to the word or says the word.

Level 2

Ask a making-connections question and expect a short phrase or sentence as a response.

- Question: "What does this part remind you of?" Point to Peter playing in the snow.
- Response: "I like play in the snow." These ELLs will need teacher support if you would like them to use one of the language prompts to respond.

Level 3

Ask a making-connections question and expect a complete sentence as a response. These students will rely less on the language prompts but may need help with academic vocabulary. They may also make common grammatical errors.

- Question: "What does this part remind you of?"
- Response: "This remind me of that day when it snowed. I was all day playing with my brother."

Levels 4–5

Ask a making-connections question and expect a complete sentence as a response. These ELLs have a broader academic vocabulary base and more complex grammatical structures to draw upon, so they can express more detailed connections (at an age-appropriate level). Questions for these ELLs can either be the same or include more academic vocabulary.

- Question: "Does this book remind you of anything else you've read?"
- Response: "It reminds me of the book *The Mitten* because they're all in the snow. But Peter wants to be outside, and in *The Mitten* the animals all want to be inside the mitten."

Monitoring for Sense (Understanding Main Idea and Details, Sequencing, Determining Word Meaning, Cause and Effect, Rereading)

Questions/Prompts

- Understanding main idea and details
  - What is this story/section/text all about? (the main idea)
  - What happened here/on this page/in this part?
  - What details do we know about (the main idea)?
  - When . . . ? Where . . . ? Why . . . ? Who . . . ? How . . . ? How many . . . ? (to check for comprehension of details from the text)
  - When did this story/event take place?
  - Reread that sentence/page/part.
- Sequencing
  - What happened first/next/in the end?
  - What happened before/after ___?
  - Retell this story/chapter/section across your fingers.
- Cause and effect
  - What happened when _____?
  - What caused _____?
  - Why did _____?
  - What made _____?
- Determining word meaning
  - What does the word _____ mean?

Responses

- Understanding main idea and details
  - This story/section/text is all about _____.
  - I learned that _____.
  - In this part, (subject) (verb) . . .
- Sequencing
  - First . . . then . . . next . . . finally . . . lastly . . .
  - Before . . . after . . .
- Cause and effect
  - (Second event) because (first event).
  - (First event) so (second event).
  - Since (first event) (second event).
  - Due to (first event), (second event).
  - (First event) which led to (second event).
  - (First event) For this reason/as a result, (second event).
- Determining word meaning
  - I think _____ means _____.

Language Structures

- Understanding details
  - ELLs need to know the difference between question words when you ask them about details from the text: *who, what, where, when, why, how.*
  - ELLs need to understand if a question is in the present tense or the past tense: Why *do* immigrants *move* to another country? (present tense); What *did* the immigrants *see* when they *arrived* to Ellis Island? (past tense); *Did* everyone *pass* the tests in Ellis Island? Why? (past tense). In these examples, the auxiliary verb *do* expresses the present tense and *did* expresses the past tense. The main verb, such as *move, see,* or *pass,* doesn't change tense.
  - ELLs need to know how to respond to questions using the present tense or the past tense. Make an ongoing chart of verbs comparing the present- and past-tense forms. You can have one chart for regular verbs and another for irregular verbs.
  - Show ELLs how to change regular verbs from the present to past tense by adding the –ed suffix (*work/worked*).
  - Point out the formation of irregular past-tense verbs (*see/saw*).
- Sequencing
  - ELLs need to know how to use a variety of transition words: *first, next, then, later, finally, lastly, before, after, until, in the beginning/middle/ end.*
  - ELLs need to use the present tense or past tense, depending on the text.
- Cause and effect
  - For explaining cause and effect, ELLs need to know how to use a variety of conjunctions: *because, so, since, as a result, due to, therefore, for this reason, consequently, thus*
  - ELLs need to use the present tense or the past tense, depending on the text.

Involving ELLs at Every English Proficiency Level in Monitoring for Sense

Examples are with the nonfiction book *Immigrant Kids* (Freedman 1995).

Level 1

Ask a sense-monitoring question to get a yes-or-no response.

- Question: "Do these children have to work? [Point to picture and act out.] Yes or no?" Show thumbs-up and thumbs-down.

- Response: Student either gives the thumbs-up or thumbs-down sign or says the word *yes* or *no*. Then have other students expand on this idea by explaining details they've learned from the text, or have the Level 1 ELL expand on her idea in the L1 and have another student translate if possible.

Ask a sense-monitoring question by giving an either-or choice.

- Question: "Is this immigrant boy in *school* or at a *factory*?" You can write the two words on the board and act them out, point to pictures in the book, or draw a quick sketch.

- Response: Student either points to the word or says the word. Then have other students expand on this idea by explaining details they've learned from the text, or have the Level 1 ELL expand on his idea in the L1 and have another student translate if possible.

Level 2

Ask a sense-monitoring question and expect a short phrase or sentence as a response. Most ELLs at this level are not yet able to use the past tense.

- Question: "Why were these children working in the factories?"
- Response: "Because they family need money."

Level 3

Ask a sense-monitoring question and expect a complete sentence as a response. ELLs at this level are typically able to use the past tense in responses but may have difficulty forming questions in the past tense or using irregular past-tense verbs.

- Question: "How did immigrant children survive in New York?"
- Response: "They helped their family get money and they worked a lot." You may want to have the student expand on this answer by helping her add more academic vocabulary, such as the types of jobs they had and places where immigrant children worked.

Levels 4–5

Ask a sense-monitoring question and expect a complete sentence as a response. ELLs at this level can typically ask questions and respond in the past tense, both with regular and irregular verbs. However, listen for any difficulties they might still have with these grammatical structures. Expect these ELLs to use a higher level of academic vocabulary, and if they don't, prompt them to expand on their answers.

- Question: "How did immigrating to New York affect these children?"

- Response: "When the families came to New York they thought they would have a better life, but what really happened is they had a lot of problems." [Prompt: "What kind of problems did they have?"] "Well, the tenement houses where they lived were really dirty and dangerous. They had to work a lot, and there was also a lot of diseases."

Inferring (Drawing Conclusions, Interpreting, Understanding Figurative Language, Author's Intent)

Questions

- Drawing conclusions/interpreting
  - What does this make you think?
  - Why do you think _____ happened? (based on clues from the text)
  - Why do you think _____ did _____? (based on clues from the text)
  - Where could this story be taking place? (based on clues from the text or pictures)
  - How do you think _____ is feeling? (based on clues from the text or pictures)
- Author's intent
  - Why did the author write this?
  - When it says _____, what is the author trying to tell us?
  - What is the author trying to show us?
- Understanding figurative language
  - When it says _____, what does that really mean?

Responses

- Drawing conclusions/interpreting
  - This makes me think that _____ because _____.
  - When I read/saw _____, it made me think that _____.
  - I think _____ happened because _____.
  - I think the story could take place in _____ because _____.
  - I think _____ is feeling _____ because _____.
- Author's intent
  - I think the author is trying to tell us _____.
  - I think the author is showing us _____ because _____.
- Understanding figurative language
  - I think _____ means that _____ because _____.

Language Structures

- ELLs need to use the present progressive tense to infer ideas from the text.
  - Present tense of verb *to be* + present participle (ending with *-ing*): The author *is trying* to *tell* us that _____; The author *is showing* us that _____; I think the character *is feeling* _____.
- ELLs may need to use a combination of the present tense and the past tense to express an inference. For example, "This makes me think that Carlos' parents knew about his problem the whole time, but they wanted him to learn a lesson." (It starts in the present tense but switches to the past tense. Changing verb tenses within a sentence can be difficult for ELLs.)
- Make an ongoing chart of verbs comparing the present- and past-tense forms. You can have one chart for regular verbs and another for irregular verbs.
- Brainstorm a list of adjectives so ELLs can make inferences about how the characters are feeling, for example: happy, excited, thrilled, sad, worried, concerned, disappointed, frustrated.
- Point out to ELLs how they should use the third person in the present tense (with an *s* or *es* at the end of the verb): I think _____ *means* _____; This *makes* me *think* _____.

Involving ELLs at Every English Proficiency Level in Inferring

Examples are with the fictional book *Carlos and the Squash Plant / Carlos y la planta de calabaza* (Stevens 1999).

Level 1

Ask an inferring question to get a yes-or-no response.

- Question: "Could this story take place in New York City? [Point to picture of the farmland, with a puzzled look, repeating 'New York City?'] Yes or no?" Give the thumbs-up and thumbs-down signs.

- Response: Student either gives the thumbs-up or thumbs-down sign or says the word *yes* or *no*. Then have other ELLs elaborate on what clues from the text help them infer when and where the story takes place. Or have the Level 1 ELL expand on his idea in the L1 and have another student translate if possible.

Ask an inferring question by giving them an either-or choice.

- Question: "Do you think Carlos is feeling *excited* or *scared*?" You can write the two words on the board and act them out.

- Response: Student either points to the word or says the word. Other ELLs can then elaborate on why they think Carlos is feeling that way, based on what's happening in the text and what they see in the illustrations. Or have the Level 1 ELL expand on her idea in the L1 and have another student translate if possible.

Level 2

Ask an inferring question and expect a short phrase or sentence as a response. ELLs at this level are able to use the present progressive tense but will probably need support to use the complete language prompts.

- Question: "How do you think Carlos is feeling in this part of the story?"

- Response: [With support to start by using the language prompt] "I think Carlos is feeling sad." [Prompt: "Why?"] "Because he have a plant in he ear."

Level 3

Ask an inferring question and expect a complete sentence as a response. ELLs at this level are developmentally ready to use the past tense in their responses, although they may not be correctly using irregular past-tense verbs.

- Question: "Why do you think Carlos lied to his mom about the squash plant growing in his ear?"

- Response: "I think he lied because he was afraid of what his mom say."

Levels 4–5

Ask an inferring question and expect a complete sentence as a response. Expect these ELLs to use a higher level of academic vocabulary and expanded details appropriate for their age level. If they don't, prompt them to expand on their answers.

- Question: "What do you think the author is trying to tell us?"

- Response: "I think the author is telling us that it's important to listen to your parents." [Prompt: "How did the author show you this?"] "The author showed that if Carlos had listened to his mom he wouldn't have the problem with the plant."

Visualizing

Questions

- When you read _____, what did you visualize/see in your mind?
- What do you see in this part? Hear? Smell? Taste?
- What picture did you get in your mind?
- What do you picture the character doing?
- What did you visualize when you read "_____"?

Prompts for Responses

- In this part I visualized/saw _____. (fill in with sensory images relating to the characters, actions, events)
- I can see/hear/smell/taste _____.
- When I read _____, I could see/hear/smell/taste _____.
- In this part/story/text I can visualize/see _____.

Language Structures

- Brainstorm an ongoing list of adjectives for colors, sizes, shapes, tastes, smells, sounds.
- Brainstorm an ongoing list of action verbs so ELLs can use them to describe what they imagine is happening in the text.
- Brainstorm an ongoing list of adverbs that describe the action (*slowly, quickly, carefully, cautiously, happily, angrily*).
- Using the present participle (ending in *-ing*) to indicate action happening in the moment. For example: "I can picture the bat *flying* with wings that look like big hands and *searching* for insects to eat."

Involving ELLs at Every English Proficiency Level in Visualizing

Examples are with the nonfiction book *Amazing Bats* (Simon 2005).

Level 1

Ask a visualizing question to get a yes-or-no response.

- Question: "Do you see the bats *migrating*? [Point to picture of the group of bats flying together.] Yes or no?" Give the thumbs-up and thumbs-down signs.

- Response: Student either gives the thumbs-up or thumbs-down sign or says the word *yes* or *no*. Then have other ELLs elaborate on what the word *migrating* means, why animals migrate, and what they envision happening when birds migrate. Or have the Level 1 ELL expand on her idea in the L1 and have another student translate if possible.

Ask a visualizing question by giving an either-or choice.

- Question: "Do you see the bat eating a *plant* or an *insect*?" Point to the object in the book, and then write the two words on the board along with a quick sketch of each one. The student will have to look closely at the book, because the insect looks a little like a plant!

- Response: Student either points to the word or says the word.

Level 2

Ask a visualizing question and expect a short phrase or sentence as a response. ELLs at this level can use basic adjectives and common verbs in the present and present progressive tense to explain what they visualize. They will probably need guidance to use the language prompts.

- Question: "What do you see in your mind after reading this first page?"
- Response: "I see the bat is flying." [Prompt: "What does the bat look like?"] "He have big wings."

Level 3

Ask a visualizing question and expect a complete sentence as a response. ELLs at this level can elaborate by using more adjectives and verbs to express what they picture happening.

- Question: "When you read this page, what did you see happening in your mind?"
- Response: "I saw the bats hanging and they're small because they don't eat food." You could help the student use the academic word *hibernating* to further describe what's happening.

Levels 4–5

Ask a visualizing question and expect a complete sentence as a response. Expect these ELLs to use a higher level of academic vocabulary, and if they don't, prompt them to expand on their answers.

- Question: "What do you visualize the bats doing in this part?"
- Response: "I visualize the bats flying all over the place in the dark, looking for six hundred bugs to eat in an hour. And I can hear them grabbing bugs with their teeth and eating them quick so they can find more bugs to eat."

Questioning

Questions

- Ask questions before reading.
  - What questions do you have before reading this text?
- Ask questions during reading.
  - What are you wondering about as you read this part of the text?
  - What do you think the answer could be? (based on the text and student's background knowledge)
  - Have you found the answer to your question? (as the student continues reading)
- Ask questions after reading.
  - Do you have more questions now that you've finished the text?
  - What are you still wondering?
  - Did the text answer any of the questions you had?

Prompts for Responses

- I wonder _____.
- Who . . . ? What . . . ? Where . . . ? When . . . ? Why . . . ? How . . .?
- What does _____ mean? (determining word meaning)

For yes-or-no questions:

- Do . . . ? Does . . . ? Did . . . ? Is . . . ? Are . . . ? Was . . . ? Were . . . ? Can . . . ? Could . . . ? Will . . . ?

Language Structures

- Many questions start with questions words: *who, what, where, when, why,* and *how.*
- These question words are followed by an auxiliary verb such as *do, does, did, is, are, was, were, can, could,* and *will.*
  - *"Why did* Sadako go to the hospital?"
  - The auxiliary verb indicates what tense the question is in. In this question the auxiliary verb *did* lets you know that the question is in the past tense.
- Yes-or-no questions don't start with a question word; they start with an auxiliary verb.
  - *"Did* Sadako finish all of the paper cranes?"

ELLs need to know the meaning of the different questions words and auxiliary verbs, and they need to know how to form questions in different tenses. Here are some of the most common tenses used to ask questions about a text.

- Present-tense questions
  - "Where *does* Sadako *live?*"
  - "*Does* Sadako *live* in Japan?"

Here the auxiliary verb *does* indicates that the question is in the present tense. The main verb, *live,* does not change tense (not "Where does Sadako *lives?*").

- Present-progressive-tense questions
  - "Why *is* Sadako *feeling* sick?"

Here the auxiliary verb *is* is in the present tense. The subject, *Sadako,* goes in between the word *is* and the present participle, *feeling* (not "Why Sadako is feeling sick?").

- Past-tense questions
  - "How *did* Sadako *get* sick?"

Here the auxiliary verb *did* indicates that the question is in the past tense. The main verb, *get,* does not change tense (not "How did Sadako *got* sick?").

- Future-tense questions
  - "*Will* Sadako *survive?*"
  - "*Is* Sadako *going to survive?*"

Here the auxiliary verb *will* indicates that the question is in the future tense, and the main verb *survive* does not change tense. The subject, *Sadako,* goes in between the word *will* and the main verb *survive* (not "Sadako will survive?"). In the second example, the future form *is going to* is also separated by the subject, *Sadako.*

Involving ELLs at Every English Proficiency Level in Questioning

Examples are with the nonfiction book *Sadako and the Thousand Paper Cranes* (Coerr 1977).

Level 1

You can ask these ELLs specific either-or and yes-or-no questions about the text, since they're not developmentally ready to verbalize their own questions in English. You can also have them share questions they have in their native language and have another student translate, if possible.

- Question: "Did Sadako make *one thousand* paper cranes? [Point to the illustration in the chapter book and write the number *1,000* on the board.] Yes or no?" Give the thumbs-up and thumbs-down signs.

- Response: Student either gives the thumbs-up or thumbs-down sign or says the word *yes* or *no*. Then have other ELLs share questions they have at this particular point in the text.

Level 2

Students at this level are typically able to use the present tense and present progressive tense. However, asking questions in these tenses is grammatically more complex. You will need to model for these ELLs how to correctly form questions in English, since the word order changes. For example, the statement "Sadako *is getting* better" changes in the question form to "*Is* Sadako *getting* better?" Level 2 ELLs will need significant support to form questions using the different question words and auxiliary verbs.

Level 3

Students at this level are developmentally able to use the past tense, but asking their own questions in the past tense is grammatically more complex and is more typical of a Level 4 proficiency. You will need to model for them how to correctly form questions they have in the past tense in English, and provide support as they form their own questions. Being able to correctly ask questions in the future tense is typical for Level 3 ELLs.

Levels 4–5

At these advanced proficiency levels, you can expect ELLs to be able to form their own questions about the text in a variety of tenses, including the present, past, and future tenses. Be on the lookout for gaps in these students' knowledge about correctly forming questions. They may still make common errors, such as using an incorrect word order or changing the tense of verbs instead of using the auxiliary verbs to indicate the tense.

Using Graphic Organizers with ELLs

I've found that using just a few basic graphic organizers for multiple purposes is very effective with ELLs. Focusing on a limited number of graphic organizers helps ELLs better understand how they can express information and ideas through the organizers and use them independently. Here I provide reproducibles of the main graphic organizers I mention in the book and a list of some of the ways I rely on them when working with ELLs. Of course, the possibilities for each graphic organizer are endless. Most of these graphic organizers are also easy for ELLs to create on their own, so when age appropriate I often have my ELLs draw them in their notebooks or on paper to express their thinking and learning.

Web with Language Structures

- Brainstorm nouns, verbs, adjectives, adverbs, or prepositional phrases that are related to a particular word (see the webs in Figure 5–6, page 149). Put sample language structures below the web so ELLs know how to combine the parts of speech into sentences.

- Brainstorm vocabulary words related to a social studies, science, or math topic. Put sample language structures below the web so your ELLs know how to use the vocabulary in a sentence. For example, if you make a web for the topic of community, with the names of people, places, and things found there, you can write language structures such as these:

  - My community has a/an _____.

  - My community doesn't have a/an _____.

  - There is a _____ in my community. (or with a contraction: *There's*)

  - There are _____ in my community.

- Brainstorm synonyms and antonyms for a particular word. You can have synonyms on the top half of the web and antonyms on the bottom half. You can also color-code them so the synonyms are green and the antonyms are red, for example, to make the difference clear for your ELLs. Put sample language structures below the web so your ELLs know how to use those synonyms and antonyms in a sentence. Following are examples for the word *trustworthy*:

- The web of synonyms could include *dependable, reliable, truthful, responsible,* and *honest.*

- The web of antonyms could include *undependable, unreliable, untruthful, irresponsible,* and *dishonest.*

- This particular example also helps ELLs see how adjectives can become negative using prefixes like *un, ir,* and *dis.*

- You can write language structures below the web such as "I am _____ because _____." You can include variations of this structure by starting it with *you are, he is, she is, we are,* or *they are.* You can also show the class how to turn these into contractions: *I'm, you're, he's, she's, we're, they're.*

- Brainstorm examples of a particular expression or idiom. The examples you put in the web should be complete sentences so your ELLs can see exactly how the expression or idiom is used in context. Here are some examples for *once in a blue moon*:

  - I go to the movies once in a blue moon.

  - We visit our family in Florida once in a blue moon.

  - This happens only once in a blue moon!

- Record what the class knows about a particular content-area topic, or record what the class has learned about the topic. The accompanying language structure could be "I already know that _____,", "I (we) learned that _____.", or "One thing I (we) learned about _____ is _____."

T-Chart

- Sort content-area vocabulary words into two different categories (see Chapter 5 for descriptions of open and closed word sorts).

- Sort words into two different categories based on spelling patterns (such as short *a* versus short *o*) to help ELLs recognize the difference between them (Bear et al. 2007).

- Compare two homonyms (words that have the same pronunciation and spelling but have multiple meanings). You can list multiple examples on each side of the T-chart. This helps ELLs expand their vocabulary base because they may know one of the word meanings but not the other. For example:

  - *bright/bright*: The sun is *bright.* / The students in our class are *bright.*

  - *blue/blue*: My favorite color is *blue.* / I'm feeling *blue* because my best friend moved to another city.

- Compare two homophones (words that have the same pronunciation but different spellings and meanings). You can list multiple examples on each side of the T-chart. This makes the different word meanings explicit for ELLs and helps them connect the correct spelling to each word meaning. For example:

  - *buy/by*: I need to *buy* groceries today. / This bilingual book is written *by* Estephani.

  - *know/no*: I *know* a lot about horses. / I have *no* idea what the answer is.

- Compare how a word is used when the part of speech changes. This helps ELLs recognize root words and see how root words can help them understand related words. This expands ELLs' vocabulary base and improves their reading comprehension. For example:

  - *admire/admiration* (verb/noun): I *admire* my mom because she works very hard to support our family. / I feel *admiration* for my mom and her hard work.

- Record thinking about reading (adapted from Harvey and Goudvis 2000). You can model these T-charts in your reading minilessons and, if age appropriate, have your ELLs use them in their reading notebooks to keep track of their thinking as they read. Ultimately I teach my ELLs how to record a combination of these strategies because readers don't use just one comprehension strategy to understand a text, but rather a combination of strategies.

  - Making predictions: what I think will happen / what really happened

  - Making connections: text / what this reminds me of; text / what I think

  - Questioning: questions / facts; what I learned / what I wonder; questions / what I think (see Figures 5–4 and 5–5 for examples from ELLs' notebooks)

  - Determining word meaning: tricky word / its meaning; tricky word / what I think it means

  - Visualizing: text / what I see in my mind

  - Determining importance: main idea / details; important event / details

  - Inferring: text / what the author is trying to say; text / this makes me think that

- Compare two different content-area concepts. For example:

  - Math: concave shapes and convex shapes (can draw examples)

  - Science: objects that conduct electricity and objects that don't (write or draw examples)

  - Social studies: rural and urban (write or draw examples of each area)

Three-Column Chart

- Sort content-area vocabulary words into three different categories (see Chapter 5 for descriptions of open and closed word sorts).

- Sort words into three categories based on spelling patterns (such as long *a*: *ai*, *ay*, *a_e*) to help ELLs recognize the difference between them (Bear et al. 2007).

- Give a list of examples to compare homophones with three different meanings. You can list multiple examples in each column of the chart. This makes the different word meanings explicit for ELLs and helps them connect the correct spelling to each word meaning. For example:

  - *there/their/they're*: Look over *there*! / *Their* prediction was correct. / *They're* working together on the project.

  - *to/two/too*: Please come *to* school on time. / I speak *two* languages. / This book is *too* easy.

- Give examples of how a word is used when the part of speech changes. This helps ELLs see the relationship between words in all of their forms and expands their vocabulary base.
  - *free/freedom/to free* (adjective/noun/verb): Before the Civil War in the United States, slaves were not *free*. / Slaves wanted *freedom*, and many tried to escape on the Underground Railroad. / The Civil War *freed* slaves in the United States.
- K-W-L chart: what I know / what I want to know / what I learned
- Compare three different content-area topics. For example:
  - Math: circles, squares, and triangles (can draw examples)
  - Science: solid, liquid, and gas (can draw or write examples)
  - Social studies: executive branch, legislative branch, and judicial branch (can write or draw examples)

Boxes and Bullets

- Record the main idea of a text and supporting details.
- Record the theme of a text and examples of that theme.
- Create an outline of a nonfiction text by keeping track of the key topics and important details.
- Plan expository or persuasive writing by recording the main topic and subtopics, or the subtopic and supporting details (see "Writing Workshop Minilesson" in Chapter 6).

Venn Diagram

- Compare and contrast two content-area concepts.
- Compare and contrast two different characters or people.
- Compare and contrast two different events.
- Compare and contrast two different vocabulary words.

Name: Date:

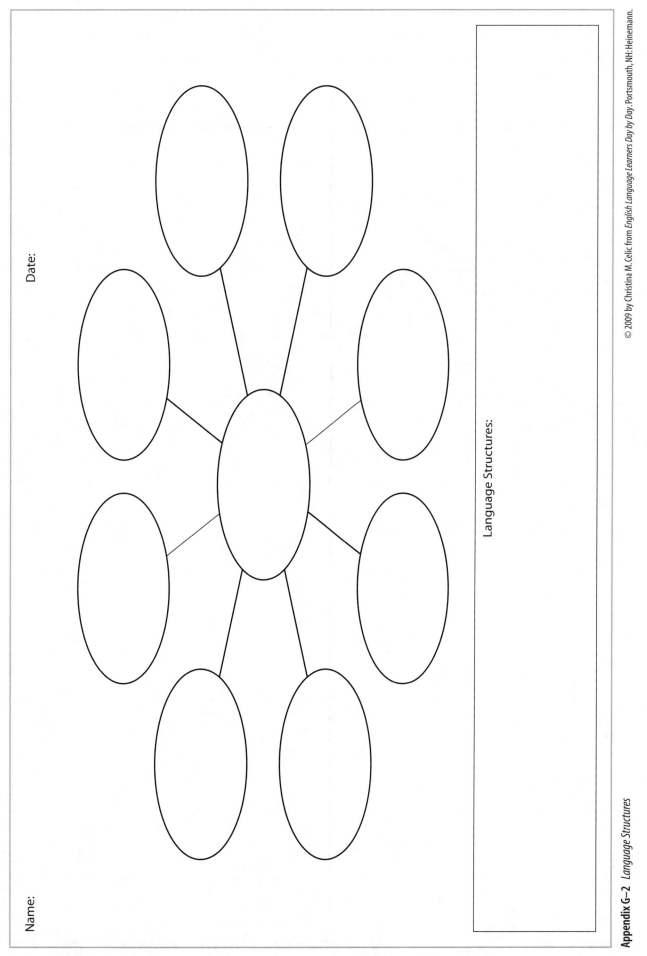

Language Structures:

Appendix G–2 *Language Structures*

Name: _____   Date: _____

Text or topic: _____

Name: _____ Date: _____

Text or topic: _____

Name: _____ Date: _____

Text: _____

```
┌─────────────────────────────────────────────────────────┐
│                                                           │
│                                                           │
│                                                           │
│                                                           │
└─────────────────────────────────────────────────────────┘
```

● _____

● _____

● _____

● _____

● _____

```
┌─────────────────────────────────────────────────────────┐
│                                                           │
│                                                           │
│                                                           │
│                                                           │
└─────────────────────────────────────────────────────────┘
```

● _____

● _____

● _____

● _____

● _____

Name: _____

Date: _____

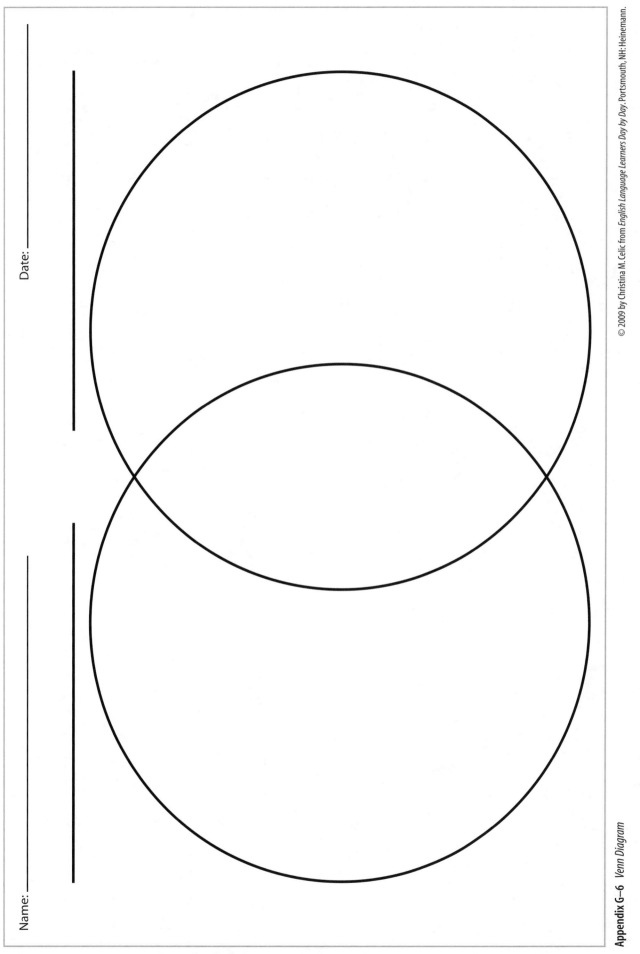

Appendix G–6 *Venn Diagram*

Study Group Discussion Questions

English Language Learners Day by Day, K–6: A Complete Guide to Literacy, Content-Area, and Language Instruction

by Christina M. Celic

Chapter 1

Setting Up a Classroom for English Language Learners

1. What do you feel are the most important aspects of classroom organization for helping ELLs develop linguistically and academically?

2. Consider each area of your classroom as a place for learning both language and content. Discuss what you already have in place that's supportive of ELLs. What can be altered to make it more supportive? You can use Chart 1 provided on page 228 to organize your thoughts.

   Pre-service teachers: How do you envision your classroom looking? Discuss what you could have in place in each area of the room to support your ELLs. You can use Chart 2 provided on page 229 to organize your thoughts.

3. Reflect on the potential changes that can be made to your classroom. Which ones are your top priorities for implementing? Are there any that could be grade-level or school-wide initiatives? Are there ways you can collaborate with colleagues to maximize time and effort?

   Pre-service teachers: Discuss your ideas for setting up a classroom. If you don't have the time and/or resources to have everything in place by the first day of school, what would your top priorities be?

4. As you consider the resources in your classroom library, discuss how you can provide multicultural and native language texts for ELLs in both the leveled and non-leveled book baskets.

5. Celic suggests ways to group ELLs based on their English proficiency levels. Reflect on how you currently seat your ELLs. Discuss the reasons for this placement and the degree of support it offers ELLs, both linguistically and academically.

6. This chapter provides examples of websites and computer programs that have supportive features for ELLs. Investigate other websites and programs you can incorporate in your instruction that have these features, as well as other ways you can use technology with ELLs.

Chapter 2

Getting Ready to Teach English Language Learners from Day One

1. What do you currently do to get to know your ELLs' abilities and needs before the school year begins? During the first weeks of school?

2. How can you get an understanding of your ELLs' abilities and needs, both academic and linguistic, in a timely way? You can use Chart 3 provided on page 230 to plan what you would like to do before the school year begins, as well as when you can fit in different assessments and instructional activities during the first weeks of school.

3. How can the idea of a whole-class profile, shown in Figures 2–1 and 2–2 (pages 29 and 30), be adapted to your classroom and/or school? What categories of important information would you include?

4. What differentiates each English proficiency level outlined in Figure 2–6 (page 40)? Think about ELLs you have worked with. Approximately where are they on this developmental chart?

5. Celic references Cappellini's work on the language structures that are typically developed at each English proficiency level. Discuss these language structures, outlined in Figure 2–6 (page 40), focusing in particular on those that are less familiar to you. How does this chart help you understand your ELLs' linguistic abilities and their developmental needs?

6. How is the development of conversational language proficiency different from academic language proficiency? What implications does this have for ELLs in the primary grades versus the upper grades? What implications does this have for former ELLs who are no longer receiving language services?

7. Writing samples are one indicator of an ELL's current English proficiency level. Using Figure 2–6, analyze several different writing samples from your ELLs.

   • What are the characteristic features of this ELL's writing in English?

   • What language structures are secure? What language structures are developing?

   • Based on this information, what English proficiency level does this one sample indicate? (Keep in mind that one sample of writing or speaking typically doesn't give a complete view of an ELL's capabilities.)

   • What does this writing sample tell you about the child's strengths as a writer? How can you support the child to continue developing as a writer?

   Alternatively, record an ELL's conversation with a teacher or with a peer during a learning activity. Do a similar analysis of the child's English proficiency level.

8. Using the Family Survey in Appendix C as a starting point, consider ways you can encourage your ELLs' families to be involved at school, including options for families who aren't proficient in English.

Chapter 3

Classroom Management with English Language Learners

1. Why is consistent classroom management particularly essential for ELLs?

2. Reflecting on what you've read in this chapter, are there any ways you can make your current daily schedule more supportive of ELLs?

3. What is the purpose of each balanced literacy component? How do they allow for a gradual release of responsibility from the teacher to the student?

4. Using the sample daily schedules in Figures 3–1 and 3–2 (pages 68 and 69), or your own daily schedule, list the routines that take place during each instructional component and during transition times. Be as specific as possible. How can you make these routines clear and consistent for your ELLs?

5. Choose a typical classroom routine and role-play how you could model and practice it with a group of ELLs.

6. What can you do to ensure that your ELLs are better prepared to complete their homework assignments?

7. Reflect on the homework assignments you are currently using. Are ELLs at different English proficiency levels able to complete them? If not, how could they be modified to be more effective?

8. Using Chart 4 provided on page 231, compile a list of appropriate homework assignments you could use for each subject area at your grade level. Draw upon homework assignments you already use that are supportive of your ELLs' needs, as well as the homework examples described in this chapter for each subject area.

Chapter 4

Integrating Instruction for English Language Learners

1. In what ways are you already integrating content area instruction with literacy components? What can you do to expand integrated instruction throughout the school day?

2. Examine the yearlong scope and sequence of your grade-level curriculum for each subject area.

   - Are there ways you can reorder certain content area and literacy units of study to maximize your ability to integrate these areas of instruction?

   - Using Figures 4–1 and 4–2 (pages 98 and 99) as a model, create a potential yearlong curricular framework that allows for the maximum amount of integration.

   Pre-service teachers: Create a similar yearlong plan for integrated instruction by identifying the programs that are used for teaching literacy and the content areas in your district. Focus on the specific units of study these programs include.

3. Choose a particular period of time in the school year and plan how you can integrate those specific content area and literacy units of study. You can use the blank planning template in Appendix E as a guide.

4. How can you maximize limited resources when integrating instruction by using them for multiple purposes?

5. Some balanced literacy components, such as shared reading, shared writing, and interactive writing, aren't commonly used in upper-grade classrooms. What are the benefits of these instructional components for ELLs? How can they be incorporated in an upper grade daily schedule in an effective, age-appropriate way?

Chapter 5

Teaching Academic Language Through the Curriculum

1. Celic provides a model for weaving language instruction throughout the school day. Compare this to the more traditional approach of teaching language during one particular block of time.

2. Share your thoughts about including language objectives for each content objective when teaching ELLs. How does this impact their ability to learn?

3. Discuss the logistics of planning for language objectives. How can you realistically incorporate this as part of your routine planning?

4. Take a content objective from a unit of study and brainstorm what your language objectives could be. Keep in mind the linguistic demands of the learning activities students will be doing and the linguistic needs of your ELLs.

5. Discuss the difference between content-specific vocabulary and general academic vocabulary. Do you agree that different teaching approaches are necessary for developing these two types of vocabulary?

6. Discuss how you could incorporate in your day-to-day instruction some of the techniques for developing language structures and vocabulary that are outlined in this chapter. From your teaching experience, are there other activities you have found to be effective for developing language with ELLs?

7. Consider what you are teaching in the content areas and in literacy at a particular time of year. Are there any language structures your ELLs would need to use across several of these subject areas? How can you model those language structures during different instructional components and how can your ELLs practice them throughout the unit of study? If you created an integrated unit of study after reading Chapter 4, you can use it as a basis for this discussion.

8. In one classroom ELLs often have a wide range of linguistic needs. Considering the examples in this chapter, how can each instructional component potentially target these different linguistic needs?

Chapter 6

Snapshots of Differentiated Instruction with English Language Learners

1. Throughout the book, Celic reflects on the *Keys to Success* that support ELLs in their academic and linguistic development. Discuss how ELLs can benefit from each one. Do you feel some are more critical to implement than others?

2. Which *Keys to Success* are you already implementing? Which would you like to use with more effectiveness in your classroom?

3. There are eight snapshots of instruction described in this chapter. Choose a snapshot and analyze the scenario. Identify the *Keys to Success* that are foundational to the instruction. (Consider doing this as a jigsaw activity where small

groups analyze different snapshots and share their thoughts with the whole group.)

4. Choose certain instructional components that you would like to focus on in your classroom. Discuss your current teaching methods and reflect on any new ideas that you gained from the snapshots in this chapter. How could you incorporate them into your teaching practice?

5. After reading *English Language Learners Day by Day*, create an action plan for implementing any ideas you would like to continue developing in your classroom, with your grade-level team, or as a school-wide initiative.

Area	What I Already Have in Place	What I Would Like to Implement for ELLs
Classroom Library/ Reading		
Math Center		
Writing Center		
Listening Center		
Science and Social Studies Centers		
Computer Center		
Desk/Table Areas		
Other		

Area	What I Would Like to Have in Place to Support ELLs
Classroom Library/ Reading	
Math Center	
Writing Center	
Listening Center	
Science and Social Studies Centers	
Computer Center	
Desk/Table Areas	
Other	

Chart 2

Before the School Year Begins:

	Date:	Date:
	Date:	Date:
	Date:	Date:
	Date:	Date:
	Date:	Date:

Chart 3 *Getting to Know Your ELLs' Abilities and Needs*

Subject Area	Effective Homework Assignments for ELLs at Different Proficiency Levels
Reading	
Writing	
Math	
Science	
Social Studies	
Word Study	

Chart 4

© 2009 by Christina M. Celic from *English Language Learners Day by Day*. Portsmouth, NH: Heinemann.

References

Professional References

Allen, Janet. 2002. *On the Same Page: Shared Reading Beyond the Primary Grades.* Portland, ME: Stenhouse.

Anderson, Carl. 2005. *Assessing Writers*. Portsmouth, NH: Heinemann.

August, Diane, María Carlo, and Margarita Calderón. 2002. *Transfer of Reading Skills from Spanish to English: A Study of Young Learners.* Washington, DC: Center for Applied Linguistics.

August, Diane, and Timothy Shanahan, eds. 2006. *Developing Literacy in Second-Language Learners: Report of the National Literacy Panel on Language-Minority Children and Youth.* Mahwah, NJ: Lawrence Erlbaum.

Batalova, Jeanne, Michael Fix, and Julie Murray. 2007. *Measures of Change: The Demography and Literacy of Adolescent English Learners.* Washington, DC: Urban Institute.

Bear, Donald R., Lori Heiman, Shane Templeton, Marcia Invernizzi, and Francine Johnston. 2007. *Words Their Way with English Learners: Word Study for Phonics, Vocabulary and Spelling Instruction.* Upper Saddle River, NJ: Pearson Merrill Prentice Hall.

Bickart, Toni S., Judy R. Jablon, and Diane Trister Dodge. 1999. *Building the Primary Classroom: A Complete Guide to Teaching and Learning.* Florence, KY: Cengage Learning.

Calderón, Margarita Espino, and Liliana Minaya-Rowe. 2003. *Designing and Implementing Two-Way Bilingual Programs: A Step-by-Step Guide for Administrators, Teachers, and Parents.* Thousand Oaks, CA: Corwin.

Calkins, Lucy. 1994. *The Art of Teaching Writing.* Portsmouth, NH: Heinemann.

———. 2001. *The Art of Teaching Reading.* New York: Longman.

Calkins, Lucy, Marjorie Martinelli, Ted Kesler, Cory Gillette, Medea McEvoy, Mary Chiarella, and M. Colleen Cruz. 2006. *Units of Study for Teaching Writing, Grades 3–5.* 7 vols. and 1 CD-ROM. Portsmouth, NH: Heinemann.

Calkins, Lucy, Leah Mermelstein, Abby Oxenhorn, Natalie Louis, Pat Bleichman, Amanda Hartman, Laurie Pessah, and Stephanie Parsons. 2003. *Units of Study for*

Primary Writing: A Yearlong Curriculum. 9 vols. and 1 CD-ROM. Portsmouth, NH: Heinemann.

Calkins, Lucy, and the Teachers College Reading and Writing Project, Columbia University. 2002. *A Field Guide to the Classroom Library: Volumes A–G.* 7 vols. Portsmouth, NH: Heinemann.

Cappellini, Mary. 2005. *Balancing Reading and Language Learning: A Resource for Teaching English Language Learners, K–5.* Portland, ME: Stenhouse.

Capps, Randy, Michael Fix, Julie Murray, Jason Ost, Jeffrey S. Passel, and Shinta Herwantoro Hernandez. 2005. *The New Demography of America's Schools: Immigration and the No Child Left Behind Act.* Washington, DC: Urban Institute.

Cary, Stephen. 2007. *Working with English Language Learners: Answers to Teachers' Top Ten Questions.* 2d ed. Portsmouth, NH: Heinemann.

Chang, Maria L. 2004. *Classroom Management in Photographs.* New York: Scholastic.

Chen, Linda, and Eugenia Mora-Flores. 2006. *Balanced Literacy for English Language Learners, K–2.* Portsmouth, NH: Heinemann.

Clay, Marie M. 2000. *Concepts About Print: What Have Children Learned About the Way We Print Language?* Portsmouth, NH: Heinemann.

———. 2006. *Running Records for Classroom Teachers.* Portsmouth, NH: Heinemann.

Coggins, Debra, Drew Kravin, Grace Dávila Coates, and Maria Dreux Carroll. 2007. *English Language Learners in the Mathematics Classroom.* Thousand Oaks, CA: Corwin.

Collins, Kathy. 2004. *Growing Readers: Units of Study in the Primary Classroom.* Portland, ME: Stenhouse.

Coxhead, Averil. 2000. "A New Academic Word List." *TESOL Quarterly* 34 (2): 213–38.

Cummins, Jim. 1981. "The Role of Primary Language Development in Promoting Educational Success for Language Minority Students." In *Schooling and Language Minority Students: A Theoretical Framework.* Los Angeles: Evaluation, Dissemination, and Assessment Center.

———. 1984. *Bilingualism and Special Education: Issues in Assessment and Pedagogy.* Clevedon, England: Multilingual Matters.

———. 1989. *Empowering Minority Students.* Sacramento, CA: California Association of Bilingual Education.

———. 2000. *Language, Power and Pedagogy: Bilingual Children in the Crossfire.* Tonawanda, NY: Multilingual Matters.

———. 2003. "Reading and the Bilingual Student: Fact and Friction." In *English Learners: Reaching the Highest Level of English Literacy,* ed. Gilbert Garcia, 2–33. Newark, DE: International Reading Association.

———. 2008. "BICS and CALP: Empirical and Theoretical Status of the Distinction." In *Encyclopedia of Language and Education,* vol. 2, ed. Nancy Hornberger, 71–84. New York: Springer Science and Business Media.

Davis, Judy, and Sharon Hill. 2003. *The No-Nonsense Guide to Teaching Writing: Strategies, Structures, Solutions.* Portsmouth, NH: Heinemann.

Dragan, Pat Barrett. 2005. *A How-to Guide for Teaching English Language Learners in the Primary Classroom.* Portsmouth, NH: Heinemann.

Faltis, Christian J., and Sarah J. Hudelson. 1998. *Bilingual Education in Elementary and Secondary School Communities: Toward Understanding and Caring.* Boston: Allyn and Bacon.

Ferris, Dana R. 2002. *Treatment of Error in Second Language Student Writing.* Ann Arbor: University of Michigan Press.

Fix, Michael, and Jeffrey Passel. 2003. *U.S. Immigration—Trends and Implications for Schools.* Washington, DC: Immigration Studies Program, Urban Institute.

Fountas, Irene C., and Gay Su Pinnell. 1996. *Guided Reading: Good First Teaching for All Children.* Portsmouth, NH: Heinemann.

———. 1999. *Matching Books to Readers.* Portsmouth, NH: Heinemann.

———. 2000. *Guiding Readers and Writers: Teaching Comprehension, Genre, and Content Literacy.* Portsmouth, NH: Heinemann.

———. 2006. *Leveled Books K–8: Matching Texts to Readers for Effective Teaching.* Portsmouth, NH: Heinemann.

———. 2009. *The Fountas and Pinnell Leveled Book List K–8+: 2009–2011 Edition.* Portsmouth, NH: Heinemann.

Freeman, David E., and Yvonne S. Freeman. 2001. *Between Worlds: Access to Second Language Acquisition.* 2d ed. Portsmouth, NH: Heinemann.

———. 2007. *English Language Learners: The Essential Guide.* New York: Scholastic.

Freeman, Yvonne S., and David E. Freeman. 2002. *Closing the Achievement Gap: How to Reach Limited Formal-Schooling and Long-Term English Learners.* Portsmouth, NH: Heinemann.

———. 2006. *Teaching Reading and Writing in Spanish and English in Bilingual and Dual Language Classrooms.* Portsmouth, NH: Heinemann.

———. 2009. *Academic Language for English Language Learners and Struggling Readers: How to Help Students Succeed Across Content Areas.* Portsmouth, NH: Heinemann.

Fu, Danling. 2003. *An Island of English: Teaching ESL in Chinatown.* Portsmouth, NH: Heinemann.

Gándara, Patricia. 1999. *Review of Research on the Instruction of Limited English Proficient Students.* Santa Barbara: University of California, Linguistic Minority Research Institute.

García, Ofelia. 2006. "Lost in Transculturation: The Case of Bilingual Education in New York City." In *Along the Routes to Power: Exploration of the Empowerment Through Language,* ed. Martin Putz, Joshua A. Fishman, and Neff-Van Aertselaer, 157–78. Berlin: Mouton de Gruyter.

García, Ofelia, Jo Anne Kleifgen, and Lorraine Falchi. 2008. *From English Language Learners to Emergent Bilinguals.* New York: Teachers College, Columbia University.

Gibbons, Pauline. 1991. *Learning to Learn in a Second Language.* Portsmouth, NH: Heinemann.

———. 2002. *Scaffolding Language, Scaffolding Learning: Teaching Second Language Learners in the Mainstream Classroom.* Portsmouth, NH: Heinemann.

Goldenberg, Claude. 2008. "Teaching English Language Learners: What the Research Does—and Does Not—Say." *American Educator* (Summer): 42–44.

Gottlieb, Margo, Lynore Carnuccio, Gisela Ernst-Slavit, and Anne Katz. 2006. *PreK–12 English Language Proficiency Standards.* Alexandria, VA: Teachers of English to Speakers of Other Languages.

Graves, Donald H. 1994. *A Fresh Look at Writing.* Portsmouth, NH: Heinemann.

Hakuta, Kenji, Yuko Goto Butler, and Daria Witt. 2000. *How Long Does It Take English Learners to Attain Proficiency?* Santa Barbara: University of California, Linguistic Minority Research Institute.

Harvey, Stephanie, and Anne Goudvis. 2000. *Strategies That Work.* Portland, ME: Stenhouse.

Hill, Jane, and Kathleen M. Flynn. 2006. *Classroom Instruction That Works with English Language Learners.* Alexandria, VA: Association for Supervision and Curriculum Development.

Holdaway, Don. 1979. *The Foundations of Literacy.* Gosford, NSW, Australia: Ashton Scholastic.

Keene, Ellin Oliver, and Susan Zimmermann. 2009. *Mosaic of Thought.* 2d ed. Portsmouth, NH: Heinemann.

Kottler, Ellen, Jeffrey A. Kottler, and Chris Street. 2008. *English Language Learners in Your Classroom: Strategies That Work.* 3d ed. Thousand Oaks, CA: Corwin.

Krashen, Stephen D. 1982. *Principles and Practices of Second Language Acquisition.* Oxford: Pergamon.

———. 1985. *The Input Hypothesis: Issues and Implications.* New York: Longman.

Marzano, Robert. 2004. *Building Background Knowledge for Academic Achievement: Research on What Works in Schools.* Alexandria, VA: Association for Supervision and Curriculum Development.

Marzano, Robert, Jennifer S. Norford, Diane E. Paynter, Debra J. Pickering, and Barbara B. Gaddy. 2001. *A Handbook for Classroom Instruction That Works.* Alexandria, VA: Association for Supervision and Curriculum Development.

Marzano, Robert J., and Debra J. Pickering. 2005. *Building Academic Vocabulary: Teacher's Manual.* Alexandria, VA: Association for Supervision and Curriculum Development.

McCarrier, Andrea, Gay Su Pinnell, and Irene C. Fountas. 2000. *Interactive Writing: How Language and Literacy Come Together, K–2.* Portsmouth, NH: Heinemann.

Miller, Debbie. 2002. *Reading with Meaning: Teaching Comprehension in the Primary Grades.* Portland, ME: Stenhouse.

Mercado, Carmen. 2005. "Seeing What's There: Language and Literacy Funds of Knowledge in New York Puerto Rican Homes." In *Building on Strength: Language and Literacy in Latino Families and Communities,* ed. Ana Celia Zentella, 134–47. New York: Teachers College Press.

Moll, Luis, Cathy Amanti, Deborah Neff, and Norma Gonzalez. 1992. "Funds of Knowledge for Teaching: Using a Qualitative Approach to Connect Homes and Classrooms." *Theory and Practice* 31: 132–41.

Olsen, Laurie, and Ann Jaramillo. 1999. *Turning the Tides of Exclusion: A Guide for Educators and Advocates for Immigrant Students.* Oakland: California Tomorrow.

Parkes, Brenda. 2000. *Read It Again! Revisiting Shared Reading.* Portland, ME: Stenhouse.

Pearson, P. David, and Margaret C. Gallagher. 1983. "The Instruction of Reading Comprehension." *Contemporary Educational Psychology* 8 (3): 317–44.

Rasinski, Timothy V. 2003. *The Fluent Reader: Oral Reading Strategies for Building Word Recognition, Fluency, and Comprehension.* New York: Scholastic Professional Books.

Rea, Denise M., and Sandra P. Mercuri. 2006. *Research-Based Strategies for English Language Learners: How to Reach Goals and Meet Standards, K–8.* Portsmouth, NH: Heinemann.

Robb, Laura. 2003. *Teaching Reading in Social Studies, Science, and Math.* New York: Scholastic Professional Books.

Routman, Regie. 2000. *Conversations: Strategies for Teaching, Learning, and Evaluating.* Portsmouth, NH: Heinemann.

Samway, Katharine Davies. 2006. *When English Language Learners Write: Connecting Research to Practice, K–8.* Portsmouth, NH: Heinemann.

Scarcella, Robin. 2003. *Accelerating Academic English: A Focus on the English Learner.* Irvine: University of California Irvine.

Shalaway, Linda. 2005. *Learning to Teach . . . Not Just for Beginners: The Essential Guide for All Teachers*. 3d ed. New York: Scholastic Professional Books.

Skutnabb-Kangas, Tove. 1981. *Bilingualism or Not: The Education of Minorities*. Clevedon, England: Multilingual Matters.

Taberski, Sharon. 2000. *On Solid Ground: Strategies for Teaching Reading K–3*. Portsmouth, NH: Heinemann.

Thomas, Wayne P., and Virginia Collier. 1995. *A Longitudinal Analysis of Programs Serving Language Minority Students*. Washington, DC: National Clearinghouse on Bilingual Education.

———. 1997. *School Effectiveness for Language Minority Students*. Washington, DC: George Washington University Center for the Study of Language and Education.

———. 2002. *A National Study of School Effectiveness for Language Minority Students' Long-Term Academic Achievement*. Santa Cruz, CA: Center for Research on Education, Diversity and Excellence.

Tompkins, Gail E. 1997. *Literacy for the 21st Century: A Balanced Approach*. Upper Saddle River, NJ: Merrill/Prentice Hall.

Trelease, Jim. 2006. *The Read-Aloud Handbook*. New York: Penguin Group.

Wiggins, Grant, and Jay McTighe. 2005. *Understanding by Design*. Alexandria, VA: Association for Supervision and Curriculum Development.

Wong, Harry K., and Rosemary T. Wong. 1998. *How to Be an Effective Teacher: The First Days of School*. Mountain View, CA: Harry K. Wong.

Wong-Fillmore, Lily, and Catherine E. Snow. 2000. "What Teachers Need to Know About Language." *ERIC Clearinghouse on Languages and Linguistics* (April): 2–40.

Zehler, Annette, Howard L. Fleischman, Paul J. Hopstock, Todd G. Stephenson, Michelle L. Pendzick, and Saloni Sapru. 2003. *Special Topic Report No. 1: Native Languages of LEP Students*. Descriptive Study of Services to LEP Students and LEP Students with Disabilities. Development Associates, Inc.: Arlington, VA.

Literature References

Aliki. 1986. *Corn Is Maize: The Gift of the Indians*. New York: HarperCollins.

Benchley, Nathaniel. 1994. *Small Wolf*. New York: HarperCollins.

Brinkworth, Brian. 2003. *Life in a Coral Reef*. New York: Rosen.

Bruchac, Joseph. 1997. *Eagle Song*. New York: Penguin Group.

Carden, Mary, and Mary Cappellini. 1997. *I Am of Two Places: Children's Poetry*. Austin, TX: Steck-Vaughn.

Carle, Eric. 2001. *The Tiny Seed*. New York: Aladdin Paperbacks.

Cherry, Lynne. 2002. *A River Ran Wild: An Environmental History*. Orlando, FL: Houghton Mifflin Harcourt.

Coerr, Eleanor. 1977. *Sadako and the Thousand Paper Cranes*. New York: Penguin Group.

Cohen, Caron Lee. 1992. *The Mud Pony: A Traditional Skidi Pawnee Tale*. New York: Scholastic.

Cuyler, Margaret. 1999. *From Here to There*. New York: Scholastic.

Erdosh, George. 2001. *Food and Recipes of the Native Americans*. New York: Rosen.

Freedman, Russell. 1995. *Immigrant Kids*. New York: Penguin Group.

Freymann, Saxton and Joost Elffers. 2004. *How Are You Peeling?* New York: Scholastic.

Gibbons, Gail. 1991. *From Seed to Plant*. New York: Holliday House.

Gibson, Karen Bush. 2005a. *Longhouses*. Mankato, MN: Capstone.

———. 2005b. *Plank Houses*. Mankato, MN: Capstone.

Hickman, Pamela. 1998. *Animal Senses: How Animals See, Hear, Taste, Smell, and Feel.* New York: Scholastic.

Hoffman, Mary. 2002. *The Color of Home.* New York: Phyllis Fogelman Books.

Hutchins, Pat. 1971. *Rosie's Walk.* New York: Simon and Schuster Children's.

Kalan, Robert, and Donald Crews. 1991. *Rain.* New York: HarperCollins.

Kalman, Bobbie. 2000. *How Do Animals Adapt?* New York: Crabtree.

Keats, Ezra Jack. 1976. *The Snowy Day.* New York: Penguin Group.

Krauss, Ruth, and Crockett Johnson. 1945. *The Carrot Seed.* New York: HarperCollins.

Martin, Rafe. 1998. *The Rough-Face Girl.* Penguin Group.

Preszler, June. 2005a. *Teepees.* Mankato, MN: Capstone.

———. 2005b. *Wickiups.* Mankato, MN: Capstone.

Rudy, Lisa Jo. 2005. *Snakes!* New York: HarperCollins.

Scott Foresman. 2004. *Social Studies: New York.* New York: Pearson Education.

Scraper, Katherine. n.d. *Earth's Water.* www.readinga-z.com/.

Simon, Seymour. 2005. *Amazing Bats.* San Francisco: Chronicle Books.

Stevens, Jan Romero. 1993. *Carlos and the Squash Plant / Carlos y la planta de calabaza.* Flagstaff, AZ: Luna Rising.

Stewart, Melissa. 2001. *Birds.* Danbury, CT: Scholastic Library.

Swamp, Jake. 2003. *Giving Thanks: A Native American Good Morning Message.* New York: Lee and Low Books.

Websites for Leveling Books

A to Z Teacher Stuff Leveled Books Database: books.atozteacherstuff.com/leveled-books

Beaverton School District Leveled Books Database: registration.beavton.k12.or.us/lbdb/

Fountas and Pinnell Leveled Books: www.fountasandpinnellleveledbooks.com/

Leveled and Guided Reading: rigby.harcourtachieve.com/en-US/lgr?=rigby

Teacher Book Wizard: bookwizard.scholastic.com/

Websites with Multicultural Resources

Celebrating Cultural Diversity Through Children's Literature (grades K–6): www.multiculturalchildrenslit.com/

Database of Award-Winning Children's Literature: www.dawcl.com/search.asp

International Children's Digital Library: en.childrenslibrary.org/

Websites for Instructional Resources

Reading A–Z (leveled books to print): www.readinga-z.com/

Raz-Kids.com (leveled books to listen to online): www.raz-kids.com/

Scholastic Mini-Books (books to print): minibooks.scholastic.com/minibooks/home

Oxford Picture Dictionaries: www.oup.com/elt/catalogue/isbn/9260?cc=gb

Wright Group (Everyday Mathematics wipe-off charts): www.wrightgroup.com
    Search keyword: "Everyday Mathematics Interactive Wallcharts"

Starfall.com: www.starfall.com/

National Geographic Kids Video Gallery (social studies and science topics): kids.nationalgeographic.com/Videos/VideoGallery

World Book: www.worldbookonline.com/

Scholastic News Online: www.scholasticnews.com/

Time for Kids: www.timeforkids.com/

Weekly Reader: www.weeklyreader.com/

Your Big Backyard: www.nwf.org/YourBigBackyard/

National Geographic Explorer!: magma.nationalgeographic.com/ngexplorer/

National Geographic Explorer! "Power Plant" (online game): magma.national geographic.com/ngexplorer/0604/games/game_intro.html

Index

International Children's Digital Library, 23
Interrupted formal schooling, 48

K-W-L chart, 216
Kidspiration program, 23

Language
    classroom resources for, 2
    figurative, 207
    incorporating into planning, 128
    See also Academic language
Language charts, 6, 20, 21
Language demands, 125
Language search, 138
Language structures, 39–43, 126–127
    graphic organizers for, 213–214
    modeling and practicing, 129–140
Letter names assessment, 50
Letter writing, 54–55
Letter-sound correlation assessment, 50
Leveled books, 6
    in classroom library, 6–8
    organizing, 8–9, 10
    text characteristics of, 9
Library, classroom, 4
    easel and whiteboard in, 4–5
    language charts in, 6
    leveled books in, 6–10
    literacy charts in, 5–6
    nonleveled books in, 6, 9–11
    physical objects in, 5
    pocket charts in, 5
Life in a Coral Reef, 172–174
Limited formal schooling, 48
Listening center, 20–21
    computers in, 22
    recordings in, 21–22
    tape players in, 21
Literacy
    charts, 5–6
    instruction in, 60, 70–74
    integration with content-area instruction. *See* Integrated instruction
Long-term English language learners, 48–49
Longhouses, 107

Main idea, 205, 215, 216
Manipulatives, for math, 17–18
Math
    effective vs. ineffective homework assignments for, 85–86
    in the L1 and L2, 55–56
    and language structures, 129–130, 215, 216
Math center, 15–18
Math charts, 15–16
    wipe-off, 16
Math manipulatives, 17–18
Math routines, 16

Miller, Debbie, 6
Minilessons
    in differentiated instruction, 167–172, 178–183
    in integrated instruction, 109, 112–114
    for reading, 49, 71
    transitioning to and from, 77
    for writing, 53, 72–73
Modeled writing, 72–73
    in integrated instruction, 112–113
Modeling
    of classroom behavior, 82–83
    of language structures, 129–140
    of rules, 80
    of supplies use, 75–76
Monitoring for sense, 205
    at all proficiency levels, 206–207
The Mud Pony, 111
Multicultural perspectives, 36, 37
Multicultural resources, 35
Music
    in the classroom, 76–77
    in integrated instruction, 119

National Geographic Explorer, 23, 178, 179
National Geographic for Kids, 23–24, 108
Native language, 32
    books in, 11
    in the classroom, xvii, 26, 60, 90, 120, 156, 188
    determining, 32–33
    and homework, 84, 85
    in partnering, 33–34
    resources in, 34
Negatives, formation of, 214
Nonfiction book baskets, 11
Nonleveled books, 6
    arranging, 121
    in classroom library, 9–11

Open sorts, 143–144
Overhead transparencies, for math, 18

Paper choice, 18–19
Parts of speech, 215, 216
Passive voice, 140
Personal pronouns, 139
Picture dictionaries, 19
Picture sorts, 143–144, 147
Plank Houses, 107
"Plant Power," 162–165
Pocket charts, 5
Possessive pronouns, 139
Predictions, making, 201, 215
    at all proficiency levels, 201–203
Primary language. *See* Native language
Proficiency, language, 36
    chart for recording, 195–196
    defined, 36, 38